Jack Benny

The Radio and Television Work

Jack Benny

The Radio and Television Work

THE MUSEUM OF TELEVISION AND RADIO

HarperPerennial
A Division of HarperCollins*Publishers*

Published in conjunction with an exhibition of the same title at The Museum of Television and Radio, New York.

The exhibition is sponsored by Jell-O Brand Desserts.

Library of Congress Cataloging-in-Publication Data

Jack Benny : the radio and television work / The Museum of Television and Radio — 1st HarperPerennial ed.
p. cm.
Includes bibliographical references.
ISBN 0–06–055209–3 — ISBN 0–06–096546–0 (pbk.)
1. Benny, Jack, 1894–1974. I. Museum of Television and Radio (New York, N.Y.)
PN2287.B4325J33 1991
792.7′028′092—dc20 90–55506

Editor: Ellen O'Neill
Art Director: Lou Dorfsman
Cover Design: Lou Dorfsman, Frank Skorski
Book Design: Paul Gamarello/Eyetooth Design Inc.

The Museum of Television and Radio
25 West 52 Street
New York, N.Y. 10019

Jack Benny had the best timing of any comedian I've ever known. He wasn't especially funny in private, though he had a very attractive, genial personality. But he loved humor, and because he understood it so well he trusted his keen instincts on what an audience would appreciate. He recognized good material and knew precisely how to lift it from the page and turn it into a marvelous comic experience. He was a perfectionist in all that he did.

Through a long broadcasting lifetime, Jack was a consummate professional who approached the comic arts with total dedication. He gave America's radio and television audiences not just great laughs, but warm and wonderful laughs. I am happy that such laughter will again be heard, at the Museum.

William S. Paley
Founder
The Museum of Television and Radio

Jack Benny by René Robert Bouché
National Portrait Gallery, Smithsonian Institution

PRESIDENT'S NOTE

This exhibition and book celebrate the comedic artistry of a man who pioneered the new forms of creative expression offered by radio and television.

First over the airwaves and then on camera, Jack Benny captured our hearts, and we welcomed him into our homes for over forty years. So seemingly indistinguishable were the man and his character, so seemingly effortless the humor and so familiar the situations that only now, many years later, do we truly recognize the singularity of his talent. On the occasion of the opening of the new home of The Museum of Television and Radio, it is fitting to salute the work of Jack Benny: he was a remarkable member of both radio and television's first generation of creative talent.

This book and the more than 150 programs that comprise the exhibition offer a comprehensive appreciation and understanding of Jack Benny's professional achievements as well as a sense of the vitality of his work.

Larry Gelbart's foreword introduces the book's themes and conveys that most abstract of concepts—the affection people have for the Jack Benny character. William A. Henry III provides the biographical details about Jack Benny, the man, as background to the genesis of the character. A reprint of Benny's 1951 article in *Collier's* magazine provides a personal account of his journey from vaudeville to radio and then television. David Marc's brings a more academic perspective to Benny's comedy and discusses Benny in relation to his comedic contemporaries and to those who inherited his legacy. And in the last essay, Peter Kaplan, using Thornton Wilder's 1938 *Our Town* as his frame, shows how Benny's comedy reflects the temperament of American society during the twentieth century.

The section provided by the Museum's curators offers a detailed analysis of the Benny oeuvre, examining how Benny fashioned the Jack Benny character and how he used it so brilliantly for over forty years. Specific radio and television programs are examined and detailed in order to provide the reader with a greater insight into Benny's celebrated use of timing and "group comedy."

An undertaking of this sort requires the cooperation, talents, and concerted efforts of numerous individuals and institutions. A complete list of these people is contained in the acknowledgments section of this book. The Museum's exhibition would not have been possible without their help. I would like to express my personal thanks to Irving Fein and Joan Benny for their enthusiasm and for supporting our efforts by granting us access to the Benny estate's collection of programs, scripts, and photographs. For their efforts in making this book possible, I also wish to acknowledge Michael Bessie, Publisher of Bessie Books and Vice President of HarperCollins, with whom we initiated our discussions for publishing the book, and Carol Cohen, Vice President and Publisher, HarperCollins Reference, for all her help. And at The Museum of Television and Radio I wish to thank Ron Simon, Curator, Television and Rich Conaty, former Associate Curator, Radio, for their tremendous contributions in research and writing the exhibition section of the book; Ellen O'Neill, Senior Editor, Publications, for her critical suggestions and continual challenges to the ideas of the manuscript; and to Lou Dorfsman for his artistic vision as Art Director.

To bring Jack Benny's work to the public again required considerable financial support. We could not have wished for a more appropriate or dedicated sponsor for the Museum's exhibition than Jell-O Brand Desserts, which also played a historical role in Benny's career, most notably as sponsor of the *Jell-O Program* from 1934 to 1942.

What is wondrous and remarkable about radio and television is that almost twenty years after his death, Jack Benny is still entertaining us; not through second-hand accounts in print or by the compilation of scripts, but by Benny himself. Because the broadcasts were recorded and preserved, we can hear and see Jack Benny today exactly as those who heard and saw the original broadcasts. The venue of the home may be different, the television set more sophisticated, and perhaps our sensibilities are different, but for a comedic artist who stands the test of time, the original character and performance is there to be enjoyed, to be admired, and to continue on in time. When this exhibition comes to a close, Jack Benny's programs will remain part of the Museum's permanent collection so that future generations will have the opportunity to enjoy his work as well as, perhaps, find the inspiration to build upon it.

Robert M. Batscha
President
The Museum of Television and Radio

FOREWORD

BY LARRY GELBART

Thirty-nine was a very good year.

Before that, Jack Benny had been thirtyeverything. Several times. When he was 51, a number totally unacceptable to the vanity of the character he had so painstakingly constructed for his audience, Benny, in a radio sketch, gave his age to an inquiring nurse as 36.

Accordingly, in the next season he became 37. It was two years later that he turned—and was to remain endlessly, shamelessly—39. It was a good year, forever set on rewind, for two reasons: it suited the fictitious Benny's ego while it revealed the youthful anxiety of the real Benny in his desire to excel, for despite his many years of success, he still needed more than anything to win our laughter and approval.

The first miracle was that Jack Benny was able to do so for well over a half century. The second that, despite his popularity (not only with his fans, who were legion—his peers idolized him as well), he remained a kind, thoughtful human being—no small trick in a business where power corrupts and absolute power is never enough.

It was a case of Dorian Gray in reverse. The public portrait, the vain, penny-pinching nicklenurser, was a pathetic mess; the real Jack Benny was an ageless prince.

So complete was his achievement, so convincingly had he painted himself as a giant of pettiness, a miser of mythical proportions, that the world paid him the ultimate compliment of coming to accept the artist as his own creation. It was as though people believed that both of Picasso's eyes were on the same side of his face.

Benny's broadcasting career began in 1932. It ended in 1974. He was a man for all forty-two seasons, each of which bore his stamp of excellence, each pitched to the highest standard he set for himself and left as his legacy.

The Museum of Television and Radio, with its collection of over 100 hours of Benny's performances on radio and television, a collection that continues to grow, offers those who knew his work (and those who one day will) the opportunity to see and hear the work of a master.

And an innovator, as well. For Jack Benny, by challenging the accepted comic conventions of the early thirties, for the most part rooted in and carried over from vaudeville, changed the nature of radio comedy, making humor far more character- and situation-oriented, which in turn influenced the most enduring of all television forms, the sitcom (so named, one begins to suspect, because if you can sit through many of them you are to be complimented).

It was the Benny radio program that pioneered "gang comedy," an ongoing company of supporting players, very much a family, each with his or her own personality and eccentricities and each given the license to assassinate Benny's character, their chief complaint being that he had none.

And what a gang they were: Mary, Rochester, Don, Phil, Dennis, Mel Blanc, and Frank Nelson, all of them merciless in their treatment of the boss (what listener did not enjoy hearing that fantasy played out without being fired for it?), a star who was so shrewdly willing to play straight man to his straight men. Their barbs drew howls but never blood, for this was a gentler time and these were

Jack and Mary rehearsing before a show from a theater

A theater appearance during the Jell-O years

gentle people. How lovingly we recall in these days of proliferating trashivision and "adult" entertainment that the only four-letter word ever heard on a Jack Benny show was "Well!"

Benny's greatest, most enduring invention was, of course, Benny himself. Born in Chicago in 1894, on Valentine's Day (even at birth he showed a flair for timing), he was giving violin concerts at the age of 8 and being hailed as a local prodigy. Hard as it is to believe that anyone could go downhill from this early age, through diligence and application Benny went on to become a consummate musical failure, the horrible violinist's horrible violinist. Happily, the man *himself* became a Stradivarius.

While he honed his craft for years as a stage comedian, it was in radio that Benny, as his own best instrument, went beyond potential to perfection. He understood instinctively, knew in his bones, all of them funny ones, the intimate nature of broadcasting, knew that the microphone was not just a piece of equipment, but that the microphone was the listener's ear.

That perception allowed him to bring to the air the style he had developed in front of theater audiences. He was a minimalist. Comics are often compared to matadors. If most funny men worked with a sword, Benny needed only a hat pin. If most needed a dozen or more words to get a laugh, Benny could get by with only three or four, the difference being made up by the audience's understanding of his attitude in any given situation. And very often even those few words could be replaced merely by a look, a look that said it all.

His great and good friend, George Burns, a legend in his own time and a half, called Benny a "quiet laugh riot."

Jack Benny could, in fact, be funny being totally quiet, absolutely mum, as he demonstrated in that memorable, seemingly endless wait before he finally, finally responded to the impatient stickup man. What other comedian before—or since—was ever able to use silence as a punch line? Before Jack Benny, who would have believed anyone could succeed as a mime on radio? What courage, what supreme confidence he displayed, not only on that occasion, but time after time, waiting until what often seemed a moment after the last possible moment before he would come in with his line. He wasn't working without a net. It's just that the net he used was maybe an eighth of an inch from the ground, and Benny knew to the millisecond how long he could wait before he delivered a payoff.

George had Gracie, but Jack had grace.

And elegance. If Bob Hope's machine-gun-like delivery made him seem a Cagney of comedy, then Benny was its Astaire, and like Astaire, Benny was able to make his exquisite expertise seem entirely effortless, despite the fact that he was a world-class worrier, a sure sign of someone who knows that you expect the best of him.

Above all, Benny had an incredible sweetness about him. Heaven knows a lot of comedians exhibit this quality, but who among them, other than Benny, portrayed themselves so relentlessly as tightfisted, selfish peacocks and still won our affection? And never, not once in his career, did he drop the pose or offer an apology or disclaimer, never stooped to telethonic sentimentality to pander for some approval of the man himself.

On March 29, 1932, in his first significant radio appearance on Ed Sullivan's show, Benny began his routine by saying: "Ladies and Gentlemen, this is Jack Benny talking. There will be a slight pause while you say, 'Who cares?' " Happily, just about everyone finally did.

Everyone who ever heard him on his radio program make change for a guest star visiting the Benny house who wanted to make a call on Jack's pay phone that was located right next to the cigarette vending machine in the Benny living room.

Everyone who ever watched him stare into a TV camera with that incomparable put-on of a put-upon face, that look of pained innocence, the expression of a calf who just found out where veal comes from.

How could anyone not care for a man who was a walking inventory of all of our failings and foolishness, who spent a lifetime holding up a mirror in which he substituted his image for ours to show us our pretentions and our shortcomings and, in forgiving him by laughing at his all-too-human frailties, allowed us to forgive them in ourselves?

On December 26, 1974, eighty years after he was born, Jack Benny passed away at the age of 39.

The good, indeed, do die young.

George Burns and Benny relive the days of burlesque, 1963

Benny "passes the hat" before a broadcast, 1939

MR. BENNY AND AMERICA— THE LONG ROMANCE

BY WILLIAM A. HENRY III

Jack Benny had style from the beginning. He stood straight and walked kind of sideways as if he were being shoved by a touch of genius—and knew it, and knew you'd know it, too, in a moment.
—William Saroyan

It is probably the best-known joke in the history of American broadcasting. A masked hoodlum, weapon in hand, accosted a fey skinflint and posed the eternal no-choice question: "Your money or your life?" A long pause followed. Tension built, punctuated by giggles. Finally the criminal, affronted at the delay, repeated his question. In an exasperated clarinet-like drone came the exquisite answer: "I'm thinking it over!" Like almost everything Jack Benny performed during his four unbroken decades of peak popularity on national radio and television, the punch line was not that funny in itself. Spoken by anyone else it would have evoked at best a gentle smile. But in Benny's delivery it was, characteristically, hilarious because of the accumulated context. Benny had been playing the Stingiest Man on Earth for so long that laughter started as soon as the stickup man said the word *money.* As the clock ticked on in silence, one by one even the slowest wits in the audience clued in to the Benny character's dilemma. To him, life was not more precious than money; life *was* money, and without it he would not care to live. He was such a miser that his avarice outstripped his fear. By the time he said, "I'm thinking it over!" at least half of the audience's gleeful exhalation was its self-congratulation on having seen the punch line coming, inevitable as an express train first glimpsed as distant headlamps.

The joke was not merely savored but repeated, in hundreds of newspaper stories and countless thousands of conversations and ultimately in innumerable memorials to the man who became perhaps the best-loved American comedian of the century, certainly the most singular. Never a clown, never antic, never gifted with sprightly slapstick or funny faces or even enticing joie de vivre, Benny was, equally, neither a beguiling monologuist nor a spontaneous wit. In fact, he had virtually none of the customary talents of a comic. As his sometime colleague and fellow radio genius Fred Allen once remarked in the midst of a publicity-stunt feud, "There are two kinds of jokes, funny jokes and Jack Benny jokes." Allen may have been teasing, but he was more right than wrong. Benny's jokes generally were not all that clever or winsome, ironic or sly. But Benny himself was, and all America thought so steadily through more than forty tumultuous years of social change, from 1932, when a successful guest appearance on Ed Sullivan's show brought him his own network radio program, to 1974, when he died and NBC devoted a half-hour news special to his passing.

Other comedians have created engagingly exaggerated archetypes. From Chaplin with his Little Tramp to Gleason with his Poor Soul, many comics have appealed more openly than Benny to the sentimentality and boundless self-pity of the common man. But with the possible exception of Bob Hope, no other performer in the history of American broadcasting has worn so well for so long. Benny died at age 80 undiminished as a star, with TV

Benny, Rochester, and Polly the parrot in the Maxwell (note director Ralph Levy's name on sign)

specials on order and his long-sought return to movies just weeks away. (He was scheduled to play the gentler and more addled of Neil Simon's retired vaudevillians in *The Sunshine Boys.* On Benny's death the role went, fittingly, to his best friend George Burns, who won an Oscar and thereby relaunched his own remarkable career.) Part of the reason for the seeming indestructibility of Benny's trademark gags was that he had so many of them. The battered, barely roadworthy Maxwell car. The vault buried so deep beneath his home, behind so many protective devices, that the government studied it to improve Fort Knox's security. The violin he played so badly and with such earnest intent. His vanity about his age, which to the end he insisted was an eternal 39. The train station announcement of departures to the preposterously named, if real, "Anaheim, Azusa, and Cucamonga." Not to mention the human foils: the pompous department store floorwalkers, the larcenous home repairmen, the pixilated mittel-European Mr. Kitzel, and the horde of rebellious subordinates, led by the wily black chauffeur/valet Rochester (Eddie Anderson). Each of these devices (and dozens more) was nurtured over decades. They were used sparingly enough to stay fresh yet repeatedly enough that, as with the celebrated stickup, audiences were in on the joke before it was well and truly begun. And while these gags were going on, Benny reinforced their seeming normalcy—the loonier the events, the more matter-of-factly he treated them—by reacting slowly, if at all. He might put his hand to his cheek (just three fingers, which he had determined by trial and error were somehow funnier than four) and he might roll his eyes after a bit and he might, just might, intone a long and long-suffering "Well!" But mostly he would wait for the laughs, and somehow the laughs would come. Critics and fellow performers invariably praised his timing, his sense of when the audience's tension had peaked without beginning to turn into tedium. The distinguished British actor Alec McCowen, who insisted that Benny was "one of the greatest comedic actors in the world," described a typical performance in terms more often used for Laurence Olivier: "His face was a mask. He never seemed to *do* anything. But you could always tell what he was thinking." Benny's own favorite review, from the British critic Beverly Baxter, said, "Jack Benny can do nothing better than any other man alive."

THE BENNY PERSONA

The oddest aspect of Benny's genius was that the persona he invented and shaped and sold through the decades would have seemed doomed to unpopularity, yet it inspired deep affection. The private Benny may have verged on sainthood: try though they might, muckrackers through the years failed to find anyone with a harsh word for the man, let alone a telling anecdote of vanity, indulgence, greed, or cruelty. The worst things that anyone came up with were his penchant for cigars, his fondness for betting on poker and horse races (with a self-imposed limit of two hundred dollars lost per session, at which point he would walk away), and the fact that he liked to change his shoes three times a day. The public Benny, by contrast, was penny-pinching and mean-spirited, petulant and proud. He was a liar and a cheat, a tinpot dictator when he could be and a coward the instant he faced a challenge. Scornful and contemptuous, he flung insults all around him—though thanks to his fractious costars, he usually got back far more billingsgate than he dished out. Nothing about the Benny persona was admirable save perhaps his loyalty, and that was more the noblesse oblige of a landlord toward his serfs.

Critics often suggested that the appeal of the character was that he embodied the main faults of practically everyone, carried to such extremes that onlookers could laugh away any discomfort about themselves. Benny certainly endorsed that analysis. He delighted, both on and off camera, in telling stories of his foul-ups and frustrations, and a favorite self-referential phrase was, "Did you ever see such a jerk?" But this notion of him as an everyman-with-egg-on-his-face fails to explain why Benny, almost alone among antiheroes, inspired such love for so long. The answer may lie in the odd yet incorruptible sweetness of the character, despite his failings—the reason and common sense, the underlying patience and serenity, above all the nonviolence that characterized the public Benny's superficially distraught dealings with an often chaotic world. A performance artist who re-created the Benny character, complete with tapes from old shows, for a 1989 new-music opera explained that he saw Benny as "a victim" dealing with a mad, mad, mad, mad world.

In all of that, some of the private man may have been seeping through. Unlike many stars, Benny was generous without seeking credit, charitable without publicity. He nurtured his colleagues as a genuine family and worked with most of them through decades. He prided himself on hiring those he considered the best and paid them accordingly. (The Benny show's four writers shared an annual total of about $250,000 a year in the late 1940s, when $10,000 could buy a comfortable suburban home. Eddie Anderson, the first black to rise to series prominence in radio, made enough playing Rochester to be cited in several black publications as one of the wealthiest of his race in the nation. His costar Dennis Day, an Irish tenor who sang and

Benny moves his vault with help from Gisele MacKenzie, 1955

also played the perpetual naïf, was a more-or-less amateur making $50 a week when Benny picked him up. By 1949, Day was able to buy a seven bedroom mansion that his widow put on the market four decades later for $4.425 million. So generous was Benny with subordinates—and with any old acquaintance in need of a hand—that his own wealth never soared. At his death at the end of 1974 his estate was valued at $5,582,025, a modest enough sum by the standards of Hollywood, where actors were beginning to be offered that much for a single role.)

At home with Eddie "Rochester" Anderson, 1963

If parsimony was the primary facet of Benny's act, a close second—in terms of jokes and particularity to Benny—was an almost ritual effeminacy. It was not just that Benny, a married man in private, remained a confirmed bachelor in his public persona. That choice, after all, could be explained: he had cast his wife Mary as his girlfriend early on, but she suffered from acute stage fright and was increasingly reluctant to appear frequently, especially during the television years, as an on-screen wife would have had to do. Besides, Benny had established a successful format and had no desire to replace it with a typical family sitcom. But there was much more to the character's effeminacy than the simple lack of a spouse. The public Benny pranced and pursed his lips and postured, flounced and extravagantly overreacted. As his colleague Phil Harris once remarked, "You could put a dress on that guy and take him anywhere." Moreover, Benny did these things without ever offering the kind of conscious gesture or word of acknowledgment that can put a knowing distance between the performer and his acts: instead, this flapping about was the only part of Benny that the public got to see.

Theories as to why the American people, not noted for kindly treatment of anyone actually homosexual during the fifties and sixties, should react so warmly to his dithery ways are few and largely posthumous—serious analysis of the subject was almost taboo during his lifetime. Appreciative audiences may have viewed the campy behavior as part of Benny's relentless inversion of all the manly virtues. Indeed, his era closely paralleled that of John Wayne, and in many ways Benny's career amounted to a send-up of the very values that Wayne's movies so humorlessly celebrated. At a deeper level viewers may have been responding from within: psychotherapists suggest that there are androgynous impulses in practically everyone. The Benny character, moreover, was carefully presented as ultimately heterosexual, if not exactly ardent in his manhood. And, of course, though the thoroughness of the Benny persona's effeminacy is remarkable, it is far from unique: cross-dressing was a staple of sketch comedy in vaudeville and of

The Gaslight *parody with Barbara Stanwyck, 1952*

early television from Milton Berle onward, while for centuries before it pervaded the theater and apparently obsessed Shakespeare.

Benny did not appear in drag as often as, say, Berle. But when he did, for instance to impersonate Gracie Allen, he shaved his legs for the sake of authenticity. Sometimes the Benny character would leer at a female guest star or make some panting gesture of desire. But the act would be so passionless, so obviously pro forma, that it only reinforced his character's apparent lack of hormones. Besides, much of his humor seemingly presupposed that he would be taken as effeminate by absolute strangers. In a Christmas episode from 1951, he walks up to a lingerie counter at Christmastime and describes what he wants to buy. The clerk takes one look and automatically responds, "What size do you wear?"

Benny as Gracie Allen meets the real Gracie and George Burns, 1952

In a 1958 episode featuring Gisele McKenzie as a guest star, she demands that Benny return her charm bracelet: it turns out that he is wearing it. Doing so, he adds with a leer, has twice gotten him thrown out of the steam room at his country club. When he and Barbara Stanwyck staged a parody of *Gaslight* in 1952, his scenes with the screen siren lacked even the faintest hint of seduction or manly appeal. Indeed, when Benny first swishes in, wearing a cape, top hat, and gloves and grimacing like a Borscht Belt version of an old auntie, even an indulgent viewer might wonder how the characters' supposed marriage was ever contracted, let alone consummated.

Late in life, Benny himself frankly discussed the matter. In a 1964 interview with the *New York Post,* when he was 70, he said, "People are always taking advantage of me, and I've always thought it's because there's a tiny bit of effeminacy in me. I don't mean I'm a pansy. But the vanity and the pouting and the sulking in the character I play—it's like a woman." These words were incendiary enough to prompt his longtime manager Irving Fein, who was in attendance at the interview, to interrupt in a vain effort to retract them, then joltingly change the subject. But as far as anyone could tell, the private man was far less exotic than the public one. He remained married to the same woman for forty-seven years, until his death, and she said that in his will he provided she be delivered a single rose every day for the rest of her life.

IT ALL STARTED IN VAUDEVILLE

The Benny persona was so enduring, its appeal so consistent, that audiences generally had trouble separating the man from the role. Benny liked to tell the story of the waitress (in some versions it was a hatcheck girl) who returned a generous tip, saying, "Please leave me at least one illusion." But as Benny himself was keenly aware, the creation of his public persona took years of experimentation in vaudeville, the movies, stage, and radio. The character did not fully emerge until its originator was nearly 40 years old. Until then, he had been a high school truant, a music hall usher, a bottom-of-the-bill touring violinist, and a knockabout comic, enjoying such moderate success that the self-deprecation of his radio debut was far from inappropriate.

Benny, Bob Hope, and George Burns bringing back vaudeville

Appearing as a guest on an Ed Sullivan radio program, Benny introduced himself to the medium with words that have became legendary: "Good evening, folks. This is Jack Benny. There will be a slight pause for everyone to say, 'Who cares?' "*At the moment, not many people did.

Benny's humor was vaudeville humor, and that meant immigrant humor. It reflected both the amused astonishment with which waves of newcomers to America viewed strange native customs and the poignant uncertainty behind their laughter, the fear among the new arrivals that they might not fit in. Nearly all the standard vaudeville routines involved a world in which logic had turned topsy-turvy, a world as baffling and arbitrary as the one that immigrants felt they faced. In no other major television series did this through-the-looking-glass perspective survive as fully and effectively as in Benny's. Surreal events took place all the time, and no attempt was made to reconcile them with known facts. An armed and masked bandit would walk unnoticed through a crowded store. An eloping couple, their every message intercepted by Benny, would nonetheless magically meet as intended at a train station. The train master, for no apparent reason, would give away a live turkey, and the "winning" ticket would of course be Benny's. These sketches and many others also touched on nepotism, petty corruption, bureaucratic impenetrability, and above all minor thievery by tradesmen—

*Editor's note: There is no known extant recording of Benny's first radio appearance on Ed Sullivan's show, and there are conflicting sources as to exactly what he said. This citation is from a 1951 CBS press release.

all standard elements of immigrant humor and of the frustrating life that inspired the jokes.

Outwardly there was not much to link the mature Benny to the immigrant experience. His accent was more Midwestern twang than shtetl slur. His stage name was bland, unlike his unmistakably ethnic birth name, Benjamin Kubelsky. His passion for music, especially the violin, was typically Eastern European but by no means a taste restricted to his ancestral people. Nonetheless, the young Kubelsky had about as typical a turn-of-the-century immigrant upbringing as could be found outside the tenements of Manhattan's Lower East Side.

His father Meyer fled the anti-Jewish pogroms of the Russian Czar's empire as a mere boy by hiding himself under a dray load of bottles. The other details of his escape to the West are shrouded in silence or contradiction but may safely be assumed to have been unpleasant. On Meyer's arrival in the United States, he launched himself in the garment business, beginning like so many of his countrymen and coreligionists by selling from a pushcart. Eventually he fulfilled the immigrant dream, opening his own business in the Chicago-area town of Waukegan, Illinois. By the time young Benjamin was born in a Chicago hospital on Valentine's Day, February 14, 1894, the family circumstances were comfortable, at least by the modest standards of that day.

Benny, who had a lifelong distaste for maudlin sentiment, generally limited discussion of any youthful privations to such clipped remarks as, "I didn't have to sell newspapers barefoot in the snow." He also apparently didn't have to work much in the store, not after such fiascos as the time he fell asleep while customers swiped merchandise or the time he took a woman's installment payment without jotting down her name. In later life Benny may have exaggerated for comic effect the degree of his ineptitude, just as he seemingly offered widely varying versions of how he fared in high school: some interviewers had him being thrown out on the eve of graduation for sassing the principal, while others had the principal laughing in delight at Benny's insurrections. In one seemingly serious conversation, Benny told a journalist, "I was very bad in school. I hated it. I had practically no education." His obituary in the *New York Times*

Benny on a vaudeville marquee in San Francisco, 1920s

described him as a ninth grade dropout. All that is certain is that at a Jack Benny Day in Waukegan in 1937, the then current principal of his old school displayed a copy of the young Benny's grade transcript while the adult comic feigned crawling in shame from the stage. In all, Benny seems to have been an ordinary student who gave few signs of future stardom, which is pretty much standard for show business success stories. His mother, who was forty-seven when she died in 1917, still thought of him as a failure, although his father lived on until 1946, proud and doting, and Benny's sister Florence survived him.

Had anyone predicted an entertainment career for young Kubelsky, it would probably have been as a musician. After his parents presented him with a pricey fifty-dollar violin for his sixth (or maybe eighth) birthday, he studied the instrument with modest seriousness for years and apparently fantasized about a concert career. Although he quickly developed a taste for the rowdy life of vaudeville once he started working at local theaters as a teenaged usher and pit orchestra musician—and thus ruled out going on for conservatory training—there seems little doubt that in retrospect he almost certainly would have preferred (or thought he would have preferred) the status and artistic integrity of a concert soloist. He retained a lifelong star-struck shyness around topflight musicians. In later years he vacillated between believing that he too might have been able to attain a classical performing career and rejecting that idea out of hand as an extreme exaggeration of his innate talent. While he exuberantly enjoyed the money, acclaim, and popular affection that comedy brought, the activity that seemed to give him the most pleasure was being able to sell out his guest benefit performances on behalf of one symphony or another. He paid twenty thousand dollars back during his radio days for a Stradivarius violin, which in his will he left to the Los Angeles Philharmonic. Musicians such as Isaac Stern praised him as surprisingly competent, with a sophisticated ear, although skeptics wondered if such pleasantries were simply recompense for Benny's great generosity with his time. (Stern also called Benny "the gentlest, least malicious man I've ever known.")

Whatever his private fantasies about music, Benny's violin quickly became just a prop, something to occupy his hands, once he set out on the vaudeville circuit. Starting at age 16 or 18 (sources differ), he initially tried to sound funny while actually playing. Then he played more or less straightforwardly in between telling jokes. While entertaining fellow sailors stateside during World War I, under the auspices of the Navy's *Great Lakes Revue,* he hit on the happy notion of being so busy telling gags that he never got around to putting bow to strings. In the early years before and after his war service he appeared under a variety of names—the penultimate was Ben K. Benny, which he gave up because of its resemblance to the moniker of the better-known comic fiddler Ben Bernie—and with a variety of partners. Among these early collaborators were two successive pianists, Cora Salisbury and Lyman Woods, with whom he toured the tank towns of the Midwest. Benny developed a fierce resentment of the cheapness and unreasonable demands of the two-bit local impresarios who booked his act, and he may have drawn conscious or unconscious inspiration from them for the miserly persona of later years. With Salisbury, he recalled, he played Storm Lake, Iowa, where the theater manager expected the duo to put on nine different acts during the course of their brief engagement. On another occasion, he claimed, he put poodles from a pet store onto the stage with him and, when they failed to perform any tricks, was confronted by an irate theater owner. "I thought you said you had a dog act," the owner stormed. "Oh, I do," said Benny, "but they usually act this way when they're only being paid twenty-five dollars."

Plenty of similar (and perhaps similarly apocryphal) stories linger from the vaudeville days. In New York City, Benny supposedly breezed in before a tough, gin-pickled crowd at the old Academy of Music. "Hello, folks," he shouted as he walked in from one side of the stage to a relentless chorus of boos. "Good night, folks," he called out

The star of MGM's Broadway Melody of 1936

to the still-booing crowd as he swept right across the stage and out the other side without breaking stride. Benny is said to have played New York's legendary Palace twice as a flop. The third time, the story goes, he got a confidence-boosting lecture from Jack Dempsey and succeeded by coming out and kidding the other acts.

Perhaps the oddest and most dubious of Benny legends is that he was invited to join the Marx Brothers at some point, perhaps in 1911 when they played Waukegan, but declined. Although Benny seems to have told this story to interviewers more than once, Groucho and company said gently that it was absolutely news to them. And indeed the mild Benny and the manic Harpo would hardly seem suited to the same routines. Benny and the Marxes definitely were acquainted, and there may have been some genuine misunderstanding between them or a memory lapse on someone's part. (One plausible version, among the several offered by Benny himself, is that he was asked by the Marx brothers' mother-manager Minnie to join them on the road as a conductor. That might well explain why the sons did not recollect it. But Benny also gave interviewers several much-different recitals of the incident.)

Jack and Benny Rubin with a member of the vault security staff, 1961

In any case, as a solo act Benny made it by 1926 to Broadway, where he appeared in *The Great Temptations,* and he then went on to Tinseltown for the film *The Hollywood Revue of 1929.* But the high of signing a studio contract was followed by the low of frequent idleness. Indeed, though Benny would eventually make more than twenty mostly profitable films, including *To Be or Not to Be, Charley's Aunt, Buck Benny Rides Again, George Washington Slept Here,* and the one he joshed about most, *The Horn Blows at Midnight,* his charms never showed to best advantage on the wide screen. He was too mannered for the screen's prevalent naturalism, too dependent on the ongoing tension between his actual and assumed personas to slip comfortably into a wholly different character, and too accustomed to sending up his own material and performances to play a full-length script with conviction. In any case, he quickly exited from his first studio contract to resume appearing on the stage, where he was an established star.

THE RADIO YEARS

By 1930 Benny was being offered a weekly salary of at least one thousand dollars—some sources say fifteen-hundred dollars, at the time a respectable full year's income for a workingman—to tour in an Earl Carroll musical revue. Yet Benny tossed the offer aside to plunge into a relatively new medium, radio. It would be poetic justice to say that Benny, who was transformed from a penny-ante celebrity into a megastar by radio almost overnight, perceived ahead of practically everyone the importance and potential of broadcasting. But he never made that claim of foresight for himself. As much as anything, he seems to have been drawn to the idea of working steadily in one place, without touring, and in an equivalent to vaudeville that would require many fewer shows per week. In some ways radio seemed ill-advised, a waste of his talents. His gift for timing was if anything more vital on stage than on the air, and his much-envied skill at double takes would count for nothing in a format where audiences could not see him.

Jack and Mary at a Jell-O *rehearsal, 1938*

Still, Benny rejoiced when his celebrated guest appearance on the Ed Sullivan show rapidly led to a series of his own. Indeed, according to one story he flew up from Miami at his own expense, in the pre-jet era when such travel was long, arduous, and costly, just to audition for NBC. Something must have told him from deep within that radio represented his big chance. He seems to have happened almost intuitively upon formulas that suited the new medium. Right at the beginning, the basic elements of his show were established as they would remain for decades. His wife Sadie Marks appeared as a character named Mary Livingstone in an early episode of the *Canada Dry Program* in 1932. Also added early were announcer Don Wilson (in a 1934 *General Tire Revue*) and bandleader Phil Harris (in a 1936 *Jell-O Program*). Eddie Anderson made his first appearance as a Pullman porter serving Benny on a purported on-air train trip to the West Coast in a 1937 Jell-O show; the public liked Anderson so much that the character became Benny's personal valet and the show's most important sidekick. Stylistically, Benny was among the first radio personalities to kid himself and, more importantly, to kid the commercials, the products being advertised (also among them over the years: Grape-Nuts cereal and Lucky Strike cigarettes), even the sponsoring corporation itself. Early on, he also experimented briefly with insult comedy directed against on-air colleagues and guests, but found that the material basically did not suit him. He did, however, continue to ride his announcers and bandleaders, from George Olsen to Phil Harris.

Benny caught the public's fancy almost instantly. The show, which began on NBC in 1932, started placing in the top three of the ratings in 1934. In 1940 Benny topped the charts to become radio's undisputed number one attraction. In a 1938 interview Benny expressed a bit of his (most conventional) philosophy of comedy. "It's easier for me to get laughs now than it was ten years ago," he said. "I don't have to hit them between the eyes. Slapstick has to be very good today to bring a laugh. Smart humor is more acceptable. But it must not be vulgar—that's dynamite. Anyway, I don't think a smutty joke is any good. For one thing, it isn't retained in the memory. It's the joke people take home and repeat that has the greatest value."

Long after the Depression had been supplanted by World War II and the postwar economic boom, a much-changed America rated Benny number one on radio in 1954 when popularity in that medium still counted almost as much as popularity on television. In an obituary tribute in 1974, critic John O'Connor of the *New York Times* described Benny as "perhaps the most enduring and astonishingly shrewd creation of radio." O'Connor expressed far more enthusiasm for the Benny of radio than for the comic's television work, which many critics saw as having slowly dissipated a comic treasure trove built up during the radio years. Argued O'Connor, "Seeing the old Maxwell was not quite as funny as hearing it. Seeing it a second time was not nearly so funny as hearing it for the hundredth time. A quality of elusiveness was lost." Fred Allen, who often appeared with Benny on radio, especially during the seriocomic "feud" between them, rated himself as a conceptual wizard of the medium but deferred to Benny even more. "Practically all comedy shows on radio owe their structure to Benny," Allen said. "He was the first to realize that the listener is not in a theater with a thousand other people but in a smaller circle at home. The Benny show is like tuning into someone else's 'home'." There were, of course, limits to this intimacy. Few homes have a tenor, a bandleader, and a small orchestra all in residence, and few households have corporate sponsors. But in essence Allen was right. When people listened to Eddie Cantor or Al Jolson or Ed Wynn, what they were asked to conjure up

Ed Wynn, Texaco's "Fire Chief," (1932–35) broadcasting in costume

in their mind's eye was an auditorium. When they listened to Benny, what they were asked to conjure up was a living room. And when they heard a sketch, it involved people they knew and places they felt they had seen. Benny was, if not the first, surely the most important figure in the fusing of stand-up and situation comedy.

The exact nature of Benny's creative contribution to the show was often debated by his contemporaries. There is no doubt that he depended hugely on his writers. At one point during the "feud" with Allen, Benny took umbrage at a series of on-air wisecracks about his baldness and, even more, at the fact that Allen, as a guest, seemed to be getting a plurality of the laughs. Benny retorted hotly, according to a newspaper account at the time, "I wish my writers were here. I'd have an answer for you, I tell you. Anyway, you mind your business. This isn't your show." People who heard him at the time were divided about whether he was kidding or not.

His posture of total dependence on others simply to be able to speak may, of course, have been just another among the innumerable Benny gimmicks. But his staff, who generally decried any suggestion of similarity between the foibles of the man and those of the character, accepted without demur his admission that he lacked spontaneous wit. Indeed, one of Benny's writers was once quoted as saying, "Jack couldn't ad lib a belch after a Hungarian dinner." Nonetheless, Benny knew what he liked. He served as an executive editor, arbitrating among proposed story lines, selecting which version of a joke to use and allocating laugh lines among the various performers. Much as he valued writers, he was apparently confident of his ability to set the show's tone and protect its quality. When in 1936 his collaborator Harry Conn, who had created many of the program's gimmicks, announced he wanted a half interest in its ownership, Benny summarily dumped him. After that, however, the creative staff remained stable for decades, though it grew slowly from two writers, Bill Morrow and Ed Beloin, to four and ultimately six. Among them, the best-known were Sam Perrin, Milt Josefsberg, John Tackaberry, George Balzer, and, especially in later years, Benny's brother-in-law Hilliard Marks.

Benny's show aired from 7:00 to 7:30 E.S.T. Sunday evenings—in 1941, NBC contractually guaranteed him a lifetime option on the time slot. The cast and crew worked six days a week, typically taking Thursdays off. No sooner was each broadcast finished than Benny was raring to go on Monday morning, planning the next. He was known as a workaholic and a notoriously early riser—so much so that when he suggested, "Boys, let's knock off until 6:30 tomorrow," one writer replied, "Is that A.M. or P.M.?" Apparently with the writers' help, Benny concocted not only shows but one-liners to be attributed to him in the gossip columns. He asserted, for example, that his new trim look resulted from a special regimen of "coffee and chewed fingernails." He hailed film studio executive Darryl F. Zanuck as "a man of courage and foresight. Courage—he hired me in 1940. Foresight—he fired me in 1942." He termed pompous, paunchy critic Alexander Woollcott "a dictionary in need of a diet" and ostensibly quipped that if he were in columnist Heywood Broun's shoes, "I would shine them."

The popularity of the show allowed Benny to buy in 1938 a two-story Georgian house in Beverly Hills with a pool and a game room for partying until dawn. The den, decorated in Old English style, featured a backgammon set and two watercolor seascapes that lifted up to reveal the movie camera in the projection room. Despite the ample space, Benny spent much of the day in his bedroom, padding around in a robe or pajamas. The bed was surrounded by bookcases with scripts, a desk littered with notes, and other impedimenta in what Benny thought of as his main workroom.

Although he thrived, Benny did not gain real wealth in a lump sum until nearly the end of the forties, when CBS chairman William S. Paley decided to strengthen his radio network and be ready for the potential explosion of television by raiding a raft of stars from rival NBC. Benny was the most important. To make the deal more alluring in the day of almost confiscatory taxes on high earned incomes, Paley's CBS accountants cunningly converted the offered salary and signing bonus, which would have been taxable as regular income, into capital gains taxable at much lower preferential rates. The network did this by purchasing Benny's production company, which had only one significant asset, the rights to his show; even that asset would have been worthless without Benny around to perform in it. The price was $2.26 million, and on Benny's personal share of $1.35 million, the tax savings amounted to almost $1 million. The Internal Revenue Service fought the issue in the courts,

The Bennys' Hollywood home—they moved in May 1938

in what attorneys described as a landmark intellectual-property case, but Benny (and Paley) prevailed. Fifteen years after the first deal, Benny and his wife sold J&M Productions, which owned his series and another called *Checkmate,* for $3.5 million, with 85 percent of the proceeds going to the Bennys personally.

THE TELEVISION YEARS

Not surprisingly for someone who had prospered so much from radio, Benny entered television cautiously. In a 1951 article for *Collier's* magazine, (see page 23) he purported to laugh off the idea of overexposure. "To me," he wrote, "the essential quality of a great comedian is humility and sincerity, and I don't feel that this type of performer will ever tire his audience." Yet when he came onto TV on October 28, 1950, he refused to appear more than once every four weeks, saying he and his writers needed the time to develop scripts properly. Gradually he increased the frequency to once every two weeks. But he also kept appearing on radio. His last original radio broadcast was in 1955, with reruns continuing into 1958. Benny was never nearly as dominant in the Nielsen ratings for television as he had been in the Hooper ratings for radio, but during the 1951–52 season his show ranked ninth; the next season it was twelfth; the season after, eighteenth; and, in 1954–55, when it seemed his popularity might at long last be fading, he surged back up to seventh. The year after, the show was rated fifth, then tenth the following season, falling to twentieth only as the Western craze took hold in 1957–58. After a couple of seasons out of the top twenty, Benny rose again to tenth place in 1960–61, then dropped again until the show was moved to Tuesday nights. In the new time slot he finished twelfth in the Nielsen ratings for 1962–63 and fourteenth in 1963–64. At the end of that season CBS dropped him, reportedly with the graceless words "You're through" from programming chief James Aubrey (although Irving Fein recounts that it was Benny's decision to leave). Benny returned to NBC after a fifteen-year hiatus for one more season, this time on Fridays, but ratings were weak and he announced his face-saving "retirement." He did not stay retired for long. For the next nine years he was ubiquitous on talk and variety shows, in personal appearances nationwide, and on televised comedy specials. In the months before his death he headlined two "farewell" specials, with more on order.

Don Wilson as ballerina, 1960

Benny's personal popularity and prestige in Hollywood lured many major stars—including Marilyn Monroe, Humphrey Bogart, and Gregory Peck—into making their TV debuts as his guests. He also attracted, among others, Frank Sinatra, Basil Rathbone, and Claudette Colbert. Guest performers could be sure that Benny would not make them look silly and would give them plenty to do. When Barbara Stanwyck, a close friend, appeared in 1952, Benny graciously introduced her by saying, "Miss Stanwyck has been in pictures almost as long as I've been out of them." Expressing envy of her dramatic career versus his own purportedly less prestigious one in comedy, he opined, "The only way you can win an Academy Award is you've got to do a picture that has absolutely no laughs in it at all. (Pause.) My last one darn near made it."

Television debut of Marilyn Monroe, 1953

But the show's appeal remained the interaction with his steady sidekicks. In a 1953 episode, Benny says he has written a special ad for Don Wilson to perform and proceeds to attach Dumbo-sized ears to the announcer, top his head with a tiny, silly hat, roll up his pants legs to show his socks and braces, then wiggle the ears by pulling a string. In a 1958 show, Dennis Day appears to protest his not having been included on-air for the past five months. During the course of conversation, he admits having skipped seeing the episodes he was not on. "You never watch any of my shows," Benny expostulates, "and you call that loyalty?" "Certainly," Day replies. "I don't want to watch an old man go downhill." On another 1958 episode, an amply padded Benny imitates Jackie Gleason in a takeoff of *The Honeymooners,* with Day twitching and fidgeting in an uncanny imitation of Art Carney's Ed Norton. Most loved of all, right up through Benny's *Twentieth Anniversary Special* in 1970, were the rolling eyes and unforgettable oboe-in-a-gravel-pit voice of Eddie Anderson as Rochester.

Benny struggled, manfully if at times a bit misguidedly, to remain up-to-date. His *First Farewell Special* featured singer-composer Isaac Hayes, performing "Shaft" shirtless amid a cascade of gold chains, and golfer Lee Trevino, who chatted with Benny about Vice President Agnew's golf game. In the *New Look* special Benny camped through the opening sequence in a Prince Valiant wig and hippie clothes, which he said he was glad he had saved from boyhood because he knew they would come back into fashion. In 1974, when he was near death (although he did not know he was ill), Benny told the *Washington Star,* "I never delve into nostalgia. I am only interested in what's happening now. Everybody is raving about radio, but if I went back, they wouldn't listen." Yet Benny did not deny the encroachments of age. Accepting an award in his late seventies, he told the audience, "I don't deserve this. But I have arthritis and I don't deserve that, either."

About the only way Benny remained old-fashioned was in his domestic arrangements. He never tired of telling interviewers that his overexcited bride fainted at the wedding, and she never tired of telling how she had fallen in love at first sight when she met him as a child. (In truth, theirs was not a whirlwind romance. Even after getting reacquainted when she was an adult, they became engaged to other people before eventually tying the

Benny interrupts Don Wilson's commercial, 1954

knot.) The Bennys were fond of entertaining and socialized frequently with such neighbors as Lucille Ball and, especially, George Burns and Gracie Allen. They would drive around with the men in the front seat talking about horse races and the women in the back talking about how they had to select all their husbands' clothing. Mary regarded her husband as hopelessly inattentive to things around the house and claimed that he looked up one night at dinner and said, "Why, doll, you removed the chandelier"—eight years after she got rid of it. The Bennys adopted a daughter, Joan, and indulgently gave her a coming-of-age party (or wedding—sources differ) reported in the forties as having cost either $25,000 or $50,000. After selling the Beverly Hills property, the family moved in the late sixties to Holmby Hills, where Mary Livingstone died on June 30, 1983.

THE CURTAIN FALLS

Jack's death came sooner, and to far more massive attention. A shocked creative community and nation learned of Benny's pancreatic cancer just hours before his death. Benny himself learned of it only a week or so before he died, when a doctor discovered an ominous shadow in an X ray. While Sinatra, Hope, Burns, Danny Kaye, and Ronald Reagan were able to visit the house, most of Benny's countless friends had to rely on viewing a massive funeral tribute, one of Hollywood's biggest ever, staged by the comedian's longtime manager Irving Fein and covered by all three networks. The list of pallbearers included, among others, Sinatra, Paley, Mervyn LeRoy, Gregory Peck, Milton Berle, Billy Wilder, Ray Stark, Robert Sarnoff, Zubin Mehta, Jack Lemmon, Walter Matthau, James Stewart, Johnny Carson, George Jessel, and all the costars of the Benny show. Words of affection gushed across the land. If Benny had been around to enjoy the tributes, he would probably have preferred two wry remembrances from close friends. Mel Blanc recalled how Benny came to visit after Blanc was injured in an automobile accident that left him immobilized in bed and encased head-to-foot in a surgical cast. Benny greeted Blanc's wife at the door with the words, "Hi. Is Mel home?" George Burns said, "We never lied to each other. I told him he was the greatest violinist in the world and he told me I was the greatest singer." But if Benny disapproved of sentiment and nostalgia, a mourning nation needed it. President Gerald Ford sent a telegram that spoke of Benny's indefinable yet undeniable ability to lighten the hearts of his countrymen and countrywomen. It read, "If laughter is the music of the soul, Jack and his violin and his good humor have made life better for all men."

Mel Blanc, "the man of a thousand voices," 1964

Of the many other tributes, perhaps the most meaningful came from the man who was Benny's only serious rival for the pinnacle of popularity among America's stand-up humorists. Bob Hope, whose career had been as enduring, as self-mocking, and as symbolic to a nation through turbulent decades as Benny's own, said in farewell, "It is a cliché to say that in times of darkness, Jack Benny brought light with his gift of laughter, making us forget our troubles. For Jack was more than an *escape* from life. He *was* life—a life that enriched his profession, his friends, his millions of fans, his family, his country. Perhaps what made Jack Benny such a great laugh-maker was that he himself loved to *laugh.*"

Jack re-creates one of his wartime USO shows, 1963

FROM VAUDEO TO VIDEO VIA RADIO

BY JACK BENNY

Two TV shows made the world's least-appreciated violinist feel like a television veteran. It's tough work, but he likes it. "After all," he says, "you can't quit when you're 39."

Before my recent television debut, a lot of my colleagues thought I was afraid of TV. They kept saying, "Jack, you're a coward. You're afraid to face those cameras." But I must say they were good sports about admitting they were wrong. After my first show, they all came up to me and said, "Jack, you had a lot of nerve."

Anyway, it's a good feeling to know that the debut phase is finally behind me. For the purposes of writing this article, however, I find that the present stage of my television career puts me in a rather awkward position. I have now completed two TV shows. This is one too many to knock television and one too few to knock radio. I say it's awkward because so long as I'm writing an article, I feel I'm expected to knock something.

Like every other performer who still hadn't made the plunge, I used to spend long hours studying television, analyzing it and theorizing about it from every angle. It was all a waste of time. Actually, doing a couple of shows on TV taught me more about the new medium than I could have learned in ten more years of watching it through all those store windows.

I learned, first of all, that if you're going to do a television show you should keep it to yourself. The minute your plans are known, all your friends generously dedicate themselves to giving you the benefit of their experience.

I made the mistake of announcing my entrance into television several weeks ahead of time. They were all ready for me. When I arrived in New York to start rehearsals, who should be at Grand Central to meet me but Eddie Cantor. Being my friend and having already absorbed the vast experience of two appearances before the video cameras, he felt it was his moral obligation to be the first to explain to me the facts of life in television. All the way through the station, he kept jumping up and down, telling me what to do and what to avoid.

When we got to the cab, Milton Berle was sitting there waiting for us. He said he'd left his rehearsal just to come down and give me some technical advice. And then, in a few thousand well-chosen words, he briefed me on the art of how to close your eyes when getting hit with a pie.

Unfortunately, as Miltie was tapering off, the cab had to stop for a red light on Forty-fifth Street. It was just long enough for Jimmy Durante to jump in with the warning that, "When youse is in television, youse is gotta speak distinkly."

By this time the taxi was so crowded I could hardly read the meter. Fortunately, the three of them were so busy expounding their theories that I was able to slip out unnoticed at Forty-ninth and Broadway.

But that was only the beginning of a siege of helpful advice that didn't let up until the curtain rose on my show. The only ones who didn't have

---

Reprinted from *Collier's* magazine dated March 24, 1951.

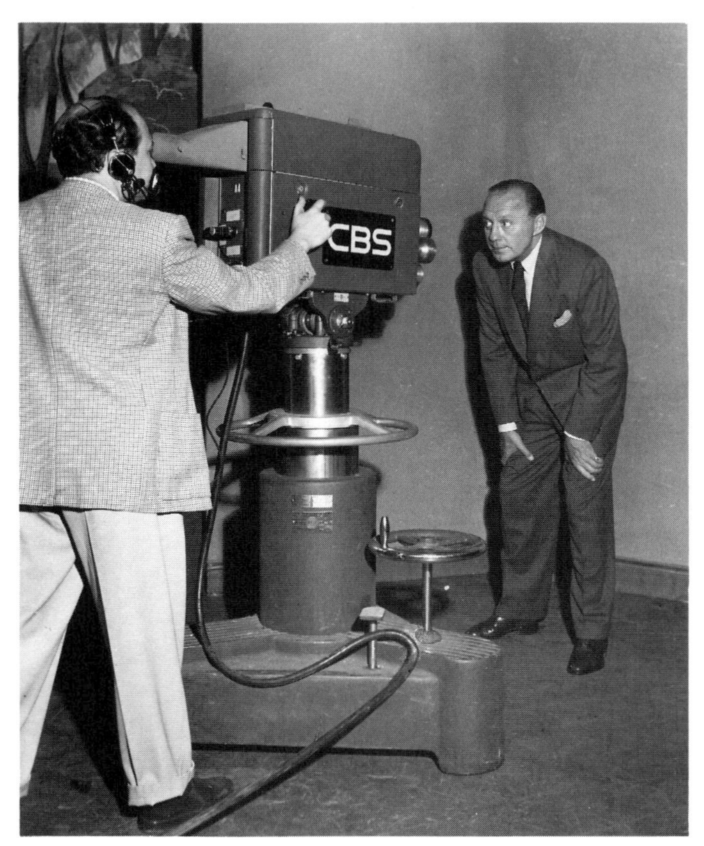

"I'd give a million dollars to know how I look"—Benny's first line on television

suggestions for my first television program were my writers.

Another thing I discovered about television is that there are far too many distractions for the studio audience. On radio comedy shows, we learned a long time ago that the laughter of the studio audience has a direct effect on the home listeners' appreciation of the program. Consequently, everything humanly possible is done to direct the attention of those in the audience to the person who is delivering the lines.

WHY CAMERAMEN SHOULD BE SMALL

On a TV comedy program, the reaction of the studio audience is equally important to its success. But with television, there is not only the frequent distraction of stagehands moving and sometimes dropping props as they get ready for the next scene, but the sets are so constructed that those in the studio inevitably miss half of what is going on. What little they might otherwise see is often obscured by the three cameramen, usually hefty, whose bulk hovers between the studio audience and the performers on stage. Fortunately I had been warned about this condition, and when the time came for me to select a cameraman for my show, my first question was not "How good is he?" but "How much does he weigh?"

The things I have just mentioned are a few of the discouraging aspects of the present television scene. But, on the whole, I was amazed at the phenomenal progress that this infant industry has already made.

I found that the technicians not only have a high degree of competence, but that they face the problems that are constantly cropping up with speed, skill, and imagination. Some of the sets that I saw constructed in a few hours would do credit to a $3 million movie production. The directors, despite a lack of time, space, and facilities, are staging scenes day after day that it would take Hollywood weeks to duplicate.

And the cameramen do more than get in the way of the studio audience. On a live television show, there is no such thing as a retake. It has to be right the first time. And yet, with a very few hours of rehearsal for their benefit, these cameramen somehow manage to shoot even hour-long dramatic shows without noticeable mistakes. If it is true that TV has borrowed from the techniques of movie making, it is also true that the movie industry would do well, even at this early stage, to adapt many of the streamlined methods of television.

Last summer, after fifty-eight weeks of putting the Goldbergs on TV, Gertrude Berg took her production crew to Hollywood to make a feature-length film version of her show. I understand that in the time it took the studio executives to complete their speech welcoming her to Hollywood, she had finished the picture and was back in New York.

It was hard at first for a radio performer like myself to realize the extent to which the entire East, and New York City in particular, has gone for television. In New York these days, a radio has two uses: as a means to advertise TV sets and as a stand to place your beer on while you're watching television. The only thing the people in New York know is TV. It was a little discouraging. The day after my video show, I was walking down Broadway and I heard a woman say to her friend, "There's Jack Benny, that new comic I just saw on television."

But whether it's for better or for worse, in New York nothing can compete with television. On "good" TV nights, attendance at dance halls, night clubs, sporting events, lectures, and every other type of public gathering falls way off. They tell me that the Saturday night of my first TV show, I practically emptied the movie theaters, a feat that hasn't been accomplished since I made *The Horn Blows at Midnight*.

A lot of people are comparing today's television with the early days of radio. I can't see any basis for such a comparison. Nineteen years ago I performed my first radio broadcast. It was done in a small room with no studio audience. The whole proposition was a hit-and-miss affair; twice during the program the transmission broke down. For my efforts I was paid $350.

By contrast, when I did my first TV show, I had a major network behind me. I was given a large studio, a big cast, a full thirty-two-piece orchestra, and I was paid $10,000. In fact, the only similarity between the two experiences was the amount of money the government let me keep. Those who saw my TV show may remember a distinguished-looking man vigorously applauding in the first row. That was Secretary of the Treasury John Snyder.

Incidentally, there were a number of distinguished figures in that first row. The fellow doubled over in fits of laughter was a professional "yakker" we had hired named Ed Sullivan. The man sleeping in the seat next to him was William Paley, chairman of the board of CBS. And the gentleman way over at the end, leaning against the "No Smoking" sign, was Paul Hahn, president of the American Tobacco Company.

I mention the latter two because it was they who were responsible for my going on television.

For several years, at various intervals, the three of us had scouted the idea. It was always the same. We were all agreed that it would be good for me to have a TV show, and that sooner or later I would want to make the plunge. But it had always seemed to me that to go on television, with all its problems, while continuing to do my radio show, might be biting off more than I could chew.

Despite my doubts, Mr. Hahn and Mr. Paley both felt that something could and should be worked out. And last spring, Mr. Hahn assigned his top assistant, Gordon Smith-Heusen, to devote all his time to this project of getting me on television. Mr. Paley did likewise with Mason Higbe, CBS vice-president in charge of Television Exploitation, Studio Facilities, and Comfort-Room Maintenance.

(The characters Gordon Smith-Heusen and Mason Higbe are fictitious. Actually, they are composites of several people named Higbe Gordon, Gordon Smith, Smith Heusen, and Heusen Mason.)

A LONG-DISTANCE CALL ON WASHDAY

Then, about four months ago, it happened. I was in my home in Beverly Hills at the time. It was on a Monday morning. I remember it distinctly because the washing machine had broken down and I was doing it all by hand.

Suddenly, in the midst of everything, the phone rang. It was Gordon Smith-Heusen calling from New York.

"Jack," he began, in a voice filled with excitement, "I just met with Mason Higbe and we decided that you're going to do a television show from New York in three weeks."

"Three weeks!" I gulped. "Does it have to be in three weeks?"

"That's right," he said. "I'll need that long to line up the commercials."

Auditioning for a role with Vincent Price and Irene Dunne, 1953

"But, Gordon—I mean, Mr. Smith-Heusen," I said. "It isn't just the commercials. I've got a lot of problems. What kind of a show do I do? How long should it run? Who do I have on it? How am I supposed to do my radio show in California and a television show in New York? When do I—"

"Pardon me, Jack," he interrupted, "but while you were talking I thought of a cute jingle for a commercial. Now what was that you were saying?"

I told him that I was trying to explain some of the problems I'd have if I were to go on TV so soon.

"I've got an idea," he said. "Why don't you hop a plane and be in New York at nine o'clock tomorrow morning? We'll meet in Higbe's office and thrash out all your problems one by one."

I don't know how I did it, but somehow I managed to catch the next plane out of Los Angeles. And at exactly nine o'clock the following morning I dashed breathlessly into Mr. Higbe's office. Two hours later they arrived for the meeting. I guess they couldn't help being late. They had to come all the way from Long Island.

THERE WERE PLENTY OF ATTORNEYS

It was just an informal gathering, typical of all our dealings together. Mr. Higbe came in with his secretary and six attorneys. Mr. Smith-Heusen was flanked by four attorneys and two vice-presidents, B.H. and G.L. (That's Be Happy and Go Lucky.) I had no one. My agent was in Alcatraz at the time.

Mr. Smith-Heusen opened the proceedings by stating that we were all there to discuss the many problems involved in putting Jack Benny on television three weeks hence. Then he began a masterful discourse on how long the commercial should run. Mr. Higbe broke in with the observation that while the commercials were a problem, we should take first things first. With this thought in mind, he brought up the question of how many ushers CBS could spare for the show.

After a half hour of tense discussion on this vital matter, I felt that it was time I raised some of my problems, so I coughed deliberately. Mr. Smith-Heusen threw me a lozenge and continued talking to Mr. Higbe. This annoyed me. I had important problems to bring up and I was determined to be heard. I raised my hand. Before I could say a word, one of Mr. Higbe's attorneys threatened to sue me.

Three hours later they had not only solved the usher problem, but had established how many puffs Snooky Lanson should take on his cigarette during the commercial and had even reached a tentative agreement on how big the letters CBS would appear on the curtain.

They were already getting up to leave, and I had yet to get a word in. It was now or never. As I helped them on with their coats, I said, "Gentlemen, I came all the way from Los Angeles to—"

Just then Mr. Higbe shouted, "There's the elevator! We'll have to run for it!"

"But, gentlemen," I said, scampering alongside, "what about my problems? I've got to fly back to California tonight."

Mr. Smith-Heusen said he was glad I had mentioned that because he'd almost forgotten. "So long as you're flying back to California tonight," he said, handing me a sheaf of papers, "you can save us a teletype by taking next Sunday's radio commercial back with you." With that he stepped into the elevator. As I watched them go I realized that these two men had something that ordinary men lacked, and I was so happy they had it instead of me.

When I got back to California, the only thing I was fairly certain of was that I had no intention of attempting a variety show. It's not that there aren't some very successful and entertaining shows of this type on television. But I just didn't think I'd be happy coming out on the stage, telling a few jokes, and then introducing the Tallahassee Tumblers or asking the audience to give a warm welcome to Ezra and Abner, the only triple-tongue yodeling brothers in America.

The more I thought about it, the more I was convinced that on television I should try to approximate my radio show as closely as possible. By this, I mean use the same cast, retain the same characterizations, and develop situations similar to what I do on the radio.

For some established radio shows, transplanting themselves to television would be next to impossible. Through the years they have created characters that the listening audience has come to visualize in a certain way. But now they find themselves with actors whose appearance on the television screen does not coincide with the public's impression of those characters. For example, on one radio soap opera, there's a woman of sixty portraying a young ingenue. And I know a man of forty-five who has made a good living doing baby cries.

NO ILLUSIONS ARE SHATTERED

In this respect, I feel that my show is very fortunate. Everyone who has seen Rochester in the movies knows that he looks exactly as we have portrayed him in radio. Dennis Day gives the appearance of an earnest but naïve young adolescent. Don Wilson weighs 230 pounds, so he's all right. Mary is definitely the desirable doll type. And, of course, I don't look a day over 39.

The only one we may have a little trouble with is Phil Harris, who hasn't yet appeared on our TV shows, but may be on a future one. Unfortunately, Phil doesn't look at all like the modest, soft-spoken teetotaler we've portrayed him to be.

Once the decision had been made to use my radio format as a pattern for the television show, I was able to begin thinking about the actual construction of the program. All along, we had automatically assumed that I would do an hour show. Now I suddenly began to have my doubts. I didn't know exactly what it was, but there was something about doing an hour show that didn't feel right.

So for the next three days I watched the film recordings of every big New York television show. And on the fourth day, while sitting in the optometrist's office, it came to me. An hour show, without dancers, tumblers, or other extraneous acts, might be too long. On the other hand, it didn't seem right to go all the way to New York, ballyhoo my television debut all over the country, and then just give the people a half hour of entertainment. So I decided on what I thought was the happy medium of putting on a forty-five-minute show.

Director Ralph Levy with Eddie Anderson and Benny, 1951

Isaac Stern with Mary Livingstone and Eddie "Rochester" Anderson, 1955

As for the cast, in addition to Dinah Shore, whom I was fortunately able to get as our guest star, we planned to use Mary, Rochester, the Sportsmen Quartet, Don Wilson, Mel Blanc, and Mr. Kitzel. At that time, however, Mary was feeling particularly tired from the grind of our weekly radio program and she asked to be left out. She said she'd come along to New York with us, but she promised that while we were working on the TV show, she would just rest. I made the mistake of giving in. Not only did everyone who saw my show miss Mary, but for weeks people constantly blamed me for keeping her off. And worst of all, from the bills she ran up in New York, I found out that she did her resting in Macy's, Gimbels, and Saks Fifth Avenue.

Even by recording one of my radio shows in advance, we were able to allow ourselves only six days in New York. So before leaving Hollywood we wrote the entire TV script, memorized all our lines, and tried to work out every possible detail ahead of time. We thought we had everything calculated down to the minute. But from the moment we arrived in New York and started rehearsals, things began to happen that we hadn't anticipated.

SO THE VAULT SCENE WAS CUT

For example, in the middle of a scene that took place in my Beverly Hills home, there was a sequence in which I was to go down to my vault. In Hollywood, when we wrote this routine, it had seemed hilarious. But now in New York, we found out that there was only one way to do the scene, and CBS refused to let us excavate forty feet under their stage so the cameras could follow me down. They all fought me. The only one who was on my side was Mason Higbe, so I gave up and eliminated the vault.

On the second day, we rehearsed a scene in which I call Dinah Shore on the phone to ask her to appear on the show, she tells me her price is five thousand dollars, and I practically faint from shock, whereupon Rochester throws a glass of cold water in my face. The very first time we tried all this, we went through the whole thing to the director's complete satisfaction. That is, until the part where Rochester throws the water in my face. *This* the director wasn't satisfied with. Every time Rochester threw water in my face, his angle was wrong or the action was out of range, and he'd have to do it over.

Nineteen times I got water in my face before Rochester finally did it right. The director went home happy, the cast went home happy, and I went home with incipient pneumonia. For three days I was in bed with a 102° temperature, and they had to go on rehearsing without me.

Another delay occurred when the stagehands moved the furniture on stage for our dress rehearsal. At this late date we suddenly found that nobody could agree on the appearance of my living room. Should it look like the living room of the cheap miserly character I portray on the radio, with four or five cigarette machines standing around? Or should it be a reproduction of the living room that I occupy in real life? After long argument, we finally decided on the latter, and that's why you saw only one cigarette machine.

Surprisingly enough, when we actually put the show on, there was only one thing that didn't go the way we planned it. But it's just my luck that this one mistake was enough to ruin my grand finale. In order to give the show a smash climax, I had saved my violin solo for the finish. I was going to play the technically difficult but deeply stirring "Hora Staccato." Then, after this selection, and purely for a gag, I was supposed to begin "Love in Bloom," and the audience would get up and walk out on me.

What actually happened was that instead of waiting for "Love in Bloom" they all started to walk out the instant I picked up my violin to play "Hora Staccato." Someone must have given them the wrong signal. By my third note the studio was cleared. And it was such an orderly exit. Women and children went first.

It still hurts me every time I think of all the people sitting at home by their sets and waiting in vain for me to play my violin. I so hated to disappoint all those lovers of good music, people like Jascha Heifetz, Yehudi Menuhin, and Mary's sister, Babe. But I guess I shouldn't feel too bad. With all the troubles we had during rehearsal, I'm probably lucky the show went off as smoothly as it did.

TV IS HARDER WORK THAN RADIO

I hope I haven't created the impression that I feel putting on a television show is necessarily confusing. It's true that a TV program will always require greater effort than a radio broadcast of comparable length and scope. The very fact that all the lines have to be memorized instead of merely read from a script, and that you are acting before a camera instead of just standing in front of a microphone, makes this inevitable. But as with anything else, experience and proper organization can and eventually will simplify the creation of TV programs.

I know that our second show was much less of a trial than the first one. We already had acquired a greater appreciation of the difference between radio and television, and we found it much easier to adjust ourselves to both the possibilities and the limitations of the new medium. Knowing from the start what we wanted to do and what we could do, we were able to go ahead with but a fraction of the problems that we had in our first attempt.

During the second show I was able just to relax and enjoy myself. In contrast to my initial appearance, I wasn't a bit nervous. The bright spotlight that they had shining directly into my eyes may have had something to do with this. It kept me from seeing Secretary Snyder in the front row.

And having Faye Emerson as my guest proved to be even more pleasant than I had anticipated. Miss Emerson is not only as charming in person as she is on her extremely popular program, but her thorough knowledge of television makes her so easy to work with. She knows exactly what to do in front of the cameras. She knows how to walk, she knows how to stand, she knows what not to wear. I'm already looking forward to having her on again in the future. However, the next time I won't bother buying her a corsage. It's a waste of money. On her, where are you going to pin it?

CONTROVERSY OVER LOVE SCENE

The only real problem we had with Miss Emerson was in trying to figure out an advantageous way of presenting her. I was anxious to do something more entertaining with her than the customary dull guest interview, something that would call forth the best of our respective talents. I figured: What could accomplish this better than if we did a romantic love scene together? My writers didn't seem to

Jack gives a golf lesson to Ben Hogan, 1951

The Maxwell rumbles into television, 1952

agree with me. They didn't feel that I would be convincing in a love scene. Finally, we reached a compromise. Half of my writers agreed with me; the other half I fired.

I did the love scene with Faye, but as those who saw the show may remember, after eight minutes of breaking down her resistance, I finally put my arm around her, puckered up—and my other guest, Frank Sinatra, stepped in front of me and kissed her. That took some nerve. I shook the tree and he picked up the apples. It happens every time. You don't pay a guy and right away he takes advantage of you.

In the midst of rehearsals for this second show, I happened to run into Frank Fontaine, whose hilarious portrayal of the character John L. C. Sivoney has become so popular on my radio program. When Frank told me that Mr. Sivoney was "just hanging around New York, not doing anything," we decided to incorporate him into the show, and wrote a scene in which he visits my dressing room.

We previewed the show several days before the actual telecast, and although it played well, I felt that the audience would miss the presence of my valet, Rochester, in this dressing-room scene. So at the last minute I called Rochester in California and he agreed to come to New York immediately.

I'm glad now I had him on the show, but it cost me a fortune: when he got to Azusa, the Maxwell broke down and he had to fly the rest of the way.

The public's reaction to my first two shows was, frankly, a pleasant surprise to me. I received thousands of letters and they were very encouraging. I even got a letter from one group suggesting that I give up radio entirely. I was considering it, until I found out that this was the same group that had suggested I give up television.

Much as I'd like to please everybody, I've already made plans for two more shows this year. Whether I actually do the last of them (which will include Mary) hinges on the increasingly difficult matter of securing network time.

As early as last fall, CBS had sold all its evening TV time for the entire year. Since my few shows this season obviously couldn't be on a regular schedule, there is always a question whether or not CBS can find a time for me.

On my first show, this problem was solved only when my good friend Ken Murray graciously offered me forty-five minutes of his weekly hour. For my second show I wanted to do forty-five minutes again, but it soon became evident that CBS couldn't clear even five minutes for me. This time it was my own sponsor who saved the day. With the co-operation of Messrs. Clifton Fadiman, George S. Kaufman, and Abe Burrows, I was able to go on in place of American Tobacco's Sunday-night program, *This Is Show Business.* It was only a half hour, but if not for Paul Hahn and the aforementioned gentlemen I wouldn't have had even that.

Arrangements have been made for the third show, but I don't know what will happen with the fourth one. If it's a warm day, I may take over the five minutes usually devoted to the frost warnings.

HOW LONG CAN AN ACTOR LAST?

This brings me to a consideration of my future in television and to a vital question that many people are asking and that I have frequently asked myself: Is it possible for any comedian, or for that matter any dramatic actor, to last in television? It is argued that audiences love Cary Grant's clowning in two or three pictures a year, but would tire of Cary Grant if they saw him every week or every other week. Can a comedian who is accepted week after week for ten or fifteen years on radio repeat the same record on television?

Only time will tell, but it is my personal opinion that a comedian can go on year after year in television and still hold his audience. To me, the essential quality of a great comedian is humility and sincerity, and I don't feel that this type of performer will ever tire his audience. I can compare this only to a friend who visits your home once a week. There are some people you're bored with after one visit—or ten visits. And there are others whom you see week after week for years and yet look forward to seeing on each succeeding visit.

For example, I don't think audiences will ever grow tired of the delightful clowning of George Burns and Gracie Allen, the perceptive pantomime of a Sid Caesar, or the warm, earthy humor of the Goldbergs.

THERE ARE MORE RADIO FANS

I feel that in the final analysis, with television as with radio, any comedian who merits an audience will have one. And I'm anxious to accept the challenge. In the immediate future the extent to which I can devote myself to television depends on my radio audience. Despite the popularity of television in the Eastern area, throughout the rest of the country, radio is still the prime source of home entertainment. The latest Nielsen figures reveal that the more popular radio shows still pull between 20 million and 30 million listeners week after week.

As long as I have a fair share of an audience of this size, I'll continue to do everything I can to satisfy my radio listeners.

It is now generally accepted that eventually television will completely dominate nighttime entertainment, at least in so far as the air waves are concerned. The rate of this evolution will depend on such factors as the completion of the transcontinental cable, the quantity of sets manufactured and sold, and so on. It may take two, three, possibly five years, but when the time comes, I imagine that I'll be devoting myself entirely to television.

Looking ahead, I can see myself doing a half-hour TV show every other week or perhaps even every week. The rehearsals may be long and tedious, the shows themselves may be a physical drain, and I'll probably long for the good old days of radio. But what can a fellow do? After all you can't quit when you're 39.

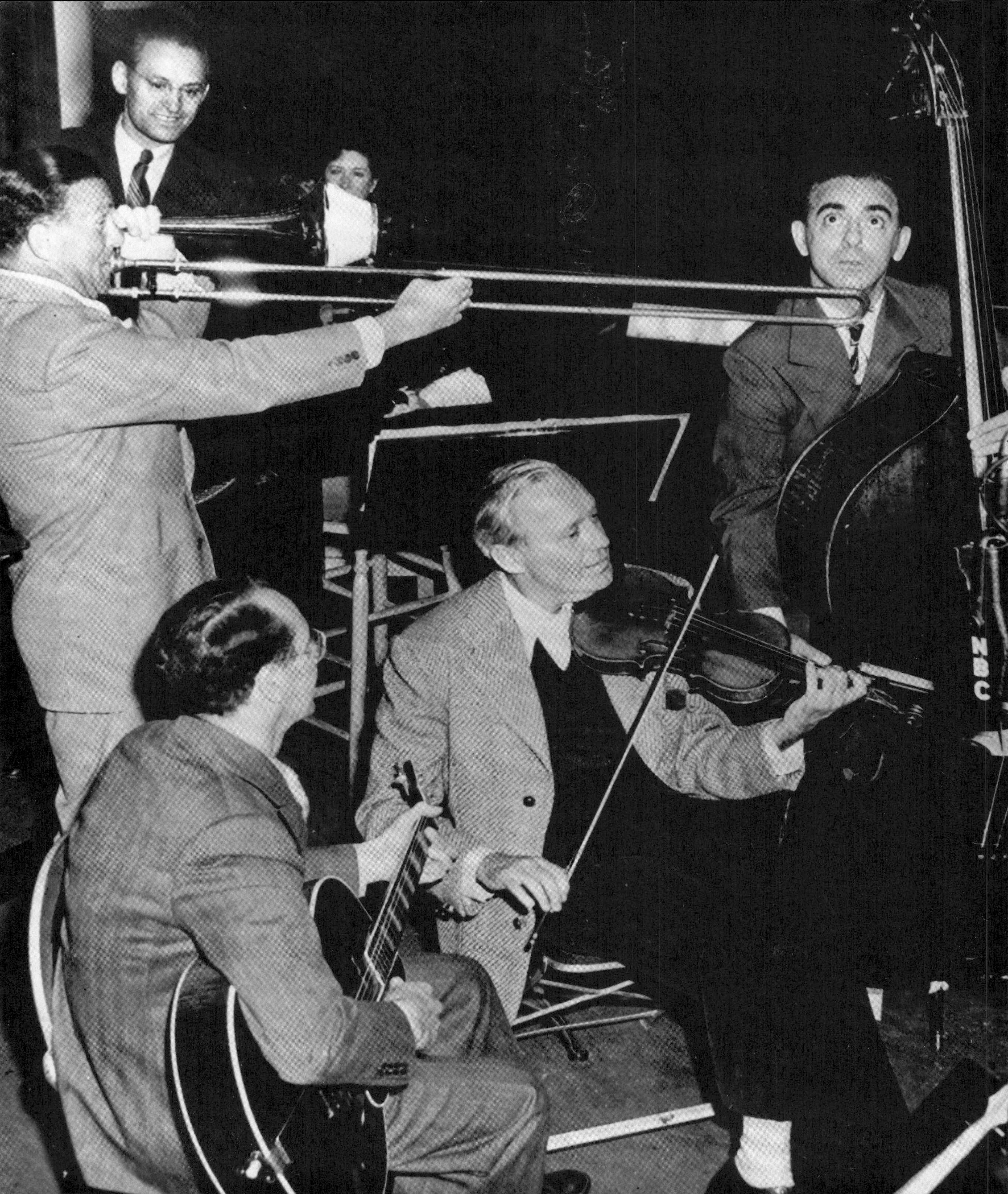
NBC

LENDING CHARACTER TO AMERICAN COMEDY

BY DAVID MARC

The generation that came to know Jack Benny by the sphinx-like perplexities of his television smile probably never realized what an extraordinary radio star the comedian had been and what a profound influence he had on the development of broadcast entertainment. For most of the period otherwise known as the Great Depression, his NBC Sunday night comedy program placed in the top three of the Hooper ratings as America's favorite weekly series. This phenomenal record led Ed Sullivan to write in his New York *Daily News* column of January 18, 1940, "Styles and fashions change in everything; residential sections that are popular one year are unfashionable the next, movie stars and movie directors flourish and disappear from the popular orbit. It is an astounding thing that in a world of flex, [sic] Jack Benny has held this position for seven years, particularly when those years were as unpredictable as 1933–39. . . ."[1]

Jack Benny, like many comedians, came to network radio from the variety stage during the early thirties. Most of his contemporaries, however, arrived with their vaudeville trunks in tow, not aware that the essential qualities of broadcasting militated against the long-term presentation of the "proven" routines that they planned to bring to the airwaves. Benny, who had traveled the tank towns and played the Palace as a pit musician and a comic actor since boyhood, was every bit as much a vaudeville veteran as Eddie Foy or George M. Cohan. But given the opportunity to work in radio, he explored and exploited the indigenous qualities of the new medium to a greater degree than any other radio comic.

Benny astutely realized that the shift in performance space from public stage to private living room had created new aesthetic conditions for comedy: radio took place not in the exotic, elevated world of the theater, but in the home, where the ordinary and even the banal took precedence. Instead of striving to wow the audience with the fantastic, he gradually built an intimate and familiar (if slightly ridiculous) world with "himself" at its center. It was a place that a listener could visit rather than attend. If a stage comic's job had been to dazzle the audience with something rare, the radio comic would depend on a recognizable persona moving through endless variations of habitual themes. Television historians Harry Castleman and Walter Podrazik describe Benny's formal innovation in serial comedy in these terms:

> *This "I-Me-Mine" sitcom approach, as it might be labeled, placed a celebrity into a setting in which the fictional character was almost identical with real life. Thus, the very relaxed and natural personality that listeners had come to enjoy could be easily recognized by the audience in each new show. Top radio comedian Jack Benny had developed this style in the 1930s by playing a comedian, surrounded by a talented supporting cast, trying to stage a radio comedy show aided by a talented supporting cast.*[2]

---

[1]Mary Livingstone Benny and Hilliard Marks (with Marcia Borie), *Jack Benny* (Garden City, N.Y.: Doubleday, 1978), p. 118.

[2]Harry Castleman and Walter Podrazik, *Watching Television: Four Decades of American Television* (New York: McGraw-Hill, 1982), p. 17.

Jack with George Burns and Eddie Cantor, 1948

Rehearsing with Burns and Allen, 1952

Having so thoroughly mastered the art—and the business—of radio, Benny was understandably less than anxious to give up the medium for TV after World War II. "Hold off television. Science be damned! Long live radio!" he told *Variety* in 1946.[3] While his friends and contemporaries, including such stars as Groucho Marx, Bob Hope, and George Burns and Gracie Allen, were abandoning Marconi's wonder in favor of the black-and-white image, Benny kept his Sunday night radio series going until 1955, making it one of the last of the classic radio comedies to leave the air. Benny's move into television was by no means a headlong leap. During the late fifties *The Jack Benny Program* was seen twice monthly on CBS television; it was not until 1960 that the show became a weekly fixture on the network's prime-time line-up.

In his book detailing the history of the Benny program, Milt Josefsberg, a staff writer for twelve years, offered this reflection on the comedian's transition from radio to television:

> *There is no doubt in my mind, and in the minds of others, that Jack Benny was bigger in radio than on television and there are many theories about why this was so. One reason is that he never established the regular family cast on television that he was so identified with on radio. True, he had Rochester and Don Wilson on almost every TV show he did, but Mary, Dennis Day, and Phil Harris made only occasional appearances.*[4]

If Jack Benny was "bigger" on radio than on television, that judgment is only indisputable in a commercial sense. Indeed, his show was never quite the dominant force in the Nielsens that it had been in the Hoopers. (Although Benny had routinely been among the top ten during his twenty-three years on network radio, he posted merely respectable numbers on TV, finishing among the top twenty-five eight times.) Artistically speaking, however, it can be argued that the comedian was never better than when he was mugging for the television camera. Far from nonplussed by the new technology, once Benny decided to commit himself to TV work he developed a unique visual style that generations of comics have revered and imitated.

On radio, Benny had constantly and casually violated the taboo against "dead air" by using long silent pauses to get laughs. Perhaps the best remembered example of this "comedy of silent reaction" was the gag in which a thief pulls a gun on Jack and says, "Your money or your life!" The demand is met by nine seconds of no dialogue and building laughter from the audience. "Look, Bud, I said your money or your life!" says the impatient thief. Jack quickly replies, "I'm thinking it over!" And then there was this scene opener: "A penny for your thoughts, Jack," says Mary. Long silence. "Well, Jack?" asks Mary. Two more beats of silence. Finally, Jack replies, "How about first keeping up your end of the bargain?"

The sheer starkness of the blank radio air created by those silences was obviously not possible on television. But Benny was able to repeat that same stickup routine on television many times by adapting it to the visual medium with facial expressions—especially the famous "Benny stare," a look of pained confusion, directed partly toward the audience and partly at the gods. It survives in public memory as the comedian's most compelling image.

As he had done in radio, Benny forged his television show out of a synthesis of elements drawn from situation comedy and comedy-variety.

---

[3]J. Fred MacDonald, *Don't Touch That Dial! Radio Programming in American Life, 1920–1960* (Chicago: Nelson-Hall, 1979), p. 146.

[4]Milt Josefsberg, *The Jack Benny Show* (New York: Arlington House, 1977), p. 390.

Performing a Tonight Show *parody with Johnny Carson, 1963*

But curiously his most enduring influence on TV comedy can be observed among performers working in a third genre: late-night comedy talk show hosts. As television historian Brian Rose has written, "Like Jack Benny, whose strong influence he readily admits, Johnny Carson [is] a master of the resigned shrug and the quick take when disaster breaks out around him . . . his comedy (like Benny's) often depends on addressing the home audience with the smallest of cracked smiles."[5] It might also be said that Carson's comic abuses of Ed McMahon and Doc Severinsen recall Benny's relationships with his announcer Don Wilson and bandleader Phil Harris.

In a special 1985 issue of *GQ* devoted to examining the historical roots of contemporary American comedy, the editors listed not only Carson, but such desk-and-sofa stars as Steve Allen, Dick Cavett, and David Letterman as heirs to "the mechanics of the Benny inheritance."[6] All developed equivalents of the "Benny stare" to economically express their personal aggravation with onstage occurrences, while creating identity with audiences and picking up laughs in the bargain.

If Benny's personal style of camera address has inspired a grand measure of imitation, the formal narrative technique of *The Jack Benny Program* has also been explored, but less widely. *It's Garry Shandling's Show,* for example, owed much to the Benny program. Making no distinction between self and persona, Shandling plays a neurotic bachelor, surrounded by a group of regular sidekicks, starring in a television show that may or may not be the very one that the viewer is watching. In *Pee-wee's Playhouse,* Paul Reubens, like Benny, never takes off his comic mask, but creates a personal world, peopled with absurd characters, and invites the viewer to visit his bachelor's "home."

The elusiveness of Benny's humor has made it difficult to categorize. Just what was so funny about watching Jack Benny mug and pout and roll his eyes on television is not easy to say. He was not a mime, yet somehow his silences were his most

---

[5]Brian Rose, *TV Genres: A Handbook and Reference Guide* (Westport, Conn.: Greenwood Press 1985), p. 333.

[6]"The Roots of American Comedy: A Family Tree," *Gentleman's Quarterly* 55 (August 1985), p. 145.

"The Benny Stare," 1963

potent jokes. If physical comedy on television is usually defined by the pratfalls and broadly played gesticulations of such clowns as Lucille Ball, Dick Van Dyke, and John Ritter, Benny's quizzical shrugs and exasperated grimaces seem like minimalist flourishes by comparison. Although rarely given to the distensive spectacle of cross-dressing á la Uncle Miltie or Flip Wilson, Benny's polymorphous affectations—the very way he walked—lampooned genteel notions of gender propriety. The violin was his trademark, but he did not use it to punctuate stand-up routines with music in the manner of a Henny Youngman or a Morey Amsterdam. His familiar tags, tight little reactions such as "Well!" and "Now cut that out!" hardly qualify as one-liners in the usual sense. Neither the seltzer bottle nor the custard pie were among his props, yet somehow the repetitive rituals of any given Benny episode—the cheapskate gags, the age jokes, the run-ins with bureaucrats, the confrontations with the one-dimensional caricatures of Mel Blanc and Frank Nelson—never stray too far from vaudeville shtick.

Perhaps it was Benny's casual attitude toward television convention that made him so original a practitioner of the art. TV comedians usually develop their personas in either of two rhetorical modes: the *representational,* in which the performer dons the mask of a fictional character to play out a drama from within the confines of fourth-wall proscenium illusion (i.e., situation comedy), or the *presentational,* in which the comedian addresses the audience as "himself" from within the context of a frankly theatrical space (i.e., stand-up comedy). Phil Silvers, putting on an army uniform to play Sgt. Bilko, is an example of the former. Milton Berle, on the other hand, whether wearing baggy pants, black tie, or evening gown, was always, quite simply, Milton Berle, the emcee, the star of the show, Mr. Television—thus epitomizing the latter. Benny and his longtime friend George Burns were perhaps the only two 1950s TV comics to utterly eschew this type of distinction.

Burns came to television first. Jumping from radio in 1950, *The George Burns and Gracie Allen Show* walked an exquisitely twisted path of narrative permutations. The show opened with George standing down left on the lip of a stage, blowing smoke rings across the fourth wall during the title credits. Over the course of the next half hour, that vaudeville stage would disappear in favor of an archetypal domestic sitcom setting. But in the middle of this sitcom, George might at any moment turn to the camera, gesture for a close-up, and give the audience a little second-person explanation of what was going on in the plot. Sometimes he would even retire to his den to watch Gracie, Blanche, Harry Morton, and Harry Von Zell on TV so he would know what to expect to happen next in the "plot." After the narrative climax, George and Gracie would reappear on the vaudeville stage that had been used to open the show and offer one of their old routines.

Jack Benny, too, worked in both of these modes at once, refusing to recognize any distinctions between life and art. He gingerly sauntered along the border between the "real world" ("Good evening, ladies and gentlemen . . .") and "play world" ("Oh Rochester, would you bring around the Maxwell?") as if the differences between these two realms of consciousness were too trivial for him to take notice of. The Benny show, more so than the Burns and Allen program, opened in the style of a strictly conventional comedy-variety format: Jack comes out onstage in front of a closed curtain to greet the audience, announce his guests, tell a few jokes, and run through a bit of radio patter with Don Wilson or Dennis Day. Although this form of presentation is not seen in prime time too often these days, there was nothing unusual about it dur-

Dennis Day plays Crazy Guggenheim to Benny's Joe the Bartender in a parody of Jackie Gleason's show, 1963

The celebration of Jack's tenth anniversary in radio, 1941

ing the 1950s. Comedy-variety stars such as Red Skelton, Jackie Gleason, and Sid Caesar all opened their shows in similar fashion. After the first commercial, however, Benny took off in a direction that was wholly his own. Whereas the other pioneer TV clowns transformed themselves into sketch characters—Skelton became Freddie the Freeloader or Sheriff Deadeye; Gleason became Ralph Kramden or the Poor Soul; Caesar became the German Professor or Charlie Hickenlooper—Jack Benny played only one character: Jack Benny. It was never quite clear whether he was the star of a comedy-variety show that showcased a sitcom or the star of a sitcom that framed a comedy-variety show.

This insistence on denying the mask of persona even extended to Benny's guest appearances on other television shows, including such sitcoms as *The Lucy Show, Here's Lucy,* and, not surprisingly, *The George Burns and Gracie Allen Show.* His 1967 guest appearance on *The Lucy Show* provides a good example. Although all the other members of the cast, including Lucille Ball, play fictional characters, Jack Benny simply comes on in the role of Jack Benny, a ready-made character. No further explanation necessary. The plot? Lucy works for a bank and she must convince Jack that it is secure enough for him to deposit his money in. She takes him to the vault, where the two slowly sink into a moat of quicksand . . . .

The result of this self-reflexive confusion of art and reality is that no single Benny gag is ever as important—or as funny—as the larger ongoing gag from which it is derived. Any particular joke is a kind of formal gesture used to conjure a grander joke. The contexts that he created over the long haul (egotism, cheapness, and so on) dominated whatever arbitrary content he happened to bump into, an observation that some critics have made about television viewing and that some philosophers have gone to great lengths to make about life itself. This absurd comic environment, which Benny was able to perfect on radio and then to adapt so smoothly to television a quarter of a century later, was a singular vision—precisely the kind of unique eccentric expression that is supposed to be impossible in a "mass culture" broadcasting industry ruled by corporate committees and dedicated to mechanical narrative conventions. Like a network anchorman or a professional wrestler, Jack Benny denied that he was ever playing any character other than himself.

All of this was accomplished with a minimum of visible effort. As George Burns observed:

> *The thing is, Jack fooled everybody . . . . On stage, on radio, in films, and on television, he seemed to be a weakling. He looked fragile with those thin little wrists . . . the way he touched his face . . . his baby-smooth skin. He seemed so vulnerable, you wanted to take him home and adopt him. But you couldn't, because, in truth, he was very strong when he was performing. He was a giant, but he appeared, instead, like a little boy. . . . And he always looked so amazed when an audience laughed at him. His expression would indicate a perpetual question: "Why are you laughing at me?"*[7]

It is all the more ironic that Jack Benny insisted on calling the fictional character he portrayed "Jack Benny" when the star's actual biography is taken into consideration. In so-called real life Jack Benny was a family man—a husband and father. By all accounts he was friendly and generous, relatively easy to work with, and active in philanthropic activities. That being the case, who was this fussbudget Jack Benny, this skinflint bachelor living by himself in a large Beverly Hills house? How

Ralph Levy directs Benny and Dennis Day, 1955

Don Wilson, Dennis Day, and Jack parody teenage music, 1960

did a Jewish comedian, born Benjamin Kubelsky to Russian immigrant parents, manage to play a penny-pinching tightwad—during the 1930s no less—without conjuring the specter of anti-Semitism? Why would a concert violinist who had shared the stage with Isaac Stern and Zubin Mehta make the mockery of his musical talents a cornerstone of his public image? If he was still "Jack Benny" when he was "at home," why was his servant, Rochester Van Jones, played by an actor named Eddie Anderson?

Walter Kerr, the theater critic of the *New York Times,* once wrote:

> *This seems unlikely, but it may have been William Shakespeare who described Jack Benny best. In one of his plays, Shakespeare speaks of a character who waits "like patience on a monument, smiling at grief . . ." No waving hello, no little hop, skip, and jump to the footlights, no mighty flourish from the brass to bring him on. He simply enters like a floorwalker who has just been promoted to the best floor, and he has come, basically, to keep an eye on you. He clasps his hands together as though to say, "What can I do for you?" He is languid and lethal and rueful and baleful and at all times ready to bite his lip in embarrassment, should anything untoward turn up. . . .*[8]

---

[7]Benny et al., *Jack Benny,* p. 91.
[8]Benny et al., *Jack Benny,* p. 231.

CBS

JACK BENNY: OUR TOWN, HIS SHOW

BY PETER W. KAPLAN

"Y'know—Babylon once had two million people in it, and all we know about'em is the names of the kings and some copies of wheat contracts . . . and contracts for the sale of slaves. Yet every night all those families sat down to supper, and the father came home from his work, and the smoke went up the chimney,—same as here. And even in Greece and Rome, all we know about the real *life of the people is what we can piece together out of the joking poems and the comedies they wrote for the theatre back then."*
—The Stage Manager, *Our Town*

"Well!" —Jack Benny

And even if all we know about the *real* life of the people in America is what we can piece together out of the joking scripts and the comedies they wrote for the radio back then, then we know that Jack Benny was great—for there is no comedy from which we can learn more about the American temperament of the twentieth century than Jack Benny's.

For more than forty years, from the Hoover through the Nixon administrations, Jack Benny swished down a street of his conception, a community that was as closely cut to his sensibility as any literary creation; a place immediately identifiable by the psyche and sensibility of its main inhabitant; a society in which people knew each other and interracted with an unapologetic lack of sentimentality; a place where the boss was the victim, the butler was the boss, the announcer was the informed one, the *tenor* had no ego (!), the girlfriend had no illusions, and where the laughs were all built on their own logic. This was Jack Benny's version of *Our Town,* the unharmonious American ensemble where democracy reigned, each voice mattered, and the star was just the Stage Manager—walking us through, presenting life to us ("Here's Mr. Kitzel!"), musing ("Gee . . . I wonder if . . ."), sputtering ("Now cut that out! Silly kid!"), listening ("Oh—really"), absorbing ("No . . ."), and talking to us ("Now, you see folks . . ."). This was Jack Benny, the fullest, most well-written creation to walk through the comedy literature of this era.

The character people called "Jack Benny" was the center of a society that was *One Man's Psyche:* fifty years later we somehow still understand that the show was almost completely subjective, an articulation of how Benny saw the world. This vision continues to teach us to see as well—through his petulance, his idiosyncrasies, his small, sudden warmths—and still evokes a peculiar empathy.

Think of the monologue up top, and put Benny's voice in it: it is not impossible to imagine him playing the Stage Manager in Thornton Wilder's play, as could have Fred Allen or George Burns, because radio's comedy greats were the narrators of American life. (Burns, in fact, said he took the amazing broken-fourth-wall technique of his TV show from *Our Town*—but the Burns and Allen show was finally a show about the ultimate rationality of love, while Jack Benny's show, like Fred Allen's, was about the American community.) In their moment the greatest radio talents talked to us about the things they saw, expressively, gently, after having listened to their neighbors. Just like *Our Town* (1938), radio's brief but brilliant moment of maturity came during this nation's most fervent affirmation of its own system—the time of the late New Deal and World War II—a moment of democratic celebration and of significant tenderness toward and awareness of the power of American individuality. And that awareness was one thing that Benny and Fred Allen, the true masters among radio comedians, shared.

They were brilliant listeners, aware that silence and sound created the contours of radio as light and shadow do in images. In one *Jell-O Program* episode from 1940, Jack's guest was Orson Welles of the Mercury Theatre, and the spoof of the show was that Jack wanted to be a great dramatic actor and do *The Hunchback of Notre Dame* (Welles, in fact, was on the show as a quid pro quo; Benny went on to act in the *Campbell Playhouse*'s radio broadcast of Ring Lardner and George S. Kaufman's *June Moon* the very next Sunday). The joke was that, of course, the cast busted Jack's considerable thespian vanity. But was it only vanity?

The real point is that Benny played Hamlet in Ernst Lubitsch's *To Be or Not to Be*, and it was funny but not implausible; playing himself, he played Hamlet as no one else had, and as no one else would. He was at once narcissistic and unconflicted, the sweet aesthetism and self-love of his violin playing entering his voice—a full range of Benny emotions, all shielded by, as Fred Allen might say, a thin layer of ham. That was for Lubitsch, and if he had ever gotten another shot at a first-rate director—Hitchcock?—there is no reason to believe that he couldn't have wrought from "Jack Benny" something altogether new.

For Benny's humanity—maybe even genius—came from his ability to truly experience the ordinary (he always wanted things to work easily), trying in all events large and small to shape human nature to his own design. Jack Benny's comedy was masochistic: the experience of his comedy was a reactive one. Sometimes with Dennis Day or Don Wilson or Phil Harris, he initiated cruelty, but mostly others pushed him to the limit, a precise boundary that showed his exact persona as clearly as a road map—explicit, specific, sketched. He walked through his formats and persisted in asking

Jack's Town: Dennis, Eddie, Phil, Mary, Don, and Mel, 1947

Jack dreams he's married to Mary (with Joan Benny at left), 1953

questions, though the answers often drove him crazy.

In radio where men walked through talking and talking, he had a great—even astonishing—power of pure absorption. Other comedians hurled their jokes at the audience with the automatic reflexiveness of the assembly line, which is what many accused radio of being at the peak of its commercial power; Benny and his great writers created something else, something that defied the cookie-cutter conformity that constituted much of radio comedy. Almost alone among radio's great stars was Fred Allen when he railed against radio's commercial slavery in the postwar years. But Allen truly admired Jack Benny, for he created intimacy on the air that stood alone among the comedy on the air; in fact, Allen said that it was only Benny who understood that a radio audience should envision a show taking place in a living room, not a theater.

William S. Paley wrote that "Jack understood that comedy was more than just being funny. The audience has to like or at least take an interest in the comedian as a person or as a character in a situation." Paley went on to remember that Benny would explain: "People tune in to me every week not because I have a great show every week. I can't and nobody can. But they get in the habit of wanting to know what I am up to."

His on-air comedy relationships with Don Wilson, Dennis Day, Phil Harris, Mary, and Rochester were dramatic *relationships,* not vaudeville devices. When the Benny ensemble walked out, audiences laughed in anticipation not at the stock stage routines but at the human qualities of Benny's created society. His great team of writers were apparently a sweet group, inspired by the boss's grateful, collegial relationship with them (they were his team, not just his laugh servants) and their memoirs indicate that they adored him. "Some of the best writers in the business were on his staff," Paley wrote. "But he himself possessed a wonderful instinct for what was good and what worked for him on the air."

Benny's repertoire fundamentally had to do with the power and the plight of the individual in America. What he said, it has been pointed out many times, was not necessarily particularly funny; it was how he said it. After all, "Well!" and "Now cut that out!" are hardly assault weapons of comedy. When used by Benny, however, what they meant was something full of nuance, promise, and intimacy. Benny was speaking to us (not at us) and *for* us with considerable affection. From his leap up during the daffy, chaotic radio of the thirties to his crest during the slower, ever-so-slightly more circumspect character comedy of the Homefront and

Fred Allen at the height of his feud with Jack, 1937

Mary's first television appearance, 1951

the sunny, fat postwar days, he struggled for equilibrium in an assaultive world. Both Henri Bergson and Freud missed the Jell-O show, but seemed to understand Benny's approach. Thornton Wilder wrote in an essay on comedy:

> *Bergson says, that we laugh when we see man—man who prides himself on living by choice, reason, and free will—reduced to being a victim of the same forces that govern things. Pretentious man reduced to automaton is funny; a scrubwoman who slips on a banana peel is less funny than a bank president in a silk hat.*
>
> *Freud says our laughter is a release of a grudge against a universe which has since infancy crossed our ambitions and defeated our egocentric wishes. Civilization, however, has educated us; we do not wish, even in our own eyes, to be transparent in the revelation of our wounded pride . . . .*

Benny fit both definitions: his ego made his falls stunning, and his wounded pride became one of our great cultural landmarks. He made fun even of his shortcomings as a comedian. That feeble laugh after a bad joke became one of his favorite techniques. And he allowed the other party, no matter who it was, to get their licks in first—then Benny would respond. He built in silence as part of his routine, and when he stood with others on his stage he never demanded the laugh himself; he absorbed.

For, among the great American comedians, Jack Benny was not only the kindest and most socialized, he was the most understated and internalized as a performer. He was, in short, radio's greatest silent actor, the Zen master of the medium; a fact that proclaimed itself instantly on TV. For a former radio audience finding Benny on television, *seeing* him was reassurance itself—it was "Garbo Talks," only the opposite: "Benny Looks." Of *course* that's what Jack Benny ought to look like; of *course* that's how he ought to hold himself.

So when Benny finally showed up on television on October 28, 1950, he asserted himself with his first line, a huge laugh that immediately reminded his audience exactly who they were with: "I'd give a million dollars to know what I look like." Among the great American comedians, in looking at himself, he told us the most about ourselves, our capacity for self-deprecation as a society (not extensive, but existent), and our gentleness as a people.

What did that *voice* mean? That warm, irritated, Midwestern-tinged instrument, somehow ruling a household in the little duchy called Beverly Hills. Jack Benny surrounded himself with, as it's often commented, a family. It was his cast, and it was us, his audience. He met them and us each week with a genuine intimacy, both casual and familial: "Hello, kids . . . ." This instant warmth was a revelation in a mass medium and part of the genius of Benny's version of American radio. Fred Allen said that "practically all the comedy shows owe their structure to Benny's conceptions . . . the Benny show was like a *One Man's Family* in slapstick." And among that family, he was the recipient of a terrific, battering punishment that was even more brilliantly comic for one reason: it made sense.

Part of Benny's leap was intuiting this amazing notion of the comedy of character—not just gags, not just boffs, nothing illogical, and no desperation for laughs. The waves of verbal and active punishment visited upon him were—consistent to his capitalist ethic—earned. Each week Jack Benny walked through his routine of life. Fred Allen's "Allen's Alley" may have been more literally a place, but it was a more cerebral one; Benny's radio family was exquisitely personal and felt. Like the Stage Manager, Jack would walk through the show unafraid to talk to his audience and break the artificial wall between himself and them.

"Y'know—folks," he would say (and if Benny created his own kind of theater by listening himself, this trait was coupled with his genius for *inspiring listening* as he paused, stammered, and took forever to get where he was going—shepherding the audience with him, no matter where), "in real life I have a seventeen-year-old daughter. Now, on the show Mary Livingstone is my girlfriend—but that's only the show, see—that's just what we—make up. In real life we're—married. And we have a daughter, and between her and Mary, they spent so much money today it made Mr. Bergdorf call Mr. Goodman and congratulate him!"

The first part of that story, the part where Jack has to explain the difference between show business and life to the audience, happened very slowly. And then the second part, the part where the joke and the outrage came in, that was the downhill part of the speech and it would happen very quickly. That was the pattern: Jack listened, absorbed facts from Dennis (about his mother) or Phil Harris (about the wet lifestyle of the band), from Rochester (about his date the night before) or from Don Wilson (about almost anything). Usually Jack would start with the most genial kind of con-

Don Wilson "saying the darndest things" to Art Linkletter, 1955

sideration, sometimes turning to us with a little amusement and repeating a few lines—until something untoward broke in and burgled paradise.

What made it work?

It did not take much to catapult Jack into a story—the character was already there. Benny did something that nobody else would risk—he would risk having no laughs at all for a while, knowing that the payoff with character comedy was greater, that the laugh (when it finally detonated) would not only be explosive, but memorable.

For instance, on one of Benny's early television shows (for New Year's week, 1954) the set-up comes like this: Jack has a hot date for New Year's Eve with an unseen siren named "Gloria"—dinner at Ciro's, dancing at the Trocadero, first-rate Eisenhower-era Hollywood glamour. The band is going to a party at Mary's (Mary is always mysteriously uncaring about Jack's other dates), and the boys ask Jack to bring his date along, but he—resplendent in white tie and tails—says no, but thanks them, and makes a very sincere and sentimental toast wishing them a Happy New Year. No caricature exists here and no gimmicks or reliable devices either—not a "Well!" to be heard; Jack just thanks his band. Then, of course, Gloria calls. She makes her excuse; she can't come, she's dropping Jack, and he, quietly on the telephone, stricken but dignified, is forsaken. The boys beg him to come to Mary's, but Jack—Chaplinesque—wants to be alone for New Year's.

He is alone at night on the town, abused, bruised. Strangers shove into him. The music is melancholy. To complete the injury, the movie marquee, half-obscured, appears to be a French-language version of *The Horn Blows at Midnight* (Benny's 1945 Warner Bros. film that he derided for years). The only reveler who wants to party with Jack is an out-of-town hick with a flask. (It is almost impossible to guess where the sketch is going.) Dejected, Jack seeks New Year's refuge in a coffee shop, where the owner—thrilled to have a formally dressed diner—offers Jack a free meal if he'll sit by the window. Jack is so depressed he even turns *this* down; he only wants a cup of coffee at the counter, where a pleasant, dumpy, middle-aged waitress in a uniform and doily cap asks if he wants anything else. "No thanks, Gloria," says Jack, petulantly.

The laugh that rises from the audience is slow, deep, and genuine. "I told you I couldn't get anyone to cover for me," she pleads. "Forget about it!" says Jack.

Act III in this play takes place at home, where Rochester is about to go out. After a few obligatory jokes about Rochester's prospective night on the town, the butler discovers that Jack's evening has been busted and he insists on staying in with the boss. Jack remembers that there's a bottle of champagne in the refrigerator, and at midnight Jack and Rochester toast each other and sing "Auld Lang Syne." Just two men together, on a stage, in front of a camera.

STAGE MANAGER (Act I, *Our Town*): *So—people a thousand years from now—this is the way we were in the provinces north of New York at the beginning of the twentieth century.—This is the way we were: in our growing up and in our marrying and in our living and in our dying.*

ROCHESTER (from offstage): *That's right, Mr. Benny.*

STAGE MANAGER: *Now cut that out! Good night, folks. I'll be seeing you soon.*

(A violin somewhere plays "Love in Bloom.")

The lights dim.

Jack and Rochester singing "Auld Lang Syne"

Selections from The Museum's Jack Benny Collection

THE CHARACTER BEHIND THE MAN

BY RON SIMON AND RICH CONATY

In 1958 Jack Benny received his first Emmy Award for "Best Continuing Performance in a Series by a Comedian . . . or Any Person Who Essentially Plays Himself." Plays himself? Nothing could be further from the truth. The Jack Benny who performed for so many years on radio and television is an artistic creation, a well-delineated character that subscribes to the rules of his own world.

This Benny character mirrors the foibles of everyman. He is known for his miserliness, his vanity, his insecurity (and being an outsider to the Hollywood community), his execrable violin playing, his "feuding," and his constant exasperation and petulance: he is a veritable catalogue of human failings. Benny's genius as an entertainer was that he used these common flaws to serve his comedy. He revealed to an interviewer way back in 1928 that "if you want the laughs you have to put something in a ridiculous light, even yourself." Benny chose himself as the victim of his jokes, and the audience laughed in delightful recognition as they saw their neighbor's (and their own) shortcomings reflected in him. Around the character, Benny and his team of writers built a repertory company of quirky individuals, each of whom had a role to play to establish and underscore the failings of the leading man. This family of characters (developed on the *Jell-O Program* between 1934 and 1939 with some changes in players over time) included Mary Livingstone, Don Wilson, Phil Harris, Rochester, Dennis Day, Mel Blanc, and Frank Nelson.

By 1940 (the year the *Jell-O Program* peaked in popularity), Jack Benny had accumulated nearly thirty years of experience as a performer, and most of that time had *not* been spent in front of a microphone. Understanding Benny's twenty years as an entertainer before his radio career even began is essential to appreciating what he accomplished on radio and television. It is difficult for those who grew up with television to imagine a time when radio was the dominant form of entertainment. It is even harder to imagine a time when Americans found their entertainment outside their homes and on a vaudeville stage.

Vaudeville was an indigenous American art form that flourished from the 1880s through the early 1930s as the nation's most popular entertainment. Unlike earlier variety shows, which were frequently presented in saloons, vaudeville catered to the entire family—acts worked clean or not at all. The weekly bill consisted of contrasting performers, including singers, actors, animal acts, jugglers, magicians, and monologuists (the forerunners of today's stand-up comics), sometimes presented by a master of ceremonies. At its height, vaudeville ran in over two thousand theaters every day.

Although the joke about who killed vaudeville lingers to this day, death notices for the old form were being written as early as 1915, when motion pictures began to supplant it as America's mass medium. Vaudeville in name continued for decades, but it wasn't the big-time vaudeville of the teens that featured eight to ten acts, two shows daily, reserved seating, and, most importantly, no movies.

Whatever its ultimate fate, vaudeville reigned during the youth of Benjamin Kubelsky, a gifted but lazy young violinist who dropped out of school at thirteen to work with a local band. By his mid-teens

39 Forever

he was in the pit orchestra of the Barrison Theatre, Waukegan's vaudeville house. It was there that Kubelsky met Minnie Marx, who, with her sons and sister Hannah was struggling with "Fun in Hi Skule," a comedy act with music. Julius, Milton, and Adolph Marx had not yet acquired the names "Groucho," "Gummo," and "Harpo," and neither Chico nor Zeppo had joined their siblings. The act was inspired by an earlier classroom routine developed by vaudevillian Gus Edwards. It featured Groucho as Mr. Green, the strict German-accented teacher, Gummo as an ethnic Jewish pupil, and Harpo as "Patsy Brannigan," a stock country bumpkin figure. Minnie Marx was sufficiently impressed with Kubelsky's musicianship to offer him a job as their music director, but Meyer Kubelsky vetoed the proposal. He felt his son was too young for life on the road.

In 1912 eighteen-year-old Kubelsky teamed with the Barrison's pianist Cora Salisbury. The duo, billed as "Salisbury and Kubelsky—From Grand Opera to Ragtime," toured the small-time Midwest vaudeville circuit for a year. During that time Kubelsky changed his name to Ben K. Benny. In 1914, Benny teamed with pianist Lyman Woods in another "dumb" act (meaning no speech), which included comedy in the form of parodies of popular melodies. On September 9, 1917, "Bennie" and Woods opened at New York City's Palace Theatre, the apex of vaudeville, in a show that was headlined by Smith and Dale, who performed their classic "Dr. Kronkite" sketch (and who were the models for the vaudevillians in Neil Simon's *The Sunshine Boys*). Bennie and Woods, following Everest's Monkeys in the unenviable "number two" spot on the bill, played to a nearly empty house. *Variety* characterized the act as a "pleasing turn for an early spot." Later in life, Benny would recall that he bombed at the Palace, but this notice, though not a rave, indicates otherwise.

The career of Bennie and Woods ended following an engagement at Milwaukee's Majestic Theatre in 1918. When the U.S. entered WWI, Benny returned to Waukegan, where he enlisted in the Navy. He spoke on stage for the first time during a camp show, when his violin solo failed to impress the assembled gobs. Benny's first planned dialogue was in *The Great Lakes Revue,* a naval counterpart to Irving Berlin's all-soldier *Yip! Yip! Yaphank.*

In 1919, out of the Navy and back on the vaudeville circuit, Benny worked alone and honed his act. Billed as "Ben K. Benny—Fiddle Funology," he sang and did ragtime violin specialties, but it was his efforts as monologuist "Jack Benny" that began to attract attention. According to *Variety*'s "New Acts" column of January 21, 1921, "Jack Benny has a violin and talk. Mainly talk," adding, "His violin playing is negligible for results." By the end of the year Benny was billing himself as the "Aristocrat of Humor." His comedy was quiet, sophisticated, and unlike the usual vaudeville fare. As Irving Fein reports in his biography on Benny, George Burns recalls that Benny's repertoire already included "cheap" stories and gags about his troubles trying to meet and keep girlfriends. In 1922 Benny worked with singer/songwriter Ned Miller, an employee of Leo Feist, Inc., a Chicago-based music publisher. Publishers would often provide vaudevillians like Benny with complimentary vocalists; the performer could get his act enhanced for free, and the publisher got its songs exposed. Miller recalled that one of the bits he developed with Benny was a naive "kid brother" routine, a vaudeville forerunner of Benny's radio exchanges with Kenny Baker and Dennis Day in the next decade. (In 1958, Miller rejoined Benny as his television stand-in and worked with him until Benny's death.)

During his vaudeville years, Benny also tried the legitimate stage, finding success as a monologuist and sketch comedian in the somewhat bawdy Shubert revue, *The Great Temptations,* which opened on May 18, 1926. It ran for a healthy 197 performances in New York, moved to Chicago in early 1927, then to San Francisco in the summer of that year. During the show's Chicago engagement, Benny married Sadie Marks. When *The Great Temptations* closed, Benny returned to vaudeville with Marks (now "Marie Marsh"), as part of the act. *Variety,* in its review of the duo's 1928 Vitaphone film short *Bright Moments,* noted that Benny gave Marsh "a chance in his act," indicating Benny was willing to share the laughs even at this early point in his career. The review also mentions Benny's subtle comedy and acknowledges his vaudeville renown. Working with and without his wife, Benny was developing a national reputation as a monologuist and master of ceremonies. In a review of a mid-1928 engagement at the Palace, vaudeville critic Larry Lawrence wrote, "An actor who can carry the difficult role of being master of ceremonies at a vaudeville show and not turn into an utter ass and bore the audience has again been discovered.

Benny stars at RKO Theatre, Los Angeles, late 1920s

Vaudevillian Benny with a song by Ned Miller, 1922

He is Jack Benny and you may listen to his drolleries this week." Other 1928 and 1929 reviews allude to Benny's "well-known suavity," note his distinctive walk, and characterize him as a "smart" monologuist.

Like many stars of the stage, Benny's success brought him the opportunity to try that new entertainment form, talking motion-pictures, and he was signed by MGM in 1929. He appeared in *Chasing Rainbows* and *The Hollywood Revue of 1929. Hollywood Revue* (in which the song "Singin' in the Rain" was introduced) was a very successful picture. Benny's performance, as "Filmland's first Master of Ceremonies," according to one review was well received. The *Buffalo Times* declared, "Jack Benny walked away with announcing honors." A mention in the *Brooklyn Times* clearly indicates another feature of Benny's radio character was already in place: "He suffers considerably at the hands of his playmates, who affect not to appreciate his stuff."

In addition to stage and screen, a third medium was burgeoning by 1929—radio. Benny's ear-

Freeman F. Gosden and Charles J. Correll

liest documented radio appearance was a result of his movie work, when, on Wednesday, August 7, 1929, he participated in the *Hollywood Midsummer Jubilee* at the Hollywood Bowl broadcast over KFWB. Also present that evening were Al Jolson, Paul Whiteman and His Orchestra, and Benny Rubin, who worked with Benny through 1970. Benny would stay in Hollywood and make one more movie called *The Medicine Man,* for Columbia. The movie was a failure, so he was more than happy to accept producer Earl Carroll's $1,500-a-week offer to appear in the next edition of his *Vanities* back on Broadway.

The *Earl Carroll Vanities* opened on June 1, 1930. Like *The Great Temptations* it was a musical-comedy with a certain amount of risqué material. Outside of Benny's participation, the show was critically lambasted. Writing in the *New Yorker,* Robert Benchley acknowledged that the show was not as good as Carroll's two previous efforts, but "Mr. Benny has long been a weakness of this department," another testament to Benny's vaudeville reputation. Percy Hammond, writing in the *Herald Tribune,* characterized Benny as "a sleepy comedian [who] draws his japes smilingly." *Vanities* managed to sustain itself for an adequate run, but it was less successful than Carroll's 1929 production. Benny was unhappy in the show, and he was not granted a release from his contract in order to join a Fred and Adele Astaire revue. Several biographies on Benny state he did not tour with *Vanities* following its Broadway engagement (choosing instead to try a career in the newest medium captivating the country, radio), but Benny was with the show in Chicago when it opened at the Erlanger Theatre on November 15, 1931. Perhaps the reason this tour is not mentioned is because Benny was not particularly well received. According to Charles Collins of the *Chicago Daily Tribune,* "The sketches represent the Broadway sense of humor, dealing with its favorite subject, which is smut, in a way that fails to be clever." As for Benny, "He acts in the sketches and serves as Master of

The star of The Fleischmann Hour, *Rudy Vallee*

Ceremonies, and is useful without being impressive." This final tour with *Vanities* only delayed Benny's destiny, and his dissatisfaction with the show and life on the road strengthened his resolve to turn his considerable talents to radio.

THE RISE OF RADIO

When Benny arrived on network radio in 1932 with the *Canada Dry Program* he was joining a cultural force less than ten years old. The rise of radio in the United States is a complex story with many threads reflecting different interests and perspectives. One thread that is important to understanding Benny's career starts with Charles J. Correll and Freeman F. Gosden, employees in the Chicago office of the Joe Bren Company, a firm that supplied everything but the performers for local theatrical productions and carnivals. Both sang and in their spare time they began creating harmony routines. In the spring of 1925 the pair took their "songs and chatter" act to WEBH, which broadcast from Chicago's Edgewater Beach Hotel, where they worked for meals. Following stays in Columbus and St. Louis, they were offered staff positions at WGN, the radio station of the *Chicago Tribune.* It was there they popularized the characters of *Sam 'n' Henry* in a daily "comic radio serial," the forerunner of situation comedy, performed by these two white actors using broad black dialects. At the time of their radio debut, blackface acts were still popular in vaudeville and on the legitimate musical-comedy stage. Even minstrel shows, which had peaked before the turn of the century, continued to exist well into the 1920s.

Following hundreds of ten-minute episodes, the team moved to the *Chicago Daily News*'s WMAQ, where *Sam 'n' Henry* was rechristened *Amos 'n' Andy* on March 19, 1928. They were enormously popular. In addition to a daily newspaper comic strip authored by the pair, Correll and Gosden were booked for five thousand dollars weekly to appear at Chicago's Balaban and Katz theater chain. Although their show was distributed by disc to numerous local stations in an early form of syndication known as a "chainless chain," *Amos 'n' Andy*'s live national debut came via NBC's Red Network on August 19, 1929. At its peak *Amos 'n' Andy* may have been the most popular radio program ever broadcast: in 1931, its nightly audience

Gosden and Correll as Amos 'n' Andy

was estimated at 40 million. While Correll and Gosden did not come out of vaudeville, their radio serial picked up one of vaudeville's traditions—the stock characters of sketch comedy—and developed it into the early situation comedy. Their success in this led to the launch of other weeknight "slice of life" serials, such as NBC's *The Goldbergs* and *Myrt and Marge* on CBS.

Other than *Amos 'n' Andy,* the weekly hour-long *Rudy Vallee Varieties* was an immensely popular show that premiered on NBC on October 24, 1929. According to Erik Barnouw, appearing on the Vallee show "had replaced the Palace Theatre as the prestige booking in vaudeville." It was the first major network variety hour and its star was the first created by radio itself, for Vallee had spent little time on the vaudeville circuit. (For the first ten years, the program was sponsored by Standard Brands and popularly known as *The Fleischmann Hour;* later it became *The Royal Gelatin Hour.*) Unlike its contemporary broadcasts such as CBS's *Old Gold Program,* starring Paul Whiteman's band, the emphasis on Vallee's show was as much on the guest artists as on Vallee's crooning. Eddie Cantor, with two decades of stage experience behind him and periodic radio appearances dating back to 1921, greatly enhanced his national reputation as one such guest on *The Fleischmann Hour* on February 5, 1931. Cantor was rewarded with his own *Chase and Sanborn Hour,* a comedy-variety show, on September 13.

The death of vaudeville and a corresponding Depression-driven downturn in the legitimate theater may have been the best things that ever happened to early radio. It created a tremendous talent pool from which the networks (and Hollywood) could draw. Increasing the demand for vaudeville-grown talent even further was a slump in the ratings for *Amos 'n' Andy,* which created room for other shows to flourish. Burns and Allen, following appearances with Cantor and Vallee, began their CBS series in February 1932. After a handful of guest appearances, Fred Allen was heard for Linit Bath Oil beginning on October 23, 1932. Dramatic and adventure shows were tried, but comedy and variety were the entertainment of popular choice.

Such was the lay of the radio landscape when *Vanities* finally closed and Jack Benny was out of a job. According to Mary Livingstone, he was frustrated that relatively unseasoned performers like Vallee and Correll and Gosden were suddenly coast-to-coast attractions. Beyond that, Benny was well aware of the phenomenal success that vaudevillian and musical-comedy star Eddie Cantor was enjoying over the ether. A 1936 *Radio Guide* article stated Benny was so impressed by the on-air efforts of another former vaudeville violinist, bandleader Ben Bernie, that he briefly led an orchestra as a route to radio. Mrs. Benny believed her husband had a marvelous voice for radio and urged him to be involved with the medium.

Gracie Allen and George Burns, 1932

Some accounts list a May 1931 Benny appearance with Ed Sullivan (the *New York Graphic*'s Broadway columnist) on WHN, a local New York radio station. That date, which falls between the New York and Chicago runs of *Vanities,* was cited in the 1941 and 1951 radio salutes to Benny's tenth and twentieth anniversaries on radio. On March 29, 1932 Benny made his first significant, confirmed radio appearance on Sullivan's *Broadway's Greatest Thrills,* a gossip and interview program sponsored by La Gerardine on CBS. Although the show was unscripted, Benny's remarks were prepared by Al Boasberg, who sold jokes to Benny beginning in 1926 and coauthored his initial MGM efforts. No recordings of the program are known to exist, but Benny's opening words, "Ladies and gentlemen, this is Jack Benny talking. There will be a slight pause while you say, 'Who cares?' " are frequently quoted. More indicative of Benny's future radio work are some of his other comments. He already characterizes himself as a Hollywood outsider. Referring to Greta Garbo, Benny says, "She and I were great friends in Hollywood. She used to let me drive her car around town. Of course, she paid me for it." The last part of the joke indicates the accentuated stinginess that is a part of his act. Benny also claims to be younger than Garbo's recent costar, Robert Montgomery. "That is," he says, "I'm younger than Montgomery & Ward." Even before he had his own radio program, Benny jokingly displayed an insecurity about his popularity and kidded about his age, cheapness, and exclusion from Hollywood, thus confirming that he brought much of his character with him from the stage.

Benny's appearance with Ed Sullivan was extremely well received, and he was signed by Doug Coulter of N. W. Ayer to be the host of a radio series sponsored by Canada Dry Ginger Ale, whose chief competitor, Clicquot Club, had been on the air since 1926. The twice weekly *Canada Dry Program,* which headlined the orchestra of George Olsen, debuted on sixteen stations of NBC's Blue Network on Monday, May 2, 1932. The character of Mary Livingstone debuted on the July 27, 1932 *Canada Dry Program.* Mrs. Benny portrayed a brash and flighty Benny fan from Plainfield, New Jersey. Although her role would develop over the next few years, the fictional New Jersey birthplace would endure. She made a handful of appearances over the next three months but did not become a permanent member of the cast until the following year.

Eddie Cantor broadcasting in 1933

The *Canada Dry Program* moved to CBS on November 17, 1932. The December 17, 1932 *New York Sun* stated, "Benny's breezy style and the informal continuity of the program" contributed to his radio success. However, his success lasted only until January 26, 1933, when the program left the air. The February 4 *Sun* claimed that the decision was Benny's. Mary Livingstone recalled that Benny was fired because Canada Dry didn't like him poking fun at their beverage. Right from the beginning, Benny's approach to his product was a major departure from radio convention. Although Ed Wynn is often named as the pioneer of weaving comedy into his sponsor's messages, his debut as Texaco's "Fire Chief" took place only six days before Benny's first broadcast. NBC's Thursday evening *Lucky Strike Hour* is a good example of the customary treatment of commercials at the time. Like the *Canada Dry Program,* it was an amalgam of dance music and

Jack and Mary at the time of the Chevrolet Program, *1933*

comedy, but its commercial announcements were insulated from the entertainment, and the performers, including Jack Pearl's Baron Munchausen, made no reference to the sponsor.

Benny was back on NBC on March 3, 1933 with a time slot (Friday night at 10:00), announcer (Howard Claney), and sponsor (Chevrolet) all inherited from Al Jolson, who had walked off his series with eleven weeks remaining in the season. In the course of the *Chevrolet Program,* writer Harry Conn introduced many elements that would be developed on Benny's subsequent series for General Tire and later emerge fully on the *Jell-O Program.* Benny, not the orchestra, was undoubtably the star of the show, and Mary Livingstone was now a permanent part of the ensemble. Tenor Frank Parker was the first vocalist to be valued as much for his personality and his relationship to Benny as for his singing. Parker, Livingstone, and orchestra leader Frank Black needled Benny about his stinginess, the first of Benny's traits to be institutionalized. Benny's ineptitude on the violin was also increasingly addressed. Movie parodies became a regular feature, and guest stars, such as Edith Evans and Edward G. Robinson, were used frequently. Announcer Howard Claney (and later Alois Havrilla) continued the novel practice of integrating the commercial into the program.

In February 1934 Jack Benny was chosen as America's favorite radio comedian in a survey conducted by New York's *World-Telegram.* Despite the honor, Benny was fired by Chevrolet. Network files indicate a "change of talent" to Victor Young and His Orchestra beginning on April 8. General Motors's president, William F. Knudsen, felt that more cars could be sold with a music-only series. Although the decision was rescinded, Benny had already accepted an offer from the General Tire and Rubber Company. Five days after his final *Chevrolet Program,* Benny was back on the air.

Although it ran only five months, the *General Tire Revue* is a milestone in the development of the Benny program. Many episodes are strikingly similar to the classic Jell-O programs. Don Wilson was heard for the first time as Benny's announcer and foil. Benny returned to a "name" bandleader, Don Bestor, and "Play, Don!" became the first Benny catchphrase to become well known: in *A Night at the Opera,* Groucho Marx uses "Play, Don!" to cue the opera's conductor. Bestor's character was the Oxford-accented know-it-all with a fondness for multisyllabic words. (Jimmie Grier and His Orchestra was used for Benny's increasing number of Hollywood-based broadcasts, as Benny's radio success re-ignited his film career.)

Story lines on the *General Tire Revue* frequently took the audience beyond the confines of a radio studio—on May 11, 1934, Benny visited Don Wilson's mother and the next week Benny and Mary Livingstone traveled to Frank Parker's home. An important member of the early Benny ensemble, comic dialectician Sam Hearn, made his debut as Irving C. Schlepperman, an ethnic Jewish character, on the August 3 program. Such exaggerated dialects were a vaudeville staple. Schlepperman always greeted Benny with "Hullo, Strayngér," and the expression caught on. The same broadcast featured a fictionalized in-show rehearsal, a plot device used repeatedly through the decades into Benny's television years. These fanciful behind-the-scenes vignettes addressed the public's fascination with the new medium.

Benny's next sponsor was Jell-O. His first broadcast for Jell-O originated from NBC's Studio 3A on Sunday, October 14, 1934. It was the first time he was heard in the 7:00 E.S.T. time slot he would occupy for the remainder of his radio career. His competition was Alexander Woollcott's *Cream of Wheat Program* on CBS. By this time, everything associated with Benny's show was news—he was a radio star. To promote the new show, Benny, Mary Livingstone, Frank Parker, and Don Wilson appeared on NBC's *Radio City Party,* a concert music program sponsored by RCA, and Benny was the guest on General Foods's popular *Maxwell House Show Boat,* featuring the original *Show Boat* star, Charles Winninger.

In reviewing Benny's Jell-O premiere *Variety* noted "the deft way [Benny] went about weaving each of the principals into the proceedings." The balance of the review focused on the adroit handling of the program's formal commercial elements: the collegiate cheer spelling out the word J-E-L-L-O, and a newsboy shouting, "Extra! Extra! The new Jell-O has extra rich flavor." Finally, it congratulated General Foods for the clever way it managed a plug for its Wednesday night *Log Cabin Syrup* program.

Harry Conn was the principal author of the *Jell-O Program* from its inception. *Variety* noted Conn's efforts in its review of Benny's September 29, 1935 season premiere, "Conn's method is to first establish his characters, then build his laughs directly through or with the character itself." As an example, it pointed to the way in which laughs were extracted from the mention of the show's new bandleader, Johnny Green. (The Harvard-educated Green, composer of "Body and Soul" and other hits, took over the condescending bandleader role played by Don Bestor.) *Variety* also praised Conn for the blending of his writing style with Benny's delivery. "No better example of perfect actor-writing mating is to be found in show business. Conn writes the way Benny talks, and vice versa." Two writing teams, Bill Morrow and Ed Beloin, and Howard Snyder and Hugh Wedlock, Jr., were Conn's permanent replacements by the launch of the fall 1936 season. One source claims that three-hundred-pound gag man, Al Boasberg (who wrote Benny's remarks for his 1932 Ed Sullivan debut), was paid $1000 weekly to shore up Benny's scripts.

The arrival of boyish vocalist Kenny Baker in November 1935 and bandleader Phil Harris on October 4, 1936 accelerated the formulation of the classic Benny ensemble. Baker was a relative unknown when he joined the program; his pliant character was Harry Conn's creation and a limitless source of exasperation for Benny. Harris, though, by virtue of his previous radio and film work, was a nationally known personality. However, his big entrances and the gags about his alleged drinking, gambling, and supposed illiteracy were the program's invention. The addition of Harris also reflected the national craze for swing music, and the Harris orchestra, though not the equal of Benny Goodman's, did successfully emulate the new sounds and kept the Benny show hip. Also in that 1936 season, Benny's musical ineptitude was the starting point for the good-natured feud between himself and Fred Allen. (See pages 128–153 for a discussion of the feud.) It became a guaranteed laugh even on Benny's professed dramatic roles on *Lux Radio Theatre* and *Campbell Playhouse.*

Phil Harris and Rochester, 1941

Like Jack Benny, gravel-voiced Eddie Anderson came to radio with decades of stage and screen experience behind him. Before joining the cast of the *Jell-O Program,* Anderson had a leading role in the film version of *The Green Pastures.* He was first heard by radio audiences in March 1937 as an anonymous Pullman porter on a Hollywood-bound train after Benny's New York encounter with Fred Allen, and he assumed the role of Benny's valet, Rochester Van Jones, on June 20. With the exception of Louis Armstrong, who was the star of a short-lived series sponsored by Fleischmann, Anderson was network radio's first regularly heard black star.

Anderson's early performances were marred by the slow talking and subservient manner typified by Stepin Fetchit, and, in fact, his character compares himself to the well-known black actor on that March 1937 show. On the first program naming Rochester, Benny asks Anderson if he has finished pressing his pants. "Yessah," he replies, "Dey is done to a crisp." Rochester's diction was upgraded by the following season, and eventually he earned a large number of his laughs by his clever use of language. A pawn shop, for example, was "Three-ball Social Security." Nevertheless, in his initial years Anderson's character was burdened with such period racial stereotypes as gambling and a fondness for liquor and the ladies. Characteristics, interestingly enough, he shared with Phil Harris. Unlike other Benny cast members, however, he was rarely heard as a guest on other broadcasts and was never rewarded with a show of his own. He wasn't even billed at the opening of the program until the 1941 season.

Though he literally shared the stage with the cast, for the most part Anderson was aurally isolated. Perhaps due to the housebound nature of his valet role as much as his race, Anderson was kept apart and his lines were usually "phoned-in" from somewhere. Far less defensible was the extension of this practice to a major black guest star, Louis Armstrong, when he was on the May 9, 1943 *Grape-Nuts Program.* Two weeks earlier, Benny had lost fifty dollars on "Burnt Cork," Rochester's horse (and the means by which white performers "black up") in the Kentucky Derby. Rochester is hiding on Central Avenue, the black section of Los Angeles, and meets Armstrong at the "Mississippi Barbecue Palace." Whether by accident or design, by placing Armstrong in Rochester's context he was segregated from the white cast: Armstrong's only lines with Benny are over the phone.

Rochester's undeniably hilarious exchanges with Benny reflect America's evolving attitude towards its black citizens. In his volume on Benny, Milt Josefsberg cites a February 1950 incident as clear evidence of the improvement in Rochester's treatment over time. Benny was visiting New York for the launch of the American Heart Association's fund drive and was to broadcast on February 5 and 12. Due to illness, the writers were unable to finish the script for the first program, so portions of the December 15, 1940 *Jell-O Program* were, in Josefsberg's words, "shoved in as an emergency measure." Rochester has disappeared upon arriving in New York, and Benny is determined to "find out once and for all whether he's California's Ambassador to Harlem or working for me!" Benny calls a number of establishments, such as the "Harlem Social, Benevolent, and Spare Ribs Every Thursday Club," in search of his valet. The broadcast was condemned by the *Los Angeles Sentinel,* a leading black newspaper, which declared, "The Harlem experience dished up clichés and horse play that we had supposed had died a quiet and unmourned death a generation ago." The furor, however, did not prevent another invocation of the Rochester-as-runaway theme eight months later, when preparations for another New York trip included Benny's warning to his valet not to "run off as soon as we get there!" and Rochester's boast, "One phone call from me and it's Mardi Gras in Harlem!"

Perhaps because his role was so tied to Benny's, Rochester, like his "boss," almost never stepped out of character. Although Eddie Anderson made records, did theater tours, and appeared in more than one dozen movies during his radio years, these facts were seldom, if ever, mentioned on the air. This is in sharp contrast to the rest of the cast, where professional matters (Harris and Day's own programs and theater dates, Wilson's other announcing jobs) and even personal ones (Phil Harris and Don Wilson's marriages, Dennis Day entering the Navy) were often incorporated into the program. Even Mary Livingstone was billed as "Mrs.

Jack surrounded by Jell-O's "six delicious flavors," 1938

ORANGE
RASPBERRY
STRAWBERRY
CHERRY
LEMON

Jell-O print ad, 1936

Benny" on her infrequent guest shots. Again, it is difficult to establish how much of this was racially motivated and how much was attributable to his role. Given the logic of the program, bandleader Harris and tenor Day *should* have outside jobs, but Rochester was Benny's servant—it would not make sense that he would be in a movie, unless it was in the company of his employer. Fortunately, television would make fuller use of Anderson's talents.

The season following Rochester's arrival found Benny second in popularity only to Edgar Bergen and Charlie McCarthy. The October 24, 1937 *Jell-O Program* is typical of Benny's shows at this time. In the episode Benny has traded in his Stanley Steamer for a new car, a Maxwell. Kenny Baker and the rest of the cast needle their boss about this wreck of an automobile, a symbol of his cheapness. A parody of Twentieth Century-Fox's *Wife, Doctor, and Nurse* features Don Wilson as a patient whose symptom is reciting the six flavors of Jell-O. Sam Hearn as Schlepperman, still a popular featured player on the program, is also heard. Hearn was the first cast member to export his Benny show character to other radio programs. On an October 1938 appearance on *Fibber McGee and Molly,* Schlepperman characterized himself as "a fugitive from six delicious flavors."

When Dennis Day joined the cast on October 8, 1939, the last of the show's principal players had arrived. The March 17, 1940 program exemplifies the period. Following an up-tempo orchestra number and Don Wilson's initial Jell-O mention, Benny is heard on the phone with that evening's guest, Orson Welles. Don Wilson, who had assumed the know-it-all role in addition to his commercial duties, characterized Welles as "a pretty smart youngster." Phil Harris, consumed by his own braggadocio, is flattered when Welles finds him "amusing in his own barbaric way." The cast was so solid at this time that the absence of Mary Livingstone went unnoticed. Shortly after this broadcast Benny was asked by the *New York Times* to explain his enormous success. "What we really try to do is take the *Amos 'n' Andy* formula, *Easy Aces,* or any good serial, make it broader and depend more on jokes. You can't go wrong with that formula. It is taken from life," said Benny.

Mel Blanc and Frank Nelson, both of whom began working with Benny in the 1930s, were heard with far greater frequency beginning in the early 1940s. Blanc was first heard as the menacing growl of Carmichael, the polar bear that lived in Benny's basement. Subsequent programs exploited Blanc's growing fame as the cartoon voice of Bugs Bunny and Porky Pig. Later in the decade he was the railroad announcer ("Anaheim, Azusa, and Cucamonga!"). He was first heard as Benny's violin teacher, Professor LeBlanc, in April 1945. These hilarious lessons with LeBlanc's excruciatingly inept pupil (and the inevitable problems he had getting paid for them) were heard for the balance of the program's run. Mel Blanc's "Little Mexican" Sy (with a sister Sue who sewed) was introduced on a May 1949 parody of *The Treasure of the Sierra Madre.* The character was not unlike Blanc's earlier "José" from Judy Canova's program and "Chico" from *The Cisco Kid.* What made a relatively slight piece of material so delightful was the effect it had on Benny. Audiences could hear, and later see, Benny doubled-over with hysterics. Frank Nelson, characterized by a squealling "Yeeeeeesss!" regardless of the role, played a myriad of unctuous and generally unnamed characters, but is best remembered in two roles: the man behind the ticket window Benny battled in numerous railroad station encounters and the hostile floorwalker Benny met on his annual Christmas shopping broadcasts.

The memorable Benny catchphrases "Well!" and "Now cut that out!" also began to be heard with increasing regularity in the 1940s. Benny also exploited pauses to greater and greater comic effect, as on a January 1943 guest shot with Burns and Allen. After Benny fails to convince the couple to order the Brown Derby's specialty of the house, crackers and milk, they order pricier fare. The waiter arrives with the bill: "Here's your check. That'll be $10.30." There is a full ten seconds of silence, which Benny breaks with, "Well, somebody say something." "That will be $10.30," repeats the waiter. "You shut up!" screams Benny. George Burns doesn't want the check either, declaring, "If you let me pay this check, you're a low, miserable, conniving miser, and I'll never speak to you again as long as I live." There's a nine second pause punctuated by Benny's "Well!" and followed by a huge laugh. Benny says he has a few words for Burns: "Pay the check!"

Long after Benny was in any real danger of cancellation, his character fretted about the sponsor, displaying the insecurity that characterized one side of his persona. Near the close of the 1941–42 season, Benny panics when he learns he will no longer be broadcasting for Jell-O. He figures his career is over until he discovers he is only switching products, not sponsors.

The sponsorship switch was about the only change in the program during the early years of World War II. Although Benny, like Bob Hope, frequently took his program to military bases, his writers—Bill Morrow and Ed Beloin—were so protective of the format they refused to change it to accommodate GI audiences. In the fall of 1943, a new writing team, made up of John Tackaberry, George Balzer, Milt Josefsberg, Sam Perrin, and, briefly, Cy Howard, joined the program. *Variety*

Benny with his writers Ed Beloin and Bill Morrow, 1939

noted the change, characterizing the team's initial effort "as explosively entertaining as anything turned out in the heyday of Ed Beloin and Bill Morrow." The new group was willing to juggle the format for its location shows, and wartime themes were increasingly heard in the studio programs.

The 1944 season saw Benny's final change in sponsorship. He was signed by the American Tobacco Company to promote Lucky Strike cigarettes. With the move came an increasingly formal approach to the commercials. Don Wilson, with help eventually from the Sportsmen Quartet, handled the in-show spots, but other announcers, as well as the Lucky Strike "auctioneers," were heard at the beginning and end of the broadcasts in commercials running as long as a minute and a half. George Washington Hill, American Tobacco's president, was known for meddling in the shows he sponsored. He also espoused the view that commercials should irritate. The commercials on the Benny program were made to sound more like *Your Hit Parade,* another show sponsored by Lucky Strike. In spite of a wartime cigarette shortage, American Tobacco stayed active in radio, if only to keep its brand names before the public. That first *Lucky Strike Program* also permanently enshrined "Love in Bloom" as Benny's theme, although he had been associated with the song since December 1935.

The first half of the 1940s saw Benny fall from first place into sixth place in the ratings. Not only was he being beaten by such radio perennials as Fibber McGee and Molly and Edgar Bergen and Charlie McCarthy, but he had fallen behind Red Skelton, a relative newcomer to the medium. The writers conceived the comical "I Can't Stand Jack Benny Because . . ." contest as a ratings booster. It ran from December 2, 1945 to January 27, 1946, when the winners were announced by Fred Allen. The promotion generated 270,000 entries and saw the series rise to fourth place in the ratings.

Fibber McGee and Molly (Marian and Jim Jordan), 1940

Another scripted device to help the show's ratings was the introduction of film stars Ronald Colman and his wife Benita Hume. They were first heard on the *Lucky Strike Program* in the midst of the "I Can't Stand Jack Benny Because . . ." broadcasts. As leaders of Hollywood's British film colony, they symbolized the movie industry's fictive disdain for Benny. After a decade of playing the Hollywood outsider, Benny now had semiregular characters to play foil to that side of his persona. His relationship to them afforded countless opportunities for Benny to display his ill-manner, for instance his habit of always borrowing things and showing up where he was not wanted. They performed with Benny more than twenty times through 1951. Their success with Benny led to their own radio program, *Halls of Ivy,* in 1950.

In addition to the Colmans, the second half of the 1940s saw several significant arrivals. Three were introduced on a single program on January 7, 1945. Benny needed five dollars to cover his expenses for a New York trip. He visits his vault for the first time, setting off a hilarious sequence of alarms, then encounters his guard, Ed, played by Joe Kearns, who greets Benny with "Halt! Who goes there?" These trips grew increasingly elaborate over the years. On a December 1948 program, Benny responds to Ed's "Halt!" with the passwords "Hair of gold, eyes of blue." Benny's railroad scenes on the January 1945 program are punctuated by Mel Blanc's increasingly desperate announcements for the train leaving for "Anaheim, Azusa, and Cucamonga!" In subsequent episodes, Blanc recalled in his autobiography, his pause between the *Cu* and *camonga* grew so long that an entirely different scene was inserted in the gap. Benny's first incongruous encounter with the character identified only as the "Race Track Tout" took place on that 1945 broadcast as well. The former vaudeville

Benny and his writers with Fred Allen (at left), 1946

star Benny Rubin was the first actor to play the part, which, regardless of setting, invoked race track terminology to dissuade Benny from his choice of train, candy, or cigarette. Sheldon Leonard eventually assumed the Runyonesque role.

Artie Auerbach introduced his Mr. Kitzel character on the January 6, 1946 *Lucky Strike Program*. Kitzel, a hot dog vendor Benny encountered at the Rose Bowl game, sang his sales pitch, which began, "Peekle een the meeddle mit da mustard on top!" Mr. Kitzel was not unlike Sam Hearn's Schlepperman, who played the hot dog man in a January 1941 Rose Bowl show. Schlepperman wasn't heard regularly after April 1939.

The Colmans were far from the only performers to parlay their success with Benny into their own radio series in early incarnations of the spinoff. Phil Harris's series, which costarred his wife, film star Alice Faye, grew out of their joint appearances on *The Fitch Bandwagon*. The program was heard Sunday evenings on NBC immediately after Benny, which guaranteed its popularity. Harris's fortunes fell when Benny moved to CBS in January 1949. *A Day in the Life of Dennis Day* debuted on NBC on Thursday, October 3, 1946. It was heard through June 1951. Even Mel Blanc had his own CBS series during the 1946–47 season. All of Benny's cast, except for Rochester and Mary Livingstone, were regularly heard on other programs. The cast of *The Judy Canova Show* included Mel Blanc, Sheldon Leonard, Joe Kearns, Verna Felton (who played Dennis Day's mother), and the Sportsmen.

Although Benny joked about his age as early as his 1932 radio appearance with Ed Sullivan, his seniority became a more frequent target in the mid-1940s. On February 11, 1945 he "proved" he was 36 years old. A June 1946 guest appearance on *The Quiz Kids* finds him declaring, "I'm 37 years old. And I was born in Waukegan in 1894," which is the actual year Benny was born. On a January 30, 1947

With guest star Jimmy Stewart, 1949

guest shot with Eddie Cantor, Benny explains, "Well, officially, I tell everyone I'm 37, but listen, I can't lie to you Eddie, I'm 32!" His 39th birthday was observed on February 15, 1948. When it was time for him to turn 40, on the February 13, 1949 *Lucky Strike Program,* he's saved by a telegram from his (real) sister Florence, who informs him he was actually born in 1910. Benny phones Rochester to have him look at his birth certificate, but there's a hole in the "Date of Birth" space. "We erased it once too often," muses Rochester.

THE RISE OF TELEVISION

Modern electronic television was demonstrated experimentally in the 1930s, but Benny addressed it tangentially. On the October 1939 broadcast that introduced Dennis Day, Benny scolds Mrs. Day for fussing with her son's tie. "This isn't television," he says. "You're quite fortunate, Mr. Benny," replies Mother Day. The gags returned when television production resumed following World War II. Benny related to the new medium in terms of his established character. On the March 16, 1947 *Lucky Strike Program,* when Don Wilson tells Benny that he has been asked to appear on a television program, Benny reacts with a "fat" joke, "They'll never get a sixty-inch beam on a ten-inch screen." On March 4, 1949, four days before his first television appearance, Benny kidded about the medium's tavern ubiquity on *The Ford Theatre* radio adaptation of *The Horn Blows at Midnight.* Radio's October 22, 1950 *Lucky Strike Program* used Benny's upcoming television show as an excuse to update his railroad station routines to an airport setting and included the anticipated encounters with Mr. Kitzel, Frank Nelson, Sheldon Leonard, and Mel Blanc's recurring characters. With the increased burden of producing periodic television broadcasts, a new writing team, Al Gordon and Hal Goldman, was added to the staff in 1950. For five years Benny was a simultaneous presence in both media.

In the 1950s the *Lucky Strike Program* alternated with *Amos 'n' Andy* as America's most popular radio program, but the overall number of radio listeners dropped dramatically as Americans spent more time in front of television sets. After fifteen years with Benny, Phil Harris left the program at the end of the 1951–1952 season, supposedly for budgetary reasons. Those same constraints reduced the number of guest stars during the program's final years. Bob Crosby replaced Phil Harris at the beginning of the 1952 season. Like Harris, his background was as a "personality" orchestra leader. Most of the humor surrounding Crosby was derived from his famous older brother, Bing, and he was never developed into a full partner on the program. On several broadcasts, the program's longtime music director, Mahlon Merrick, filled in for Crosby.

With the diminution of the bandleader's role, along with Mary Livingstone's decision to prerecord her lines at home due to "mike fright," the program's final radio years saw Frank Nelson and Mel Blanc given greater prominence. To their credit, the writers continually developed innovative approaches to comic devices entering their third decade. On the first show of the last season, September 26, 1954, Benny tells Bob Crosby, "Money isn't

Ed Wynn moves to television, 1949

Milton Berle with French singing star Jean Sablon, 1949

everything," then explains he has a new writer who hasn't grasped his character yet, indicating that the Benny persona lived a life of its own. When he runs into Frank Nelson, who is playing the broadcast's chief engineer, Nelson sneers, "May I shake your hand? I've already *grasped* your character."

Although the Jack Benny program on radio acknowledged the existence of television for many years, Benny himself lagged behind his fellow comedians in embracing the new medium as it became more prevalent. When the Benny show was first televised as a special in October 1950, four networks (ABC, CBS, DuMont, NBC) had been broadcasting almost full prime-time schedules for several seasons. By the end of the following year television had exhibited tremendous growth: in 1948 less than one half of 1 percent of all households had television sets; by 1951 the number approached 25 percent, leading advertisers to spend more money on network television than network radio. In September 1951 the coaxial cable link to the West Coast was complete, and television was broadcast nationwide.

The first stars to make their mark in television were already familiar to audiences who had enjoyed their work in both vaudeville and radio. Veteran entertainers Ed Wynn and Milton Berle, both exemplars of visual humor, were able to transfer their talents to the new medium. Wynn and Berle hosted their own variety shows, whose series of contrasting acts were a throwback to the early vaudeville circuit. Both were recognized as television's "most outstanding" personalities of 1949 by the Academy of Television Arts & Sciences.

Ed Wynn was a favorite comedian of Jack Benny. During the vaudeville era Wynn had created a naive, bumbling character, the Perfect Fool, whose comedy relied on funny hats and silly costumes. Although the act was developed for the stage, Wynn is credited with being one of the first established comedians to appear before a radio microphone. He achieved popularity during the early days of radio, but it was in television that Wynn could once again utilize his outlandish props. Wynn's character was one dimensional, but it was the innocence of his humor that must have appealed to Benny. For Wynn, like Benny, was noted for never telling a risqué joke.

Berle (also an ex-vaudevillian) found some success on radio and in nightclubs and headlined *Texaco Star Theater,* which from its 1948 debut helped galvanize public interest in television. Berle became popular because he injected himself into every act; people tuned in to see Berle's response

Burns and Allen successfully made the move to television

to the performances surrounding him. He expanded the traditional master of ceremonies role until it was the dominant focus of all attention. Berle did not create an identifiable character, but this "whirling dervish" of television seized the spotlight with his unpredictable antics.

Benny's closest compatriots on radio, George Burns and Gracie Allen, had dropped their radio show and committed to a biweekly television series in 1950. They made a smooth transition to the new medium, adapting the characters they had developed on stage and radio to the nascent domestic comedy format on television. George played the tolerant husband and straight man opposite his zany, scatterbrained wife. Although they portrayed entertainers who performed a weekly show, most of the comedy was restricted to the home. The show's format harkened back to the earliest progenitors of the radio situation comedy, *The Goldbergs* and *Amos 'n' Andy.* What was unique on television about the Burns and Allen show was that the character of George Burns assumed the role of narrator as well as participant in the action. He acknowledges that the cast was performing a comedy show and makes frequent asides to the audience, thus adapting the concept of master of ceremonies to the limited world of his comedy family.

Benny bridged the world of the variety show and the situation comedy to create a distinct format. In contrast to Milton Berle's spontaneous antics as host of his own variety show, Benny brought to television a defined, identifiable character forged during his vaudeville and radio years. Benny also expanded the role George Burns played (as affable straight man/narrator of a situation comedy) to encompass the hosting of an actual variety show. The Benny program was both a variety show and the comic adventures surrounding the production of such a series. He was an adept master of ceremonies, never relinquishing his role in front of the curtain (even when the focus of the program shifted to the situation comedy behind the curtain). His major concession to the visual medium was to add a deliberate performance to the role—he not only had to tell the joke but also underline it with gestures and facial expressions.

Unlike Milton Berle's grand comic gestures, directly derived from a vaudeville act, Benny mini-

Imogene Coca and Sid Caesar became stars on the new medium

Ernie Kovacs as Percy Dovetonsils—he appeared on Benny's television show in 1959

mized his performance. He suited his character for the intimate requirements of the small screen. Instead of slapstick contortions, he evoked his character's time-honored exasperation with a stare. The stare became Benny's visual signature—it was the pause in radio and more. When he gazed at the audience for several seconds, the audience completed the joke and, more importantly, identified with the character. This letting the audience in on the joke was a big part of Benny's continual success.

The great success of Berle, Burns, and Benny does not imply that television was an easy medium for all former vaudevillians to conquer. Fred Allen, Benny's "rival" for so many years, had witnessed an ignominious end to his own radio show in 1949. He held a dour view of television and was forced into formats that did not fit his personality. Allen was never comfortable with the visual medium, and he died before his talents could be put to proper use. If Fred Allen was *too* verbal for television, veteran showmen Ole Olsen and Chick Johnson were too noisy and chaotic. Olsen and Johnson were not able to adapt their madcap Broadway revue *Hellzapoppin'* to the small screen in their series *Fireball Fun-for-All.* The unremitting bedlam of one-liners and seltzer bottles had no focus and exhausted audiences as much as entertained them. In short, Allen was an identifiable character in search of a situation and Olsen and Johnson created only pandemonium in search of a structure.

It is also important to recognize that not all early television was created by radio stars en route from vaudeville. At the time Benny and his colleagues were translating their older formats to television, a new generation of performers was beginning to create its own imprint. These performers were untrained in the traditional forms of mass entertainment. Comedians Sid Caesar and Imogene Coca brought a fresh sensibility to the variety show, first on the *Admiral Broadway Revue,* and a year later on *Your Show of Shows.* They imbued their sketches with a topicality and a sophistication that was a conscious move away from the broad humor that characterized Berle's show. Caesar and Coca's humor recognized the increasing affluence and education of their audience. Sketches revolved around buying a first car or tipping in a fancy restaurant. At the same time Ernie Kovacs was expanding the vocabulary of television expression. During his live variety show in Philadelphia he integrated zany off-screen situations into the flow of the program. He incorporated the process of making a television show, discussions with directors and cameramen, into the actual show. In many ways, Kovacs was building on a comic tradition that the Benny radio program had begun.

As well written and performed as the *Your Show of Shows* routines were, they have not found the immortality in syndication that *I Love Lucy* and *The Honeymooners* have. In 1951 Lucille Ball, an established movie actress, found stardom in a situation comedy; that same year Jackie Gleason created the character Ralph Kramden on *Cavalcade of Stars.* Both Ball and Gleason discovered that audiences crave characters, fictional representations of their own desires and fears. The audience would forgo the surprise of new acts and sketches each week, the essence of any variety show, for the comfort of continuing characters.

Benny defined his character through rituals that were repeated during almost every show. Vir-

Jack and his writers Sam Perrin, Hal Goldman, Al Gordon, and George Balzer, 1955

tually each episode opens with Benny in front of a curtain, welcoming the audience and telling a few jokes before Don Wilson does the obligatory commercial. The curtain harkens back to Benny's earliest days in vaudeville, where his act was most likely always performed at the foot of the stage while stagehands adjusted scenery behind the curtain for the next act. Perhaps the curtain was a touchstone for Benny because he rarely deviated from the standard opening: Benny enters in his inimitable manner stage left to right to start the monologue. Perhaps the curtain also served to place Benny and his regulars in an artificial context. When the curtain parted, the viewer entered a world based on Benny's own logic.

Benny and his writers warmed slowly to the visual possibilities of television. The debut program is set for the most part in Benny's Beverly Hills living room. The sketch is performed on a proscenium stage, framed with a curtain. Rochester performs a little dance as he dusts, and as a visual joke there is a pay phone on Benny's wall. Every joke in this episode, however, is possible to re-create on radio with sound effects, including the pay phone. Although the actors seem comfortable on camera, what they are essentially doing is performing a choreographed Benny radio program. Jack Gould, in his review of the premiere program in the *New York Times,* observed, "The major part of the presentation was largely a revival of one of Jack's favorite radio formats—the program devoted to telling how the program is going to be done. . . . Visually, there was very little excitement. . . ."

The subsequent programs of the first and second seasons are similar, with the exception of one program featuring champion golfer Ben Hogan that closes the first season and features Mary Livingstone's television debut. In it, Benny, not recognizing Hogan, comically contorts his body as he demonstrates the proper form for a golf swing to someone he assumes is a rookie. Benny is surprisingly adept at physical humor, but such displays of action do not fit the constraints of his character. Perhaps the first episode that forays completely into the realm of visual humor is "Jack Falls Asleep and Is Robbed" (November 30, 1952) in the third season. The final sequence is set entirely in Jack's bedroom and is conceived of as a silent movie. The episode's humor is almost completely reliant on a series of visual jokes that underscore the Benny character's petulance and stinginess.

The Benny team becomes more visually adventurous as the seasons progress, innovating new uses of dream sequences, flashbacks, and even flashbacks within flashbacks. While never experimenting conceptually with the limits of film and videotape as Ernie Kovacs did, the Benny program takes an essentially traditional format and subtly bends the boundaries.

In his memoir *Jack Benny: An Intimate Biography,* the entertainer's former publicist and manager Irving Fein writes, "In searching for plots and ideas for television, Jack and his writers utilized every possible radio program that was adaptable to the new medium. . . ." Early television plots directly descended from radio include remakes of "Buck Benny Rides Again" (which had also been made into a feature film) and "Gaslight," a parody of the MGM film that on radio had featured the film's star, Ingrid Bergman, and in its television version starred Barbara Stanwyck.

In television there is less emphasis on stereotypical situations with Benny's regulars, and rarely do we see the entire gang from radio on the same show. Group reunions would be reserved for reprises of classic radio sketches, most notably the train/airport and Christmas routines. If any of the Benny regulars changed in their television incarnation, it was certainly Rochester. There is a deepen-

Twilight Zone *sketch with Rod Serling and Dennis Day, 1963*

Jack Benny's First Farewell Special, *with Dean Martin in 1973*

ing of the emotional bond between Benny and his servant. In many skits Rochester serves as both valet and protector to his boss. In one episode he rocks him to sleep; in another they celebrate New Year's Eve alone together. Rochester's role on camera helps to bring a humanity to the more negative characteristics of the Benny persona.

Since the program did not become a weekly series until 1960, there was a desire to generate audience appeal with special guest stars. The guests came from a variety of endeavors: motion picture, vaudeville, and the musical stage (Maurice Chevalier, George Burns, Ben Blue); popular and classical music (Isaac Stern, Johnnie Ray, Spike Jones); and television itself (Jackie Gleason, Red Skelton, Ed Sullivan).

Moreover, an unusual number of major motion picture stars appear on the show in their television debuts. According to Fein, the Benny format was a known quantity to the stars, and they knew that Benny would make them look good. Some of these stars adapted easily to series television and even became ubiquitous on the medium (Barbara Stanwyck, Fred MacMurray); others never returned (Marilyn Monroe, Gary Cooper). The reason so many celebrities appear with Benny can be traced to his radio years, where the same conditions prevailed: all jokes where guests are concerned are made at Benny's expense.

While there were some changes in the "regular" cast from the radio years, the Benny persona entered television unfazed. He upsets Mr. and Mrs. James Stewart's New Year's Eve by boorishly horning in on their plans, with shrill-voiced date Mabel Flapsaddle in tow. He upsets a rehearsal of a live television drama starring Claudette Colbert and Basil Rathbone by insisting that he should play Rathbone's part. In a plot worthy of an *I Love Lucy* episode, he dons six-inch cowboy boots to audition for a role as Gary Cooper's twin brother: he wants to leave when physical action is required. He sports a false moustache to win money on Groucho Marx's *You Bet Your Life.* And, as a meek Tarzan, he startles the animals by playing his primitive violin.

THE LATER TELEVISION WORK

One of the chief achievements of Jack Benny's creative team is that they made the familiar attributes of the Benny character continually new and alive. Adjustments had to be made if Benny was to remain vital to younger television audiences and in tune with the times. In the late fifties television was undergoing a major transformation, and Benny's team responded by incorporating contemporary situations and topical references into the trusted formula.

Keeping the Benny persona fresh might mean looking for the right headline around which a series of running gags could be constructed. While most television comedians steered away from joking about the 1959 quiz show investigation that scandalized the whole industry, Benny seized the opportunity for comic self-examination. He stated that to conform to the network's new policy of forthrightness, his show was going to be truthful. Waiting a beat, he announced that he, too, was coming clean—he was not really 39 years old.

The end of the fifties proved a difficult time for many of Benny's compatriots who had learned their craft in vaudeville and became pioneers in radio and television. George Burns's career faltered after the retirement of his wife Gracie Allen in 1958. The comedy of Milton Berle, Mr. Television himself, was decidedly out of fashion by the end of the decade. Indeed, the landscape of television was rapidly changing. During the mid-fifties there was a major shift in programming strategies by television executives. Live television, exemplified by the variety show and the dramatic anthology, was deemphasized and the networks began to produce filmed series in conjunction with the Hollywood studios.

Benny's production company, J&M Productions, produced several comedies outside his own series during the mid-fifties. These programs were filmed with the traditional single-camera technique. In these outside projects, there were attempts to modify the Benny persona. Director Frank Tashlin, known for his irreverent comedies *The Girl Can't Help It* and *Will Success Spoil Rock Hunter?,* worked on two such episodes for *General Electric Theater.* It is interesting how the Benny character, so well-defined within his own family, was integrated into different supporting casts. In the two Tashlin episodes Benny plays an innocent caught up in the intrigues of mobsters. In "The Honest Man" Benny plays a humble piano tuner, who becomes the courier of stolen jewelery. In "The Face Is Familiar" the joke is that no one can remember Benny's countenance. The humility of these characters is at odds with the established Benny ego.

One may suspect that Benny was uneasy in these filmed comedies. Since they were shot on the Universal backlot, Benny was not able to savor audience reaction. A laugh track was utilized, prominently underlining all the Benny phrases and mannerisms that were not really pertinent to the plots. During each program there developed a distinct dichotomy between the Benny character and the character Benny was playing. Even with the talent of Frank Tashlin it was probably recognized that Jack Benny was at his best in his own universe.

As television developed through the fifties, the Benny character could no longer guarantee an audience, even in his own universe. The popularity of

Jack and Billy Graham on the first show of the 1963 season

Sheldon Leonard as the Race Track Tout, 1957

the series had waned; for three seasons (1957–59) it did not place among Nielsen's top-rated shows of the year. Benny had first suffered in the ratings when scheduled opposite the Warner Bros. series *Maverick,* a humorous Western starring the easygoing James Garner. In order to make Benny's show more contemporary, the program underwent restructuring, and during the 1960–61 season a decision was made to produce *The Jack Benny Program* more in the style of a weekly West Coast situation comedy. Instead of underlining the series's connection to the live variety series, such as *Texaco Star Theater* and *Your Show of Shows,* Benny's program would be filmed in front of an audience by the three-camera technique developed by Desi Arnaz for his *I Love Lucy* series. Previously, the Benny series had been either performed live or recorded on videotape in order to preserve the immediacy of an East Coast show. There had been experiments in one-camera filming, but the audience rapport was missing. Now the show would have a polished Hollywood look as well as a potential afterlife in syndication.

The Benny writers also made changes in the content of the series. They recognized the shift in the taste and composition of the viewing public and incorporated cultural references that might appeal to the new television constituency. Such references were increasingly based on television itself. When Benny began on television only 9 percent of households had receivers; ten years later the figure approached 90 percent. One 1960 episode had a baffled Benny seeking advice from the youthful Dick Clark of *American Bandstand* fame on how to attract teenagers. On many occasions these youth-oriented shows would end with Jack donning a wig with guitar in hand. In fact, the final skit that Benny performed on television was as a leader of his own rock group, "Jack Benny's Rolling Pips." But it was still just Jack, desiring to be eternally young.

As the Benny program evolved, there were more sketches devoted to television. Instead of relying on the motion picture community for guest stars, the Benny show welcomed celebrities created by the new medium, including Ernie Kovacs, Mike Wallace, and Jack Webb. In the 1959 Webb program there is a subtle commentary on the new personalities of television. Benny is startled to discover that the star of *Dragnet* cannot sing, dance, or tell jokes. Webb's training was in episodic television, not vaudeville. But Webb was willing to make fun of his stoic persona, and the writers spoofed television's detective genre.

There had always been an inherent anxiety in the Benny character, who assumed he was losing his audience appeal. A recurring sketch at the end of many seasons had Benny negotiating his contract with a skeptical sponsor. Just as the sponsor worried about finding a way to sell his product to a younger audience, the writers also knew they had to sell the character to a generation growing up with television that was not acquainted with Benny's radio work. There was a conscious effort to broaden Benny's appeal by employing contemporary guests, such as Peter, Paul, and Mary and the Smothers Brothers.

While the Benny television program bridged the two genres of the variety show and the situation comedy, it also anticipated the development of a third category, the talk show. The comfortable informality of the Benny program, with its comic banter between Benny and his cast of real-life entertainers, served as a model in 1950 for the creation of the first late-night talk and variety series, *Broadway Open House.* Network executive Sylvester "Pat" Weaver specifically stated he was searching for "a zany lighthearted show" that captured Benny's sense of fun and spontaneity. *Broadway Open House,* a freewheeling revue starring the frantic comic Jerry Lester, became the predecessor of *The Tonight Show.* Two of Jack Benny's protégés, Jack Paar and Johnny Carson, later emerged as the quintessential hosts of the talk show. Both adapted components of the Benny style, especially the crafted pauses and the long takes. Benny, who always reacted to situations with aplomb and perfect timing, could be seen as a model of the successful talk show host.

As talk shows became more popular, the Benny writers looked to the new television form for inspiration and comedy. Talk show parodies became a standard device on the Benny program. In several episodes exact replicas of *The Tonight Show* were built. Benny, not known for his comic impersonations, performed a witty and incisive mimicking of Paar. Throughout the *Tonight* take-off with Rock Hudson and Paar's sidekick Hugh Downs, the viewer becomes conscious of the tics and mannerisms that Paar had borrowed from Benny to create his own style. During his 1959 guest appearance Jack Paar acknowledged that he learned how to perform in front of an audience from Jack Benny; in fact, in 1947 he starred in a situation comedy overtly based on the Benny formula that was a summer replacement of Benny's radio show.

Jack, Dennis, and Don parody Peter, Paul, and Mary, 1964

Mel Blanc as Sy, 1957

Johnny Carson first appeared on the Benny program in 1955, the year he hosted his first network variety series. Benny had always been Carson's idol, who ostensibly appeared on the program to receive advice on comedy from the master. The writers created a nifty reversal of expectations when the sketch ended with Carson complaining about the length of Benny's pauses and the slowness of his delivery. Carson returned in 1963 as a full-fledged entertainer and, to the amazement of

A pair of Jacks, Benny and Paar, 1959

his mentor, demonstrated his talents as a magician, drummer, and song and dance man. Benny is surprised that a talk show host must have such multiple skills, somewhat akin to a vaudeville showman. It is noteworthy that the director of many Benny episodes, Fred de Cordova, left the series during the 1962–63 season and later became the producer of *The Tonight Show Starring Johnny Carson.* In his biography of Jack Benny, Irving Fein revealed that Jack was offered the guest host spot on *The Tonight Show.* Jack eventually turned it down because he was scared of working before a live audience night after night without a prepared script.

In 1961 Benny self-consciously adapted one of Jack Paar's favorite techniques and ventured into the studio audience for the first time. The initial foray consisted of mostly staged routines and Benny himself was somewhat tentative. As part of his "One Man Show" during his final 1964–65 season, Benny engaged the audience in conversation and displayed the casual air of a talk show veteran. There was an obvious empathy between Benny and his audience, and there was little need for prerehearsed sketches.

Throughout the fifties Benny stayed close to his theatrical roots by hosting the variety series *Shower of Stars*. In 1959 he hosted his own special, *The Jack Benny Hour*, which became the prototype of specials to follow. Produced and directed by Bud Yorkin, the initial outing features Bob Hope, Mitzi Gaynor, and Señor Wences performing with and without Benny. The cold opening of the show finds Benny warming up the audience in shirtsleeves; at the director's behest he runs backstage to officially open the program and is then introduced in one of the most hilariously overblown openings ever produced on live television. But the animals and marching bands would not get the laugh without the ultimate payoff, the Benny stare.

When Benny's weekly series ended in 1965, he returned to comedy specials. The programs harkened back to the early days of vaudeville, with Benny serving as host and emcee. There were comic monologues, songs, and typical sketches. Benny and his staff engaged the turbulent sixties with the material they knew best. Yet Benny tried to remain current and imbue his persona with a contemporary appeal. His Maxwell was painted in psychedelic colors, and the Benny character identified with the hippy ethos of the "free" lunch.

It is hard to imagine that one single character could experience both Prohibition and psychedelia. But Jack Benny did. Jack Benny played a major role in every development of twentieth century entertainment: he created his persona in front of a live audience on the dusty vaudeville circuit; his voice was transmitted over the airwaves; and his image beamed electronically across the nation. But it is not the technological advances that are important. It is the enduring quality of the Benny character—so vain, so petulant, so insecure, but so identifiable to his audience. In the century of continual progress, modern America chose the most imperfect of characters to adore.

The following selected radio and television programs from The Museum of Television and Radio's collection illustrate the themes discussed in this essay.

Mentor and protégé, Jack and Johnny

Broadcast Overview

Canada Dry Program	May 2, 1932–October 26, 1932	NBC-Blue, New York
	Monday/Wednesday 9:30–10:00 P.M.	
	October 30, 1932–January 26, 1933	CBS, New York
	Sunday 10:00–10:30 P.M.	
	Thursday 8:15–8:45 P.M. (Through 12/29/32)	
	Thursday 8:00–8:30 P.M. (1/5/33–1/26/33)	
Chevrolet Program	March 3, 1933–June 23, 1933	NBC-Red, New York
	Friday 10:00–10:30 P.M.	
	October 1, 1933–April 1, 1934	
	Sunday 10:00–10:30 P.M.	
General Tire Revue	April 6, 1934–September 28, 1934	NBC-Red, New York
	Friday 10:30–11:00 P.M.	
Jell-O Program Starring Jack Benny	October 14, 1934–July 14, 1935	NBC-Blue, New York
	September 29, 1935–June 21, 1936	NBC-Blue, Hollywood
	October 4, 1936–May 31, 1942	NBC-Red, Hollywood
Jack Benny Program for Grape-Nuts and Grape-Nuts Flakes	October 4, 1942–June 4, 1944	NBC-Red, Hollywood
Lucky Strike Program Starring Jack Benny	October 1, 1944–December 26, 1948	NBC, Hollywood
	January 2, 1949–May 22, 1955	CBS, Hollywood
	Sunday 7:00–7:30 P.M.	

Producers

Tom Harrington (1934–38)
Murray Bolen (1939–42)
Robert Walsh (1942–43)
Walter Bunker (1943–44)
Robert Ballin (1944–46)
Hilliard Marks (1946–55)

Writers

Harry Conn (1932–36)
Al Boasberg (Intermittently, 1932–36)
Arthur Phillips (1935–36)
Bill Morrow (1936–43)
Ed Beloin (1936–43)
Howard Snyder (Intermittently, 1936–55)
Hugh Wedlock, Jr. (Intermittently, 1936–55)
Cy Howard (1943)
Sam Perrin (1935–36, 1943–55)
John Tackaberry (1943–55)
George Balzer (1943–1955)
Milt Josefsberg (1943–55)
Al Gordon (1950–55)
Hal Goldman (1950–55)

The Radio Work

MAY 2, 1932

Canada Dry Program (PREMIERE)

Surprisingly, Jack Benny is not the star of his own first network radio program. The featured attraction is George Olsen and His Music, and it is Olsen's theme, "Beyond the Blue Horizon," that opens the show. Announcer Ed Thorgersen introduces Benny as a "suave comedian, *dry* humorist, and famous master of ceremonies." Although delivered with tongue in cheek, Thorgersen's remarks are accurate. Benny was nationally known through his vaudeville, musical comedy, and motion picture appearances, as well as his recent national exposure on Ed Sullivan's CBS program *Broadway's Greatest Thrills.* Benny explains that a master of ceremonies is "really a fellow who is unemployed and gets paid for it." Even at the outset of his radio career, there is combative banter with the orchestra leader and nasty asides about the vocal group. There are cheap jokes, too, but they are directed at maestro Olsen. Benny teases his sponsor and dismisses the commercials as a waste of time. "You drink it, like it, and don't want to hear about it." Later he expresses the fear of cancellation in a display of the insecure side of his character, "I hope you'll be with us again next Wednesday. In fact, I hope I'll be here Wednesday."

MARCH 31, 1933

Chevrolet Program

The *Canada Dry Program* ran until January 1933. Six weeks after its demise, Benny was back on NBC with a time slot, sponsor, and announcer inherited from Al Jolson, who had left in mid-season. The orchestra was led by Frank Black, James Melton sang tenor, and the announcer was Howard Claney. The format of what was now clearly Benny's show was starting to evolve: guest stars, usually drawn from musical comedy, were featured; movies and plays were parodied; and as character foils such as Mary Livingstone were added, Benny was increasingly the victim of the jokes.

Following Howard Claney's announcement that April is "National Drive a Chevrolet Month," Benny greets the audience with "Hello, optimists," then goes into a formal opening monologue, a convention that would be dropped during the course of this series. A dispatch from "King Kong, Africa" manages to incorporate a Chevrolet plug, "Missionaries find natives wilder than ever. Howard, what are they wild about?" "They're wild about the new Chevrolet. . . ." Mary Livingstone sings on the program. By the end of the half hour, Benny asks Livingstone, Frank Black, and James Melton what each thought of his violin solo on the previous Friday night broadcast. "What gives you the courage to sing?" Benny asks Livingstone. "I heard you play the violin last week," she replies. The balance of the show is devoted to a parody of Mae

West's Paramount picture *She Done Him Wrong,* with Mary doing a commendable West, and Benny, already his own established character, making no attempt to sound like Cary Grant.

Chevrolet Program

DECEMBER 10, 1933

The program opens with new announcer Alois Havrilla introducing Benny as "America's outstanding false alarm." Benny is offended. He wishes to be introduced with a little dignity. "Well, Jack," Havrilla explains, "I'm using as little as possible"—an example of the classic put-downs Benny's own cast continually inflicted upon him. Benny "quits," and bandleader Frank Black takes over, doing a parody of Benny's style, "Did you hear the one about the peacock? It's a wonderful tail!" When Benny returns and orders "Play, Frank!" a fight breaks out between the pair, which includes some sophisticated sound effects, such as crowd noise and a bell announcing the first round. Mary Livingstone enters to thank Black for knocking out Benny. Frank Parker, the tenor replacing James Melton, arrives. He thanks Mary for the great time he had at her house the night before. "Sweetheart," he asks, "What do your folks think of me?" "They didn't like you very much, but that's only one family's opinion," Mary replies. Although the public knew that Livingstone was Mrs. Benny, her unmarried character flirted shamelessly. Her romantic interlude with Parker is punctuated by the groans of the semiconscious Benny. Following an orchestra number, Benny announces their presentation of *Uncle Tom's Cabin,* with Benny as Uncle Tom and Mary Livingstone (as Liza) playing Uncle Tom's secretary. When Benny hears that Simon Legree is selling him to the "show boat," he muses, "Well, that's a good program." The *Maxwell House Show Boat,* an early variety series, had debuted on NBC in October 1932. Much of the comedy of early radio was derived from allusions to popular songs, movies, plays, and other radio shows. At the end of the program, Benny asks Mary, "Can I take you home tonight for a change?" "No, I'm sorry," she replies. "Foiled again!" says Benny, in keeping with the evening's melodrama.

FEBRUARY 18, 1934

Chevrolet Program

Benny tells the audience he's happy since Mary Livingstone, toward whom he frequently feigns irritation, is in Miami. He has just returned from his unspecified hometown, where he celebrated his birthday. Benny, who had just turned 40, doesn't specify his age, telling Frank Black, "A man is as old as he looks." "So, you're 55, eh?" cracks the bandleader. Benny asks Alois Havrilla, "Did you hear any other programs tonight? Did they say or do anything that we're going to do?" The exchange establishes the evening's running gag: each time Benny starts a joke, another cast member cites the radio program that was its source. There are mentions of fellow radio comedians Eddie Cantor, Joe Penner, and "Freddy" Allen. When a young lady interrupts Benny's conversation with Frank Parker, Benny tells her, "If you had a brain, you'd be a half-wit!" "I heard that on Burns and Allen's program," she retorts. In another overt acknowledgment that he is doing a radio show, Benny reads his fan mail. One listener asks for an autographed picture of Amos 'n' Andy. Another letter turns out to be a poem from Mary Livingstone. The final letter requests a mystery sketch, so Benny presents "The Green Room Murder." Benny adopts the name he would use in many future programs, Detective O'Benny, "the William Powell of the Air." (In 1934 the suave actor was known for his film role as detective Philo Vance.) When Benny makes the "Calling all cars!" announcement, announcer Havrilla interrupts, "And when calling for cars, ask for the new Chevrolet!" Benny resumes irritatedly, "Calling the whole thing off!" On the way to the crime scene, Benny is stopped by a traffic cop in an episode not unlike his future encounters with ensemble

member Frank Nelson. "Where's the fire?" the officer demands. "In your eyes," coos Benny. "Heard it on the Rudy Vallee program," responds the cop. At the closing, Benny reads a telegram from Mary Livingstone. " 'Just heard your program. I better be back with you next Sunday night.' Goodnight, folks." Benny's last Chevrolet broadcast was heard on Sunday, April 1, 1934.

General Tire Revue

JULY 20, 1934

Benny's weekly *General Tire Revue* premiered on NBC's Red Network on Friday, April 6, 1934, five days after the final Chevrolet program. Three sponsors in two years was not unusual at that time. This program originates from Hollywood with Jimmie Grier's band, and Benny's monologue has a West Coast slant. For example, he announces the arrival of twins in the Bing Crosby household. The continuing sketch "The Stooge Murder Case; or, Who Killed Mr. Stooge" is used to present comedian Phil Baker, whose NBC broadcast is heard one hour before Benny's. Baker is joined by his own fellow cast members, Bottle (who is his butler) and Beetle (who is a ghost). Baker, known as the "Armour Jester," plugs his sponsor. Don Wilson, who first worked with Benny on this series, turns Baker's plug into a commercial for General Tire. Benny and Mary Livingstone appeared on Baker's next program.

General Tire Revue

AUGUST 3, 1934

Don Bestor, the new bandleader, makes the opening announcements. Benny is supposedly on a train en route back to New York from Hollywood, where he had been making *Transatlantic Merry-Go-Round,* in which cast members Frank Parker and Jimmie Grier and His Orchestra also appear. Sam Hearn, a dialect comedian who had previously performed on several Chevrolet broadcasts, as well as this series, makes his debut as Irving C. Schlepperman, a recurring character on the Benny program through 1939. (He appears with Benny in Paramount's *The Big Broadcast of 1937.*) The repeated onboard announcement for "Poughkeepsie! All out!" at a variety of points in the journey presages the popular "Anaheim, Azusa, and Cucamonga" catchphrase of the next decade. This broadcast also includes an early example of an in-show rehearsal, another Benny trademark. This popular series was canceled after its September 28, 1934 broadcast.

NOVEMBER 3, 1935

Jell-O Program

In September 1935, at the beginning of his second season sponsored by Jell-O, Benny moved the base of his program to Hollywood, and composer Johnny Green became the orchestra leader. (No complete copies of the first Jell-O season, from October 1934 to May 1935, are known to exist.) An opening sequence set in a barber shop plays off Benny's stinginess. He grumbles about paying twenty cents for a haircut, shampoo, hair tonic, shave, and hot towel. Following plugs for his two recent films, *It's in the Air* and *Broadway Melody of 1936,* Benny meets vocalist Kenny Baker, who is introduced on this program. "Tell me, what kind of a voice have you?" Benny inquires. "I'm a tenor singer. I'm sorry," replies Baker, much in the humble and apologetic manner that Dennis Day would later follow. Baker became an excellent foil for Benny's egocentric character. Benny explains to Baker, "This is one big happy family, depending on options, of course," referring either to Benny's contracts with the cast, which became a running gag, or his professed fear of cancellation.

OCTOBER 4, 1936

Jell-O Program

Phil Harris joins the cast as bandleader, bringing the program one step closer to the classic Benny ensemble. Harris's career goes back to the 1920s. He began as a drummer, then coleader, then sole leader of his own orchestra, most notably at the famous Cocoanut Grove of the Ambassador Hotel in Los Angeles. By 1936 he had appeared in several movies and starred in his own NBC series, *Let's Listen to Harris,* from June 1933 through December 1934. Harris was an established personality, hired for the *Jell-O Program* more as a character than maestro. Mahlon Merrick was the program's actual music director for many years.

Benny opens the show with his characteristic greeting, "Jell-O again," and welcomes the cast. He tells Don Wilson he looks "fit as a bass fiddle," an early "fat" joke of the type that Benny would hurl at Wilson for the next three decades. Mary Livingstone counters with the observation that Benny appears "tan and ragged." By this time Livingstone's characteristic sarcasm has fully supplanted the girlish innocence she displayed earlier. Benny deliberately fumbles Harris's introduction with "Play Don, er, John," a reference to predecessors Bestor and Green. He follows the band selection by saying, "with John Green at the piano . . . on another program." The other program was NBC's *The Packard Show,* starring Fred Astaire. Benny and Mary Livingstone had substituted for Astaire on the September 8, 1936 premiere broadcast.

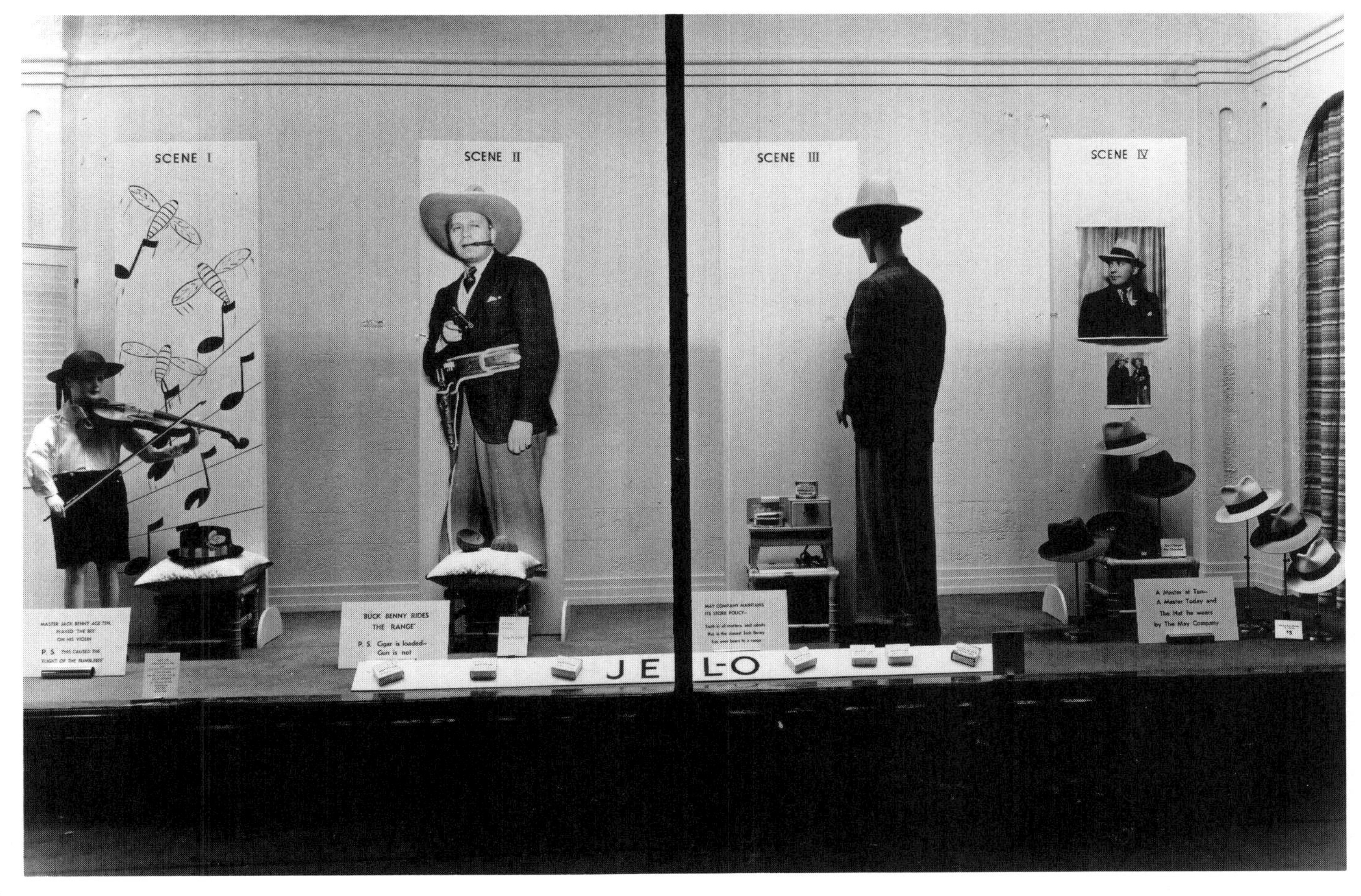

Jell-O Program *NOVEMBER 15, 1936*

The show opens with a re-creation of the closing of the previous week's broadcast. Later the cast reminisces about their school days: Benny claims he walked through ten miles of snow; Phil Harris says he walked through ten miles of cotton, a reflection of his exaggerated Southern roots. In an early example of one of Don Wilson's characteristics—affected sensitivity—he is hurt that he was left out of the conversation about school days. When asked, he says that he had to "eat through ten miles of Jell-O to get to school," inserting the commercial reference that characterized much of his dialogue. The Western serial parody, "Buck Benny Rides Again," to which Benny returned all the way through to his television years, begins on this date. It was made into a film starring the Benny cast in 1940.

On his *Town Hall Tonight* broadcast of December 30, 1936, Fred Allen unfavorably compared Jack Benny's skill on the violin with ten-and-a-half-year-old Stuart Canin, who had just completed an impressive performance of "The Bee." This event officially launched the Jack Benny-Fred Allen "feud," which peaked in the first three months of 1937. See pages 128–153 for the full story of this radio phenomenon.

MARCH 28, 1937

Jell-O Program

This program, set in Chicago's Dearborn Station, is notable for the arrival of Eddie Anderson. Zany train announcements, much like Mel Blanc's "Anaheim, Azusa, and Cucamonga" of the next decade, are heard throughout the broadcast. The first, "Train leaving on track seven for Kansas City, Sioux City, Dodge City, Carson City, Salt Lake City . . . and Pottstown!" is followed by "Train leaving for San Pedro, San Diego, San Jose, and *San Francisco,* starring Clark Gable and Jeanette MacDonald!" Benny meets Kenny Baker carrying a bucket of snow. Baker explains, "My mother never saw any." Benny tells him it will be water by the time they get to California. "My mother will believe me," reasons Baker. Another train announcement incorporates the six flavors of Jell–O (strawberry, raspberry, cherry, orange, lemon, and lime), much to Don Wilson's delight. As Benny boards, he is to give the porter fifty cents. "This is a dime," the Red Cap complains. "Look at your script, not the coin," squawks Benny. The scene changes to the second day on the train. Mary Livingstone makes several attempts to recite an Easter poem, but is interrupted by the first appearance of Eddie Anderson on the program. "Hey porter, porter," asks Benny, "What time do we get to Albuquerque?" "Who?" responds Anderson, who has not yet acquired the name "Rochester Van Jones." (He would not assume the part of Benny's valet until June 20.) While on the train, Benny asks Kenny Baker to "rehearse" his song for the upcoming broadcast. When the music starts, Baker is startled. "Where'd we get the orchestra?" he asks. After, Benny tells him, "I'm sure your song will be a big hit Sunday." "It sure was!" responds Baker, whose character is even too dumb to play along with one of the program's conventions. The show concludes with Andy Devine waiting in the studio with Phil Harris for the rest of the cast to return. Devine has a "swell present" for Benny, "If he got me one."

Jell-O Program

APRIL 11, 1937

George Burns and Gracie Allen, whose program sponsored by Grape-Nuts debuts the following evening, are the guests. Both Grape-Nuts and Jell-O were products of General Foods. Mary Livingstone arrives with a letter from her mother. These fictional missives and her poetry (the latter beginning with her first *Canada Dry Program* appearance) annoyed Benny and were early devices to fuel his characteristic exasperation toward those around him. As Benny announces his "symphony of the great outdoors," "Buck Benny Rides Again," Gracie Allen enters. She has come with a message from George Burns that she cannot remember. She is reminded of their own new program "tomorrow night for Grape-Nuts." Gracie comments on "Buck Benny" throughout its presentation. The action is interrupted by Burns and Allen going into their act, but Benny admonishes them. "Save that for tomorrow night!" Phil Harris's "Buck Benny" role as the inebriated Pappy is an early instance of a gag regarding his alleged drinking. Gracie comments, "Isn't he cute?" "No!" barks George. "I am, too!" counters Harris, demonstrating the Harris vanity that played counterpoint to Benny's own arrogance.

Jell-O Program

OCTOBER 24, 1937

Don Wilson brings on Benny as a "favorite of men, women, and children. Especially men and children," comparing Benny to Jell-O and tweaking his lack of sex appeal. Benny says he's like a kid with a new toy. He has traded in his Stanley Steamer for a "new" car, a Maxwell. "It's in swell shape," he claims. It doesn't have a radio, "but there's a Victrola on the steering wheel." Kenny Baker enters laughing. There's a crowd gathered downstairs around the Maxwell waiting "to see the guy that would ride in it." Gags revolving around Benny's rattling transportation are among the program's most enduring. Benny announces their version of Twentieth Century-Fox's *Wife, Doctor, and Nurse,* which starred Loretta Young. Don Wilson is a patient whose symptoms include reciting the flavors of Jell-O. Dr. Benny asks if he's still seeing "those big red letters on the box?" "Oh, all the time! All the time!" Sam Hearn as Schlepperman recounts a lengthy menu of ills, prompting Benny to end the sketch by singing "You Can't Have Everything."

JANUARY 16, 1938

Jell-O Program

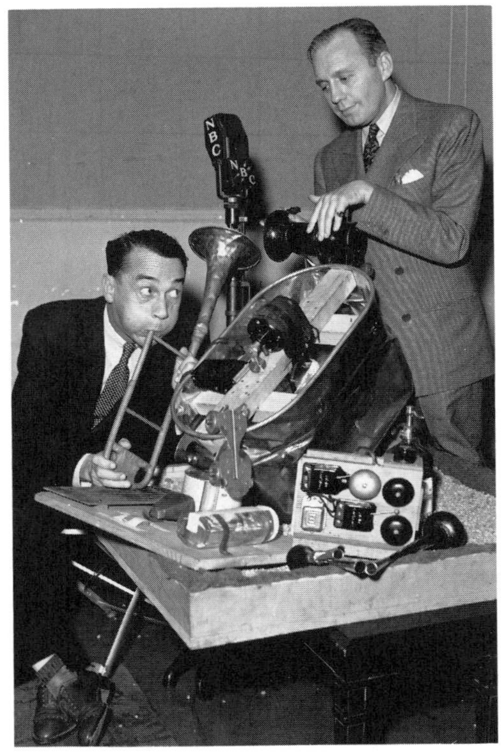

Don Wilson opens the program with letters of praise for Jell-O, then turns things over to Benny and Mary Livingstone, who are supposedly in the Maxwell en route to Hollywood from San Francisco, the actual site of the previous broadcast. "Take it away Highway 99!" Wilson exclaims. The program played with radio's ability to transport listeners across great distances by only pretending to go somewhere. Mary is complaining that they are in the fourth day of what should be a ten-hour drive. When they stop for gas, Benny asks for only three gallons. "Is there anything else?" asks the attendant. Says Mary, "Yeah. Squeeze the hose." They decide to stop at a lunchroom near the gas station. The food is no good, the attendant tells Benny, "But you'll like it. The second cup of coffee's free," reflecting that the "public" knew Benny's character. During their meal, Benny turns on the radio right at the end of Don Wilson's Jell-O commercial and just in time for Kenny Baker's song. Then, Baker, Wilson, and Phil Harris discuss what could be keeping Benny. "He probably had trouble with that gasoline snail he drives," Harris speculates.

Benny and Mary Livingstone finally arrive at the studio with Rochester, who has brought Benny's suitcases but failed to pack them. Kenny Baker offers Benny a suit, and Don Wilson offers a shirt. With Wilson's shirt, says Benny, "I won't need your suit, Kenny." "If you need a slip, let me know," adds Mary. Benny discusses the rumor that he's planning on retiring from radio. "I expect to be working for a long time yet, and on radio, too," says Benny, "Even television!" This is a relief to Phil Harris. "If I worked for any other guy, I'd have to learn music," he says. The discussion sets the stage for a sketch projecting the program forty years into the future. With a quavering voice, Don Wilson introduces Benny with "Wheel him in, boys!" Kenny Baker is now the father of five boys. "Let Bing Crosby top that!" he boasts.

Jell-O Program *NOVEMBER 27, 1938*

Benny is suffering from a cold. Phil Harris quickly points out that he visited him at home, but Benny dismisses him: "You knew I had a cold, so you figured I'd have a bottle of whiskey around." Harris needles Benny about his nightgown. Benny defends himself. "Of course, I was wearing a nightgown. It creeps up around my neck where the cold is and keeps me warm." Benny grumbles that he couldn't sleep a wink. "How could you," asks Mary Livingstone, "With all those silver dollars in your mattress?" With their next program originating from New York's Radio City, Benny boasts he'll be seeing a producer about appearing in a production of *Romeo and Juliet.* "You couldn't be a flower pot on the balcony," scoffs Harris. Counters Benny, "Quite possibly I'm going to be Romeo." Adds Mary sarcastically, "With my nightgown, you could be Juliet."

Benny announces their "annual drama of the gridiron: 'Hold That Line! or, One Moment, Please.' " Benny portrays "Flash" Benny, the coach. Before the sketch, Rochester phones to warn Benny that he mixed the cold medicine with the hair tonic, "You ain't never gonna have dandruff in your stomach!" Phil Harris offers that hair tonic won't hurt Benny, "Look at my guitar player, he's the picture of health." "Yes," agrees Benny, "but if you ever take that stool out from under him, watch out!" This is an early example of a "Frankie Remley" gag. Remley, the band's actual guitarist, was the source of one of the program's longest running gags, as Benny and Harris (and much later Bob Crosby) would banter about the musician's perpetual inebriation. The gag became so closely associated with Harris's act, that when he got his own program actor Elliot Lewis was cast to play "Remley," and the guitarist was given dialogue for the first time.

Once the game starts, Frank Nelson is heard as the play-by-play announcer. (Nelson first worked on Benny's *General Tire Revue* in 1934.) "Wilson missed the ball and kicked Baker!" he exclaims. Benny gets the ball. "Wow! Can that boy run! Look at him go! Twenty yards! Thirty yards! Forty yards!" Nelson's exclamations are interrupted by the sound of hoofbeats. Suddenly, it's a horse race. "And here comes Sea Biscuit!"

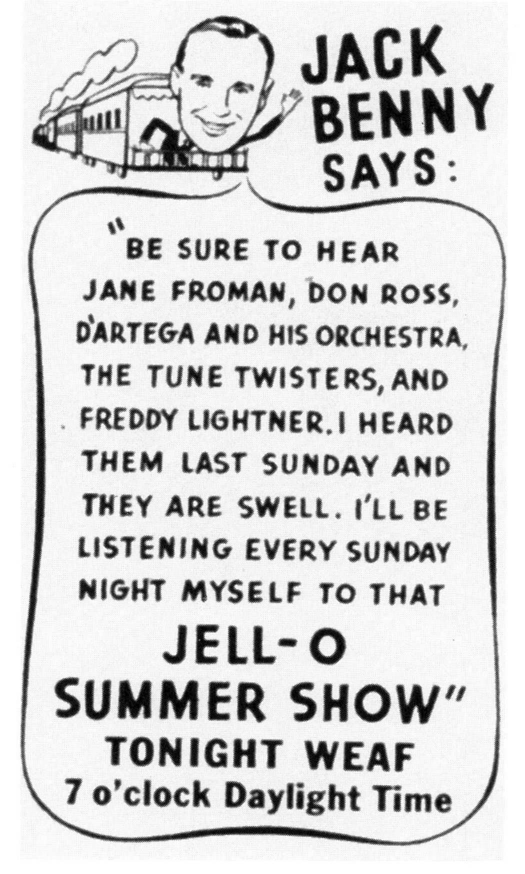

DECEMBER 4, 1938

Jell-O Program

The program originates from New York's Radio City, and Don Wilson introduces Benny as "that little ray of California sunshine. That shimmering, quivering, ice-kissed comedian, Jack Benny!" Benny gripes about the cold New York City weather. "I slept under six blankets. I felt like the bottom wheat cake!" Although he says they're "pretty good friends," Benny complains about his dinner at Fred Allen's. Even though the meal was attended only by Benny, Mary Livingstone, Portland Hoffa, and Allen, Allen insisted that Benny make an after-dinner speech. "He was hoping I would say something that he could use on his program next Wednesday." Benny is extremely loose and relaxed on these New York programs. He teases Mary about her hat, saying it looks "like something a bride would bake" and gets a big laugh when he bills the band as "Phil Harris and His Van Steeden Orchestra"—Harris was using Fred Allen's group rather than taking his band East.

Don Wilson presents Benny and Mary in a parody of the popular vignette-style commercials, where a married couple exchange remarks about a product over an imaginary dinner table. Benny's version concludes, "I have an appointment at the office." Mary asks blankly, "Where is your office?" "It doesn't say here," says Benny. Kenny Baker tells Benny it's the first time he's seen snow, "forgetting" his own snow jokes of March 1937, adding, "It tastes good, too." Benny's lecture on the formation of snowflakes is ended by Mary: "Now, why don't you tell him about the stork?" Benny presents "Murder at the Movies," another detective-story parody. Its conclusion indicates that Benny's derision of his film efforts didn't begin with *The Horn Blows at Midnight.* Captain Benny, Lieutenant Wilson, and Sergeant Harris have tracked the killer to the theater's loge section, but Benny delays his capture to watch *Artists and Models* (Benny's 1937 movie), which infuriates the felon. "I confess! I killed him! I'm the murderer! But I'm not gonna sit through this picture! I'd rather hang!"

DECEMBER 11, 1938

Jell-O Program

Don Wilson teases Benny about not having an overcoat for his New York visit. "Listen, Don, are you selling clothing or Jell-O?" "Jell-O," says Wilson. "Stick to it or I'll fatten up [announcer] Graham McNamee for your job!" threatens Benny. The conversation turns to the band borrowed from Fred Allen. Says Benny, "I don't mind Allen telling them when to laugh and applaud, but when he throws lighted matches around to get them to stamp their feet, that's going too far!" Mary Livingstone has a letter from her mother, whom Benny characterizes as the "Noël

Coward of Plainfield." The missive concludes with bad news about Mary's cousin Otto. The police "caught him on a ladder the other night and he wasn't eloping." In Kenny Baker's absence, Benny offers to play the violin, causing the orchestra to scatter—a radio "sight gag" later used in television. Instead, Phil Harris sings "I've Got a Pocketful of Dreams," which Benny punctuates with a "Yeah, man!" in the final chorus. Benny turns the show over to Don Wilson, while he and Mary leave to do some Christmas shopping. But first Rochester calls from Harlem, where he's enjoying "a little Southern hospitality." Benny asks him three times what has become of his dress suit before Rochester confesses, "Well, I'll be doggoned, I've got it on!"

The scene switches to the department store, where Benny haggles with the woman at the perfume counter until she screams, "Why don't you just run some violets through a wringer and make it yourself!" "Well! Of all the impertinence," Benny huffs with characteristic exasperation. This episode is followed by an encounter with a floorwalker (not played by Frank Nelson), who barks, "Go back to Hollywood and squeeze an orange!" The program concludes with Benny arguing with two salesmen who are trying to sell him an overcoat. When Benny complains, "I've been in shower curtains that fit better than this!" the salesmen shoot at him in a classic example of the Benny character pushing those around him to extremes because of his own petulance.

FEBRUARY 12, 1939

Jell-O Program

The program opens with the cast and audience singing "Happy Birthday" to Benny, who adds his own "Happy Birthday to me!" Benny speaks of all the great men born in February but adds, "I don't want you to think I'm comparing myself to Lincoln or Washington." "Washington wore a wig too," counters Phil Harris. Don Wilson theorizes that Benny is "somewhere between 34 and 37." Mary arrives with two presents for Benny: a necktie and a poem, but first she has to guess his age. "30?" "No," Benny replies coyly. "31?" "No." "32?" "No." "48?" "Shut up!" He had actually turned 45. Mary presents her poem: "Oh, Jack Benny / Oh, Jack Benny / You've had birthdays / but how many? / So happy returns / and all good wishes / from us and Jell-O / so delicious / The end." Rochester phones to wish Benny a happy birthday and to inform him that a polar bear has arrived at Benny's home. At the moment, the bear is taking a cold shower. A growl is heard, but it is from a sound effects device, not from Mel Blanc, whose first role on the program would be the "voice" of Carmichael. Benny theorizes the beast was sent by Fred Allen, then wonders how much it would cost to send an alligator to New York. The "Benny Art and Bingo Players" present a Valentine's Day drama, "Love Finds Annie Hardy; or, It's About Time." (*Love Finds Andy Hardy* was a successful 1938 MGM motion picture starring Mickey Rooney and Judy Garland. Benny's sketch has nothing to do with the movie.) It's about a rural couple's forty-year-old unmarried daughter whom they variously try to marry off to "Tubby" Wilson, "Daffy" Baker, and "Twitch" Harris.

Jell-O Program *OCTOBER 8, 1939*

Dennis Day, the last of the classic Jell-O ensemble, joins the show as the new tenor on the first program of the season. The program opens with Benny picking up the cast in his Maxwell en route to the studio, a pre-show plot device used often. Rochester grumbles about the extra stops. "What are you, a mother hen?" Benny derides Phil Harris because they're meeting him at a beauty parlor. Mary Livingstone says, "You're jealous because Phil's handsome and you're you." Replies Benny, "If you think I'm homely, why don't you come right out and say so?" "It was perfectly clear to me," says Rochester, an exchange that clearly highlights how Benny was the target of his own cast's jokes. Rochester beeps the horn when they spot Kenny Baker in front of his house, but as Mary explains, "He can't answer, he's on another program." Baker had left the *Jell-O Program* shortly before the end of the previous season. Only after this scene does the show "open."

Don Wilson describes Benny without naming him and asks the audience to guess, "Who is he?" Benny clears his throat and hums "Love in Bloom" for six seconds before exploding in exasperation, "For heaven's sake, Jack Benny!" Benny tells Wilson that he and Rochester spent the summer touring the country and leading the gypsy life, explaining, "Rochester read tea leaves and I played the fiddle." Phil Harris arrives to the accompaniment of his theme song, "Rose Room," and refers to himself as "Smiling Phil Harris." He tells Benny he's an actor and says, "I'm not playing a number until I get a couple of laughs here." "The easiest way for you to get laughs is to play a number," replies Benny in one of his frequent attacks on Harris's competence. Benny tells his cast that their new tenor, Dennis Day, is due. He asks his troupe to show him courtesy and respect, since "I'd like to get this kid started out on the right foot." Dennis Day arrives with his mother, played by Verna Felton, who had previously portrayed Phil Harris's and Don Wilson's mother. Felton appeared as Mrs. Day intermittently for the next twelve years on both Benny's and Day's programs. Mrs. Day is extremely hostile to Benny, who can't understand how "a basso profundo like that can have a tenor for a son." Day asks, "When do I get some funny lines?" "I know how you feel, Bub," counsels Harris. Mrs. Day tells Benny that her son is nineteen and was born in Cairo, Illinois. In fact, Day, whose real name was Edward McNulty, was twenty-two and born in the Bronx. When Mrs. Day adjusts her son's tie before his song, Benny scolds, "This isn't television." "You're quite fortunate, Mr. Benny," says Mother Day. (Television sets became commercially available after the New York World's Fair in April 1939, when NBC began providing regular television service.)

MARCH 17, 1940

Jell-O Program

Benny explains to Don, Phil, and Dennis that Orson Welles is going to be his acting coach. Dennis Day tells Benny, "You're a swell actor now. You don't need any coaching." "Yes I do, Dennis," says Benny. "That's right!" Day responds sunnily. Don Wilson characterizes Welles as a "pretty smart youngster." Benny adds that as a baby Welles wore "diapers with cuffs on them." Welles meets the cast. He finds Phil Harris "rather amusing in his own barbaric way." For their lesson, Welles suggests a scene from *The Hunchback of Notre Dame.* "The Charles Laughton part?" inquires Benny, who then quotes Laughton's lines from *Mutiny on the Bounty.* In keeping with his "boy wonder" image, Welles dictates a letter, is fitted for a suit, and takes an overseas phone call during Benny's lesson, which consists largely of groaning. When he finally arrives at Quasimodo's soliloquy, Benny is drowned out by tower bells and another phone call. The broadcast concludes with Welles extending an intra-network invitation to "come over to my show next Sunday. We're going to do *June Moon,* and there's a swell part in it for you." Benny's last word is to Mary, who is ill, "Good night, Doll."

Jell-O Program *OCTOBER 20, 1940*

Benny tells Don Wilson, "This is the busiest week I've ever had." Following the broadcast, he's appearing on CBS's *Screen Guild Theatre,* having dinner, "then back here to do our repeat Jell-O show, and then back again and do the second program for the Guild." With recorded programs prohibited by NBC, many shows were done twice to accommodate different time zones. "And at 11 o'clock," Benny adds, "I've got to emcee the opening of that new Chili Bowl in Tarzana." Phil Harris enters with a joke. "This'll kill you, Jackson! What's a twack?" Benny doesn't know. "It's something a twain wuns on!" Dennis Day asks Benny the same question minus the answer because "Mr. Harris won't tell me." Benny asks Dennis if he had registered for the draft, telling him if he is inducted his salary would be twenty-one dollars a month. "Grab it, kid. It's a raise," advises Livingstone. Day's song is introduced as "Twade Winds," and Don Wilson's Jell-O commercial touts "six dewicious fwavors." Benny gets a ficticious call from Mark Sandrich, the director of *Love Thy Neighbor,* the film Benny made with Fred Allen. Benny insists that he be billed ahead of Allen. "I don't care what that worm said! He's in New York and I'm here! Take care of the local boy!"

When Benny "leaves" for his *Screen Guild* appearance, Mary Livingstone tells how she convinced Benny to trade in his Maxwell. The scene switches to the previous week, with Rochester driving Benny and Livingstone to the dealer. They are stopped by a policeman. Benny insists on doing the talking. "What can you say without your writers?" asks Mary. They visit a Packard dealership. Benny wants seven hundred dollars for his Maxwell; they offer forty dollars. "Confidentially, boss, snap at it," offers Rochester. Benny accepts the deal until he learns they plan on junking his old car. Near tears, Benny declares, "I'm sorry, Mr. Collins, the deal is off!" Back at the studio, Phil Harris suggests to Mary, "Let's go home and hear Jack's *Screen Guild* show." Benny was featured that evening in a sketch with Claudette Colbert directed by Ernst Lubitsch, who would be Benny's director for *To Be or Not to Be.*

DECEMBER 15, 1940

Jell-O Program

The program originates from New York's Ritz Theatre because Benny is in New York for the premiere of his film with Fred Allen, *Love Thy Neighbor.* He takes an opening shot at Allen: "There's a guy living in this town that makes me look like Diamond Jim Brady." For protection against Allen, Benny has hired a bodyguard, Killer Hogan, a lisping, effeminate character. Don Wilson is honeymooning in New York, so Benny offers to pay his hotel bill. "Where are you living?" Benny asks. "At the Ritz-Carlton," replies Wilson. "Yipe!" responds Benny, who hands his announcer a handful of nickles, telling him, "you *know* where to eat!" (meaning the Automat). When Wilson tells Mary Livingstone that Jack is paying his expenses, she cracks, "That's great! Jack who?" Dennis Day tells Benny he's got nothing to fear from Fred Allen, since his uncle, Tip-Toes McNulty, is the house detective where Benny is staying. Phil Harris arrives late. "Hiya, Jackson! Look what I found in the hall!" "Phil!" yells Benny, "put Hogan down!" Frank Nelson, an increasing presence on the program, makes his second appearance as Dr. LeRoy, a medical quack, who checks Benny's lungs. "Take a real deep breath," he tells his patient, "Now, hold it!" This is Don Wilson's cue, "While Jack is holding his breath, why don't you run down to your grocer and ask him for a package of Jell-O?" Mancel Talcott, the mayor of Waukegan, arrives to convince Benny to move the premiere of *Love Thy Neighbor* to Benny's hometown. Talcott visited the program in March 1937, and Benny had broadcast from Waukegan in 1939. Talcott mistakes Dennis Day for Kenny Baker, which doesn't bother Day, who reasons, "What's the difference? A tenor's a tenor." Benny begins calling around for Rochester, who has been missing in Harlem since the previous program. Benny calls one place where he asks, "Was he shooting craps?" "He must have been, we ain't much for backgammon up here."

Jell-O Program *APRIL 20, 1941*

See pages 164–181 for the complete script with annotations by Rich Conaty.

Jell-O Program *MAY 11, 1941*

Benny is introduced as "an actor whose roles extend from leading man in *Love Thy Neighbor* to leading lady in *Charley's Aunt.*" The latter film was still in production at Twentieth Century-Fox. Benny's female impersonation act was so convincing, he claims he was picked up by comedian Jack Oakie. "I walked home from Santa Monica," Benny gripes, "He can keep his mink coat!" Dennis Day extends Mother's Day greetings and thanks Benny for all he's done, including saving his money for him. "It's nothing at all," Benny says modestly. "I'm keeping track, Bub," warns Dennis, switching moods.

Phil Harris apologizes for missing NBC's tenth anniversary salute to Benny aired the previous Friday. Don Wilson turns the program over to *Kraft Music Hall* announcer Ken Carpenter, who presents "The Life of Jack Benny in Music," a portion of the tenth anniversary salute. The story, with actors portraying Benny, Livingstone, and others, follows the facts of Benny's career closely, but occasionally blends in show devices, blurring the distinction between fact and fiction. His real age of 47 is given, but his father is called Meyer Benny rather than Kubelsky, and Mary Livingstone is called Mary rather than Sadie Marks. Benny's life is traced from Waukegan to an initial try at vaudeville, then back home to his father's store. As the chorus explains, "Selling men's apparel only filled young Jack with loathing / He wanted to be next to closing / instead of next to clothing." Benny gets back into vaudeville, bombs at the Palace (untrue), joins the Navy, emerges as a solo performer (true), marries, and eventually winds up on Broadway in the *Vanities* (true). The story simplifies his entry into radio, but states the date of his first Ed Sullivan appearance as May 1931, a year before the frequently cited 1932 show. It credits early writer Harry Conn and the current team of Ed Beloin and Bill Morrow. It praises the cast, though unfortunately refers to Rochester as a "Dusky Devil" and adds, "Jack and Mary do all the work / and he gets all the laughs." Benny returns to thank NBC, Ken Carpenter, and conductor Gordon Jenkins. He also thanks those who participated in the Friday night salute: Claudette Colbert, Herbert Marshall, the Quiz Kids, Ed Sullivan, Ole Olsen (of Olsen and Johnson), and Benny's earliest announcers, Ed Thorgersen and Alois Havrilla.

FEBRUARY 1, 1942

Jell-O Program

Frank Nelson, portraying the show's actual sound effects man, Virgil Reime, does an opening monologue that is heavily punctuated by the sounds of his craft. Benny is not amused and berates "Virgil's" efforts. The balance of the program is devoted to the conclusion of a mystery, "The Frightwig Murder Case; or, That Rug Will Have to Go to the Cleaners," featuring guest star Humphrey Bogart. Virgil wants to meet Bogart, who, it turns out, is a fan of the sound effects man. Bogart refuses to play Phil Harris's assistant in the play. Then he insists on announcing the play and amends its title to include ". . . or All Through the Night," a Bogart picture then in release. Benny is exasperated at Bogart's demands and can't understand why he doesn't slug him. "You're a coward," Phil Harris explains. "Oh, yes," Benny realizes. Mary Livingstone's character is done in the manner of Mae West, whom she impersonated on a 1933 *Chevrolet Program.* Virgil refuses to supply the sound of a door breaking down until Benny apologizes for yelling at him. "O'Benny" confesses to the murder and is accused by Bogart of doing so merely to build up his part. As the other cast members exit, Benny is left behind to play gin rummy with Dennis Day, who played the corpse.

MAY 10, 1942

Jell-O Program

As part of the war effort, Benny, like Bob Hope and many others, took his program to military bases. This one, originating from Mather Field, incorporates "The Army Air Corps Song" into the opening theme, which now includes "Love in Bloom" (though not on every program). Dennis Day's naïveté is amply displayed. He is embarrassed by the word "sexton." When Benny learns he will not be broadcasting for Jell-O next season, the balance of the program is devoted to his fear that he's been fired. "Goodbye, Benny! Hello, Skelton!" he frets. (In its first season, Red Skelton's Tuesday night Raleigh-sponsored program was nearly as popular as Benny's.) Benny and Don Wilson drive over to see their sponsor, Mr. Mortimer. Charles Mortimer was, in fact, General Foods's chairman of the board. Wilson offers comfort. "You're a great comedian!" "I stink and you know it!"—another glimpse of insecurity. Eight years after Benny had genuine sponsor problems, he continued to mine humor from his unfounded fear of cancellation. Following the meeting, Benny explains to Wilson that they are not being fired, only broadcasting for another product of General Foods. Wilson, with so much of his character tied to Jell-O, is near hysteria: "I won't do it, I tell ya! I won't do it!" After Benny calms him down, Wilson asks, "As long as they're at their grocers, can't they buy a little package of Jell-O, too?" Due to

wartime sugar shortages, production of Jell-O was cut severely and any that was available sold regardless of Benny.

Grape-Nuts and Grape-Nuts Flakes Program

OCTOBER 4, 1942

The show opens with the Jell-O theme and Don Wilson announcing, "The Jell-O Program. Starring Jack Benny, with Mary Livingstone. . . ." Benny interrupts, "No! No! Don! It's not Jell-O! It's Grape-Nuts Flakes this year!" Wilson panics and mispronounces the product as "Grapes-Nuts." The clock is turned back to an hour before the broadcast for a pre-show sketch. Once again Benny has volunteered to collect the cast in his Maxwell. Mary Livingstone scolds Benny for having a sign advertising his new picture, *George Washington Slept Here,* on the back of the car. When they arrive at Dennis Day's house, Day refuses to get in unless Benny gives him a raise. "You better get in this car!" Benny threatens, "Kenny Baker is in the tool chest!" When the gang arrives at NBC, Benny drops in on the rehearsal of the fictitious soap opera, *The Heartaches of Sally Sutton,* which he and Rochester listen to every morning. Frank Nelson is the announcer. Benny is stunned to find Dennis Day in the cast. "Well, I gotta make some money someplace!" Don Wilson continues to have trouble with the Grape-Nuts announcements. He advises listeners to "be sure to look for the red letters on the box" in the manner of Jell-O. As the show closes, Benny and Rochester are discussing *Sally Sutton.* Rochester is unaware that Benny had heard the rehearsal. Says Benny, "I'll bet you five bucks they're going to get a divorce!"

FEBRUARY 21, 1943

Grape-Nuts and Grape-Nuts Flakes Program

Benny describes the audience for this Chicago-based program as "boys who are studying to be Army Air Force technicians." This leads to a Fred Allen gag, "Every time I tune in to Fred Allen's program, the aerial coils up and strikes at me like a rattlesnake." Benny then describes his local accommodations, saying, "I'm at the Stockyards Plaza. I have a lovely room overlooking Armour and Company. On a clear day you can see meat." Dennis Day enters boiling mad. "You hired Bing Crosby, and this program isn't big enough for the both of us!" Benny explains that it is not Bing, but Bob Crosby, who is the guest bandleader. As Benny points out, "This fellow here is wearing a necktie." (Bob Crosby would succeed Phil Harris as bandleader at the beginning of the 1952 season.) After Don Wilson describes his dream of being a Grape-Nuts flake, Day quips, "Wilson in a twelve-ounce package, that's a hot one!" Benny tells the military audience that in the Navy he was known as the Skipper. "And you still walk that way," cracks Mary Livingstone. Bob Crosby asks Benny for a tour of nearby Waukegan, "especially that log cabin where you were born." Rochester telephones (as usual) to tell Benny he's been taking advantage of Chicago cultural life. Wednesday was the museum, and Thursday he went to the planetarium. Friday, though, "I met a gal and culture went out the window." Benny concludes, "Well, I've got to run along now and be a judge on the Quiz Kids show. Good night, folks."

MARCH 14, 1943

Grape-Nuts and Grape-Nuts Flakes Program

Orson Welles substitutes for Benny, who is ill. Phil Harris returns after an absence of three months. Although not mentioned on the air, at age thirty-nine he was deemed too old for the Merchant Marine. Harris is very anxious to see Welles. "When I put on the dog, you'd think I was graduated at Oxnard." Miss Harrington, Welles's private secretary, arrives. She disinfects the microphone Welles will use, then sprays Harris. These preparations are reminiscent of Welles's 1940 Jell-O appearance. Welles is preceded by a fanfare, then intones, "Good evening. This is Orson Welles." He notices Dennis Day is terrified and reassures him, "*All* tenors shouldn't be killed." Welles dictates a letter to Harvard: "I have recently come upon a specimen that should prove of great interest in your study of subnormal extroverts. At present, he is conducting the orchestra on a well-known radio program." Harris is ecstatic, "Wow! I'm getting a build-up at Harvard!" Dennis Day requests a raise. Currently he's making twelve dollars, but when he does Benny's laundry he gets fourteen. "Some weeks, it's only a pair of socks, but it ruins me socially." Andy Devine enters with a couple of steaks for Rita Hayworth. "Is she your girlfriend?" Welles asks. "She will be till the meat's gone," says Devine, in reference to wartime shortages. Welles suggests they all have dinner together. "I'm not a genius, Orson," says Devine, "but I can see through that!" (Welles married Hayworth on September 7, 1943.) Welles places a call to General Foods. Welles says, "I'd like my picture put on the box," a reference to the fact that a sketch of Jack Benny was actually on the box of Grape-Nuts Flakes. Welles invites the cast to visit him the next week at Orson Welles Productions. After lunch, "I'll make a picture for you." Not an epic, he explains, "just a good solid drama with a message." Rochester phones in a status report on Benny, who is recuperating in Chicago. Don Wilson concludes with a chuckle, "In spite of Orson Welles, this program is written by Bill Morrow and Ed Beloin."

APRIL 11, 1943

Grape-Nuts and Grape-Nuts Flakes Program

Benny returns after a five-week absence. The program is set in the bedroom of Benny's Beverly Hills home with Rochester preparing a cold remedy. Benny is surprised to learn the formula includes gin. He catches Rochester sampling the "medicine"; the valet claims he was "holding it up to the light and some of it ran down my throat." Mary Livingstone praises Orson Welles's recent job filling in for Benny. Benny grumbles that Welles didn't even send him a basket of fruit, "I finally had to wire him!" When Phil Harris visits, he sneaks in a plug for his wife: "Alice Faye, now appearing in *Hello, Frisco, Hello,* made a dozen donuts for you with her own little hands." Benny's doctor, played by Frank Nelson, enters. "I gotta go down to NBC and do a broadcast today," Benny tells him. "Why? Is Orson Welles sick?" Nelson asks. Dennis Day, too, is shocked that Welles will be absent: "Gosh! The 'Orson Welles Program' without Orson Welles! I worry about things like that." As before, Miss Harrington precedes Welles, who enters with much fanfare. "Gee, you'd think he was [guitarist] Frank Remley or something the way they're jumping around here!" says Benny. Even though Welles is not on the program this week, he wants to stay to watch the rehearsal. He spots a draft of Benny's ficticious autobiography, *From Rags to Radio.* Welles begins to recite sections of the book, but is interrupted by Don Wilson, who must deliver his commercial. Welles joins in. Things get chaotic, and when Benny addresses Welles, "But, Oswald . . . ," the cast breaks up. Frank Nelson returns. He gives Benny a sleeping pill instead of an aspirin, which kicks in rapidly, so it looks as though Welles will be doing the show after all.

Grape-Nuts and Grape-Nuts Flakes Program

DECEMBER 19, 1943

The show opens in the home of Mary Livingstone, who returns following a three-week absence due to laryngitis. Butterfly McQueen, who joined the program earlier in the season, is heard as Livingstone's maid. McQueen is best remembered for her role as "Prissy" in *Gone with the Wind*, which also included Eddie Anderson in the cast. In 1943 she was a featured player in *Cabin in the Sky*, in which Anderson costarred. In the 1944–45 radio season, Doris Singleton took over the role as Mary's maid, and McQueen went on to work on Danny Kaye's CBS series.

Benny visits bearing a box of candy "with over a hundred pieces in it"—a package of Sen Sen breath fresheners. Mary's mother calls to find out if Livingstone will be paid for her missed programs. This sparks an argument with Benny that fades as the orchestra enters. After, Benny apologizes. "Let's kiss and make up," he suggests. The sound of kissing is heard, then "How was that?" asks Benny. "Let's argue," counters Livingstone. Dennis enters during the fight, which concludes with the pair conceding they are dopes. "It's nothing to be ashamed of," offers Dennis Day. Rochester arrives with Benny's "new" car, a taxicab, complete with meter. "You never know when he's gonna give a friend a lift," explains Rochester. He has come to take Benny Christmas shopping. En route, they pick up a passenger, whom Benny ejects when he learns the man is rushing home to hear Fred Allen. Benny has an encounter with Frank Nelson as the floorwalker, who explains, "I'm not rugged enough to be a customer." Benny and Rochester meet Phil Harris, who gives Benny his usual greeting, adding, "Hello, Chester!" When Benny learns that Don Wilson is playing Santa Claus, he convinces Phil to dress up like a kid. Benny goes off to dress like the boy's mother. While waiting for Benny, Harris exclaims, "Oh boy, look what Jack's missing! Hiya, Babe!" "Shut up, it's me!" hisses Benny. Harris plays "Clearwater Clapsaddle," a takeoff on Red Skelton's "mean widdle kid," who tells "Santa" Wilson that he wants Grape-Nuts Flakes for Christmas. "You should be proud of him, Mrs. Clapsaddle," Wilson tells Benny.

APRIL 23, 1944

Grape-Nuts and Grape-Nuts Flakes Program

The program originates from Vancouver Municipal Stadium. Vancouver is the actual hometown of Mrs. Benny. "Mary Livingstone" was born in Plainfield, New Jersey, but that issue is sidestepped on this program. Instead, Livingstone reminisces about her hometown, saying, "Just think, Jack, right here in Vancouver I spent my girlhood days. Gee, Vancouver, 1928." Benny counters, "I spent my boyhood days in Waukegan." "Gee, Waukegan, 1883," cracks Livingstone. Benny recalls playing in vaudeville at the Orpheum Theatre. Mary asks him if he remembers seeing a little girl with blonde curls in the audience. "Was that you?" Benny asks. "No, that was my mother!" "Now cut that out!" commands Benny. Phil Harris and Mary sing "You, You, You." After, Mary scolds Benny, "You see, Jack, you were wrong. Phil *can* do something!" Harris teases Don Wilson during the Grape-Nuts commercial, asking, "Did it ever occur to you that someone might want an egg for breakfast? One little egg?" Wilson is unfazed, "It's perfectly all right to have an egg as long as you have your Grape-Nuts or Grape-Nuts Flakes first!" After an awkward exchange with Vancouver's mayor, Dennis Day enters for his song, then Benny announces that Day is leaving the program. "If you were leaving for any other reason except to join the Armed Forces," says Benny, "I'd hate to lose you." Benny then tries to sell his singer his old sailor suit for ten dollars. Day offers Benny his civilian wardrobe. "All you have to do is keep up the payments," he says. Rochester's phone call gets a big reaction from the crowd. He tells Benny that he received eleven Canadian dollars for ten American ones. "Sounds like something you might have started," says Rochester, who adds his congratulations to Day. In a touching moment Dennis Day steps out of character to say, "Jack, I can never thank you and Mary for all you've done for me, and for the five most wonderful years of my life."

Lucky Strike Program *OCTOBER 1, 1944*

This is Benny's first program for the American Tobacco Company. Unlike the Jell-O and Grape-Nuts shows, Don Wilson is not heard until after announcer Basil Ruysdael and the two Lucky Strike auctioneers, F. E. Boone and L. A. "Speed" Riggs, present a one-minute and ten-second opening commercial. Wilson's first words are followed by Benny's new theme song, a medley combining "Love in Bloom" and "Yankee Doodle Dandy." Although Benny's association with "Love in Bloom" goes back to 1935, it was not a formal part of every broadcast until this show. The program opens in Benny's Beverly Hills home, where Rochester is preparing breakfast. He answers the telephone with Benny's usual billing as a star of stage, screen, and radio, but adds, "Whether you go out or stay home, he's got you trapped." When the milkman arrives, he asks Rochester about Benny's new sponsor. Says Rochester, "From now on he's gonna be with L.S.M.F.T.!" ("Lucky Strike Means Fine Tobacco" was the company slogan.) Mary Livingstone arrives, kissing Benny twice. "My, for heaven's sake, put me down!" Benny implores. Don Wilson and Phil Harris arrive. Don Wilson is worried that the new sponsor may not like him. Livingstone tells Wilson he's a natural to represent Lucky: "You're so round, so firm, so fully packed." Benny panics when he gets a call to visit his sponsor.

Following a Harris vocal, the scene switches to the offices of the president of American Tobacco, G. W. Hill. (See page 244 for the April 1953 television version of the following sketch.) Benny announces to Hill's secretary, "The star of his Lucky Strike radio program is here!" "You're not looking so well today, Mr. Sinatra," she replies. (Frank Sinatra was then the singing star of Lucky Strike's *Your Hit Parade* on CBS.) Benny paraphrases the company slogan to provide another clue: "With men who know comedians best, it's Benny two to one!" The scene switches to inside Hill's office. "Well, first of all Mr. Hill—" Fred Allen's unmistakable voice is interrupted by applause, "I don't want you to think I have anything against Benny personally." When Allen is greeted with an additional round of applause, he quips, "With Allen, it's two receptions to one." Allen is setting Hill straight on the subject of Jack Benny. "Anyone can get laughs who tells a joke, wiggles his ears, drops his pants, and then shows a Bob Hope movie on the seat of his underwear," he says. Hill, who is impersonated, tells Allen he thinks Benny is a good choice for his product, since people smoke while listening to the radio. Allen counters, "How can anyone smoke and hold his nose at the same time?" Allen exits before Benny, now a nervous wreck, enters. Hill begins to tell Benny about his conversation with Allen, but Benny explodes, "That's a lie!" Upon his return, Allen greets Benny with, "Jack, old pal, it's certainly good to see what's left of you." He tells

Benny he is making a film at United Artists. "I heard that Boris Karloff isn't there anymore," responds Benny. An argument erupts and Hill intercedes, "Jack, why don't you and Fred shake hands—" "You shut up!" barks Benny, whose apologies fade as the music swells. After another commercial, Benny returns to announce that Frank Sinatra will be next Sunday's guest. He tells Mary Livingstone he is considering him for the singing spot. Mary informs him Sinatra already has two shows. "Maybe he'll hire me," concludes Benny.

Lucky Strike Program *JANUARY 7, 1945*

This program introduces three memorable comic devices: a trip to the vault; an encounter with the race track tout; and the "Anaheim, Azusa, and Cucamonga" refrain. Benny is preparing for his trip to New York for a broadcast the following Sunday. He sings "Sidewalks of New York" and reminisces about such old vaudeville acts as Fink's Mules and Fred Allen. Benny estimates his expenses for the trip as nine meals at fifty cents each. He considers having Rochester pack sandwiches, but concludes, "Nah. How often do you go to New York?" He decides expenses will be five dollars to be on the safe side, which prompts a visit to his safe. Benny's footsteps are heard, then a door is opened, then more footsteps, then another, noisier door is opened. "Wonder if that door is heavy enough," Benny muses. He meets Ed, who guards the safe. "Shall I turn my back?" Ed asks. Benny opens the safe, which sets off an alarm, a siren, then a slide whistle, and finally the bellow of a steamship, which is referred to in the script as a "B. O. foghorn." After the withdrawal, Benny says his goodbye to Ed, "I'll see you in the spring." Back upstairs, Rochester reacts to the alarm. "Everybody in Beverly Hills is digging foxholes!" Rochester packs Benny's toupees, including two fur-lined ones and another with a cowlick that makes him look like Van Johnson.

Benny's arrival at the railroad station is accompanied by the first announcement for the train leaving for "Anaheim, Azusa, and Cucamonga," delivered with increasing desperation throughout the scene by Mel Blanc. Former vaudeville star Benny Rubin is heard as the race track tout. He tries to talk Benny out of taking the Chief to New York. "The El Capitan beat the Chief into Kansas City by three lengths." But Benny counters in equally conspiratorial tones, "I found out the Chief . . . is a sleeper." This episode is followed by an encounter with Frank Nelson, who is working behind the ticket counter. "What do you think I am in this cage, a canary?" he asks. When Benny informs him he's traveling one-way, Nelson snaps, "Good!" However, Nelson has no ticket for Benny. "There must be one train that has room for me," he pleads, cueing "Anaheim, Azusa, and Cucamonga."

FEBRUARY 11, 1945

Lucky Strike Program

The program originates from the Glenview Naval Air Station in Glenview, Illinois. Don Wilson points out that Benny's birthday is coming up Wednesday, adding that some babies are born with silver spoons in their mouths, but Benny was "the only baby that was born with a toupee on its head!" Benny insists it was the doctor's fur-lined glove and, "My mother thought the thumb was a cowlick." Mary Livingstone greets the audience upon arriving and claims to have gone on a flight with a young pilot with "a medal for good behavior, but I made him give it back," her flirtatious side surfacing. Benny claims he is turning 36 and proves it by taking the year of his previous birthday (1944) and deducting the number of letters in Waukegan. Using the same formula, Livingstone proves she is four months old. Larry Stevens, the stand-in crooner while Dennis Day served in the Navy, wishes Benny a happy birthday. Stevens's father turned fifty-four yesterday, "but he tells everybody he's forty-two." Livingstone says of Benny, "He's 23, but he tells everybody he's 36." The news frightens twenty-two-year-old Stevens, "Look what's going to happen to me in just one year!" Phil Harris greets Benny with "I hope you live to be as old as you look!" Don Wilson presents Benny with a gift, a picture of Whistler's mother smoking a Lucky Strike. Benny plugs Harris's upcoming appearance on the *Fitch Bandwagon* broadcast. "The way you congratulated him," says Livingstone, "I thought he was going on the water wagon." "Mary, stop being ridiculous!" scolds Benny. "Yeah!" adds Harris.

Benny announces a nautical sketch, "Boy! Was I Seasick; or, You Can't Take It with You." Captain Jack McBenny is the commander of an aircraft carrier heading for a secret destination.

Ensign Harris delivers a coded message, "L.S.M.F.T.," or "Load supplies, move for Tokyo." The sketch is interrupted by Dick Powell, who explains, "We're going to broadcast from here, too. I'm on the *Fitch Bandwagon!*" Suddenly, McBenny spies "a hulking shape looming through the mist!" The hulk is Andy Devine, whose greeting, "Hiya, Buck!" gets a huge reaction. Benny decides, "We'll finish the sketch in St. Joe. They love me there!" The next program was broadcast from St. Joseph, Missouri, before an audience of 4,000 Red Cross blood donors.

Lucky Strike Program

APRIL 29, 1945

The broadcast opens with Benny relaxing in his library. He spots *Forever Amber,* commenting, "No pictures. This book's on the wrong shelf." Of a missing volume he says, "Ronald Colman took that one two weeks ago. Say, that little book is going to pay for itself in no time!" Spotting *My Diary* by Rochester Van Jones, he reads the April 2 entry. "Two nights ago I dreamed that Lena Horne fell madly in love with me. Last night I dreamed she threw her arms around my neck and kissed me. Right now I'm drinking Ovaltine as my dreams are getting better all the time." Mary Livingstone arrives with the current *Look* magazine featuring Benny on the cover. He instructs Rochester to put it on the bulletin board in front of the house. "Should I put it above or below the reviews for *The Horn Blows at Midnight?*" asks Rochester. Next to them, says Benny, "And while you're out there, throw those rocks back off the lawn." This is one of the first gags about the then-new Benny film.

A new Mel Blanc character, violin instructor Professor Andre LeBlanc, is introduced on this program. After an excruciating attempt to play the scale, LeBlanc suggests, "Perhaps if you held the violin upside down." "But Professor, I can't play that way," pleads Benny. "Let's try anything!" counters LeBlanc, who sings along with the practicing, "Hold your bow so strokes are littler / They should make you play for Hitler." When Phil Harris enters, LeBlanc greets him with "Ah, a fellow artiste!" and kisses Harris twice. "Funny. He didn't do that when I came in," says Benny. LeBlanc concludes that he might be able to do something for Benny, but first wants to know how old Benny is. "Why?" asks Benny. "How much time have we got left?" says the Professor.

DECEMBER 2, 1945

Lucky Strike Program

The details of the "I Can't Stand Jack Benny Because . . ." contest are announced on this program, which begins with Benny boasting that his career has "covered show business from *A* to *Z.*" "From actor to zombie," cracks Mary Livingstone. Benny asks Don Wilson to define a "zombie." Explains Wilson, "A man with hollow eyes, a vacant stare, and, although he's really dead, he still walks around." "Mary!" exclaims Benny, "How many times have I told you not to mention Fred Allen on this program!" Frank Nelson is Westbrook Shlogglemeyer, a columnist syndicated throughout "Anaheim, Azusa, and Cucamonga," doing a story on the $10,000 contest. "Are you a reporter?" Benny asks. "Well, what do you think I am with this pencil in my ear, *a desk set?*" is Nelson's characteristically hostile reply. Mary is skeptical that Benny would be willing to part with such a large amount, but Don Wilson says, "I think the whole idea about you being cheap is just a gag." Counters Mary, "When he goes to bed at night he puts his money in his mouth and rubs alum on his lips." Benny waits ten seconds for the laugh to build and then retorts, "I only did that once!" Phil Harris gets a call from his "daughter," played by Jeanine Roose, who tells Harris she has been bad: "I broke twenty-six records of 'That's What I Like About the South.' " Harris used to sing it to her when she was a baby. "I could hardly wait to grow up," cracks Jeanine, who would later play Harris's daughter on his own series.

Mabel and Gertrude, the NBC switchboard operators introduced at the beginning of the season, are heard discussing the contest. Gertrude (played by Bea Benaderet) speculates, "I'll bet he marries the winner." Even if a man wins, "He'll dress up like Charley's Aunt, have an early ceremony, and make a quick trip to Reno!" Benny's fast-talking press agent, Steve Bradley, a character played by Richard Lane and introduced on September 30, explains the $10,000 giveaway: "This is the greatest thing to hit radio since L.S. was introduced to M.F.T.!" Bradley reasons that since only 30 million people listen to Benny, "100 million don't like you. And that's only in this country!" A total of $10,000 in Victory Bonds will be awarded to the winners, who will be selected by the Supreme Judge, "the Honorable Fred Allen." After the final commercial, Harris tells Benny 3,000 entries have already arrived. "That's my regular fan mail!" Benny quips.

Lucky Strike Program *JANUARY 6, 1946*

Artie Auerbach's Mr. Kitzel, a Jewish caricature much like Sam Hearn's Schlepperman, is introduced in a flashback sequence. The program opens with Mary Livingstone complaining about the bad time Benny showed her on New Year's Eve, "It's the first time I've ever done the Minuet!" Don Wilson tells a corny joke about being stuck in the chimney, "I was lucky enough to catch the flue!" "Don," says Benny, "I have an arrangement with Abbott and Costello. We leave them alone and they leave us alone!" At the time, the brash comic duo was heard Thursdays on NBC and sponsored by Lucky Strike's competitor, Camel cigarettes. Benny welshes on a fifty-dollar bet he made with Phil Harris on the previous week's Rose Bowl game because he did not see it: "I don't care if a hundred thousand people saw it! I'm not taking the word of a lot of strangers. That's how rumors get started." The story of how Benny missed the game follows, in a variation of a January 1941 program. (This annual New Year's story would be re-created several times on television.) Benny is in the company of Gladys, played by Sara Berner, whom he met at Simon's Drive-In. "Yeah, it was chicken gumbo night," she explains. Artie Auerbach plays a hot dog vendor whose "Peekle een the meeddle" song became quite well known. He charges only three cents for his "puppies." "How come you sell them so cheap?" Benny asks. "Taste 'em!" explains Auerbach. In 1941, Sam Hearn as Schlepperman had played the vendor, and at least one line is identical; commenting on the hot dogs' toughness, both said, "What suitcases they would make."

APRIL 14, 1946 **Lucky Strike Program**

Benny takes another violin lesson with Professor LeBlanc, who is puzzled that with only four strings and only five fingers, "the nine of you make so many mistakes." Benny asks the professor if he'd like some lunch, but LeBlanc prefers money. "That gag alone ought to get you a summer show," Benny quips. In fact, Blanc did get his own CBS series in September 1946. LeBlanc's plea for payment is incorporated into the Lucky Strike commercial that follows. He shows up again when Rochester goes over to the Colmans to borrow some butter. (Ronald Colman and his wife Benita Hume would make more than twenty appearances on the program over the next four years.) "How long you been waiting?" Rochester asks. "Since 12 o'clock," LeBlanc replies. Rochester, it turns out, has been waiting to get paid since 1937. Ronald Colman is stunned by Rochester's request: "Butter? Butter! What does he think this is, Shangri-la?"—a combined reference to Colman's role in *Lost Horizon* and lingering postwar food shortages. Rochester leaves, and Colman returns to rehearsing his "If I Were King" soliloquy from *The Prisoner of Zenda,* which Benny interrupts with his violin playing. "Would you please put the cat out!" an exasperated Colman asks his wife. When he learns it is Benny, he declares, "Call the police! Call the fire department! Call Petrillo!"—the latter being the head of the Musicians' Union. Colman's shouting prompts a complaint from next-door neighbor Benny. As the program ends, Professor LeBlanc shows up at the Colmans to enlist their help in getting paid.

Lucky Strike Program *MARCH 16, 1947*

Don Wilson uses the previous Thursday's Academy Awards presentation to introduce Benny as "the man who had the hat check concession." "I was master of ceremonies, too," Benny adds. Benny reviews the tipping habits of the stars, "Margaret O'Brien, a nickel! I felt like throwing it back in her face!" Don Wilson tells Benny he has been asked to appear on a television program. Benny is skeptical of Wilson's claim: "They'll never get a sixty-inch beam on a ten-inch screen." Mary Livingstone supplies a poem on the subject, "Television is here to stay, and it won't be hard to sell it / Now you can hear and see Jack's show / and soon you'll be able to smell it!" (Benny's first television appearance was still two years away, when he participated in the dedication of the Los Angeles Station KTTV.) Phil Harris arrives late, a curler still in his hair. He woke up on the wrong side of the bed, and he has got his wife Alice Faye's shoes on. Harris explains that he will need sight gags when he makes the inevitable move to television. He's not egotistical. "I'm much better looking than I think I am," he says, a classic Harris vanity line. Don Wilson informs Benny that the sponsor insists they get a new group to replace the Sportsmen Quartet, the vocal group introduced at the beginning of the season which Benny had "fired" three weeks previously. Wilson has found another group. Lucky Strike's *Your Hit Parade* vocalist Andy Russell is the first to arrive. Next is Dick Haymes, then Bing Crosby, who incorporates Lucky Strike's slogan into his theme, "Where the Blue of the Night Meets the Gold of the Day, L.S.M.F.T." With the addition of Dennis Day, the quartet sings a special version of "Always": "L.S.M.F.T., Always. That's the smoke for me, *Always.*" The last note is too high for Crosby, who ad libs, "Who the hell picked this key, Dennis Day?" Such language was strictly forbidden on the air, and the remark gets a huge audience reaction. When the group sings "Ragtime Cowboy Joe," tenor Dennis Day wants to sing bass "to get down where the money is." At the close of the show, Crosby returns to congratulate Benny on the award he has received from *Daily Variety.* "On behalf of my cast and writers who have been with me so long, I want to thank the *Variety* for this honor," says Benny, who admonishes Crosby, "The next time you come over, tuck your shirt in."

FEBRUARY 15, 1948

Lucky Strike Program

The Beverly Hills Beavers, the Boy-Scout-like troop introduced earlier in the season, are depleting their entire treasury, $1.43, to celebrate Benny's 39th birthday. A new member doesn't know who Benny is. "He's only the greatest fullback Yale ever had," responds a veteran member. Benny even loaned the club money for their baseball uniforms, "And my father says 4 percent is reasonable." Even Benny's age proves how smart he is. "He was in my uncle's class in school," a Beaver offers, "and my uncle's fifty-five!" The scene switches to the home of Mary Livingstone, who is planning her own party for Benny with her maid Pauline, played by Doris Singleton. Next, Phil Harris is heard in the midst of a game of pool discussing his party plans for Benny, and then we learn that Dennis Day is planning a party. At the Wilson home, Don is wrapping his gift for Benny. He tells his wife that the present is "round and firm and fully packed." Mrs. Wilson guesses a box of Crayolas, so he gives her another clue, "L.S.M.F.T." "Long silk muffler from Tubby?" she ventures. Benny, thinking his birthday has been forgotten, has locked himself in the den. Mary calls Rochester to clear things up: everyone is coming to Benny's for a party, but Rochester needs to get Benny out of the house so he can get things ready. Benny enters a theater showing *The Horn Blows at Midnight.* "Guess they're running it again on account of the Academy Awards," he speculates. Four hours later, the exasperated manager, Frank Nelson, is trying to get Benny to leave. The cast is gone when Benny returns home and he considers firing them. In this typical periodic outburst of insecurity, he rails, "If I had any talent, I would!" When Rochester explains the next morning that the gang had been there, Benny weeps with joy. Rochester observes, "That rainbow's coming back in your little blue eyes!"

Lucky Strike Program

FEBRUARY 29, 1948

Benny and his plumber girlfriend, Gladys, played by Bea Benaderet, stop in the drugstore near the studio. (In 1946, Sara Berner was a "Gladys" who worked in a diner.) Benny orders the cheapest thing on the menu, a sardine sandwich. "Would you like the domestic or the imported?" asks waiter Mel Blanc, who explains that the imported comes from Sweden, Norway, and Holland while the domestic comes from "Anaheim, Azusa, and Cucamonga." At the studio, Benny finds Phil Harris rehearsing his signature tune, "That's What I Like About the South." Harris first recorded it in 1937, and the song was the subject of a Benny sketch at that time. A new version was a hit in 1947. Benny tells Harris he has heard him sing the song "fifty times a year for the last twelve years, and I defy you to show me where those lyrics make one bit of sense!" Benny analyzes the song line by line. When Harris comes to the mention of Doo Wah Ditty, Benny exclaims, "Where in the name of Stephen Foster is Doo Wah Ditty?" The Sportsmen Quartet do a version of "Sonny Boy" that incorporates the names of the two Lucky Strike auctioneers, Speed Riggs and F. E. Boone. Rochester asks for the night off to show his aunt around Los Angeles. She's from Mississippi, explains Rochester, "little place called Doo Wah Ditty." Benny is stunned and goes to the telephone: "Hello. Rand McNally? I'm going to sue you! Imagine! Leaving off an important place like Doo Wah Ditty!"

Lucky Strike Program

MARCH 14, 1948

This program features an appearance by the winner of "The Walking Man" contest. This parody of giveaway shows ran on NBC's *Truth or Consequences* from December 20, 1947 until March 6, 1948. Listeners had to identify a mystery celebrity, Benny, based only on his footsteps and a weekly clue. Following a spirited rendition of "MacNamara's Band" by Dennis Day, Benny wishes him a happy Saint Patrick's Day. "Good yontiff to you!" he responds. During the Lucky Strike commercial, Benny insists that Don Wilson wear a straw hat: "It'll be great on television!" Ralph Edwards, the host of *Truth or Consequences,* explains that the contest raised over $1 million for the American Heart Association. When Edwards expresses satisfaction that $100,000 in prizes were given away, Benny sniffs, "Well, to each his own." Finally, the contest winner, Mrs. Florence Hubbard, is introduced. She's a Chicago resident, but was born in Doo Wah Ditty, continuing the new round of gags about Phil Harris's song that began on February 29.

MARCH 28, 1948

Lucky Strike Program

This episode contains Benny's most remembered scene, the "Your money or your life?" skit. It begins with a segment built around Benny as a Hollywood outsider. Benny receives a script and note from Harry Warner of Warner Bros. "Dear Jack," Benny reads, "Enclosed find script and contract for your next picture as agreed upon. And it's the last time I'll play gin rummy with you!" Benny is very enthusiastic about the script, *The Bad Man of Bullock's Basement.* (Benny's previous film, *The Horn Blows at Midnight,* was released in 1945, but his subsequent film work was limited to cameo appearances.) The scene switches to the home of Ronald and Benita Colman. Ronald Colman is reminiscing about his early days in England, where his mastery of the banjo earned him comparisons to the legendary vaudevillian Eddie Peabody. Arriving in America, though, he was billed as "England's answer to Frank Remley." (The guitarist in Phil Harris's band.) The Colmans gripe about Benny's behavior at the Academy Awards ceremony and his habit of borrowing things. Benny has decided to ask Ronald Colman to costar in his movie. He convinces Colman to read a scene. "Bow your legs a little," Benny instructs Colman, who concludes that the part isn't for him. As he leaves, Benny spots Colman's Oscar, which he borrows to show to Rochester. As he returns home, his journey is interrupted. "Hey, Bud . . . Bud, got a match?" asks a menacing voice, provided

by Eddie Marr. "Match? Yes. I have one right here. . . ." "Don't make a move! This is a stickup!" Benny is in shock, "Mister, put down that gun!" "Shut up!" says the thief, "Now, come on! Your money or your life!" The laughter begins to swell after only two seconds of total silence; seven seconds later the thief demands, "Look, Bud, I said, 'Your money or your life!' " "I'm thinking it over!" wails Benny. The thief takes Benny's wallet and "that package you're holding, too." He instructs Benny to lie down and count to one hundred. The count resumes after a Lucky Strike commercial, with Don Wilson concluding, "Will Jack Benny recover the stolen Oscar? Will Ronald Colman sue him? Will Bing Crosby be our guest next week? Tune in and find out!"

Lucky Strike Program *APRIL 4, 1948*

This program picks up where the previous one ended. Benny repeats the story of the robbery, making himself increasingly heroic with each telling. He claims he dropped Ronald Colman's Oscar while beating up the crook. When Rochester hears that the Sportsmen Quartet won't be making the broadcast, each of their wives having given birth simultaneously, he suggests using his friends, the Ink Spots. They sing the weekly Lucky Strike commercial to the melody of their hit "If I Didn't Care." Benny decides to acquire another Oscar to give to Colman in the hope that the stolen one is recovered. He decides to drive over to Bing Crosby's house to borrow the Academy Award Crosby won for *Going My Way*. Benny is reluctant to admit why he has dropped by, so he and Mary Livingstone get a tour of the house. Crosby takes a phone call about a guest for his radio program who is coming from Doo Wah Ditty, extending the running gag from the show of February 29. Crosby agrees to lend Benny the Oscar, and Benny retells the robbery story, increasing the number of thieves to ten. His story is accompanied by the sound of machine guns.

JANUARY 2, 1949

Lucky Strike Program

Benny returns to CBS after sixteen years. He is very nervous. Rochester says that Benny didn't sleep a wink the night before. "I tried everything," he says. "I even threw him over my shoulder and burped him twice." CBS President William S. Paley has now replaced Heddy Lamarr in Benny's dreams. "All night long," Rochester explains, Benny kept saying, "P.A.L.E.Y., P.A.L.E.Y.!" in the manner of the Lucky Strike commercials. On their way to the studio, Benny, Rochester, and Mary Livingstone are pulled over by a traffic cop, played by Frank Nelson, who gets a big laugh with the snide way he delivers his opening line, "Caught you, didn't I?" The conversation is interrupted by the police radio. Mel Blanc supplies the voice. "Investigate a double murder at Hill and Grand. Only two more hours and Jack Benny will be on CBS," spoofing the network's heavy promotion of Benny's move. Rochester restarts the Maxwell, with the sound effects supplied by Blanc. Arriving at CBS, Benny and Mary Livingstone meet Amos 'n' Andy, whose broadcast now follows Benny's. As they part, Amos says Benny isn't too funny. "He ain't nothing without Rochester," Andy adds. In his search for Paley, Benny meets Mr. Kitzel, who is perplexed by CBS's efforts to promote Benny. "With all this fuss they were making, you'd think they were getting Al Pearce!" Pearce was an early radio comic whose radio career peaked by 1940 and was over by 1946. The comment is doubly inside, since in the mid-1930s Auerbach played Mr. Kitzel on Pearce's program. Benny meets Don Thornburgh, the head of CBS's Western Division, who explains that Mr. Paley is in New York. He "only comes out here on urgent business." "Well," says Benny, "Do you have the authority to validate my parking lot ticket?"

Lucky Strike Program *SEPTEMBER 11, 1949*

The first show of the 1949 season is notable for the fact that Benny is not heard until the program is two-thirds over. Don Wilson takes the audience back to a few hours before the broadcast, all aboard a free sightseeing bus midway on its tour of Beverly Hills. As they pass the home of Orson Welles, guide Frank Nelson explains that except for the trees everything is "conceived, designed, constructed, decorated, and furnished" by Welles. Next is the home of "Miss Mary Livingstone." The scene switches to inside the house, where she is talking about Benny. She saw him once a month over the summer, "when he came for the rent." Dennis Day and his mother are next. Mrs. Day, portrayed by Verna Felton, wonders why Dennis doesn't "get married and leave home like other boys do." Phil Harris is heard in a conversation with his gardener, talking of how he irrigates his cabbages with bourbon. Nelson observes Don Wilson "waddling up the block," then points out the home of Ronald and Benita Colman, and, across from it, Benny's residence. Rochester is on the phone with a girlfriend. He says that Benny was so nervous about his first show of the season, "He combed his hair three times, then left without it." When the bus arrives at CBS, more than twenty minutes into the program, Benny is finally heard saying, "This is where I get off, Driver." Shortly after "arriving" at the studio, Benny realizes that he has left this week's scripts on the bus. He chases it, but learns that Nelson has thrown them into "the blue goo of the La Brea Tar Pits."

APRIL 9, 1950

Lucky Strike Program

The program opens in the drugstore near the studio. Mervyn the soda jerk, portrayed by Mel Blanc, greets the cast with "Good Health to All from Rexall," the slogan of Phil Harris's sponsor on NBC. Harris can't play gin rummy with the cast tonight because he has to wash his wife Alice Faye's hair. Since Harris and Faye's previous sponsor was Fitch shampoo, they have to use it up. "Slip yours off. I'll wash it, too," he offers Benny. On his walk home, Benny meets a panhandler, John L. C. Sivoney, played by Frank Fontaine. (Sivoney is essentially the same character Fontaine would call Crazy Guggenheim on Jackie Gleason's television series.) Benny gives him fifty cents. "Gee, that was nice of me," Benny says of himself. "Wonder if it's deductible." He tells Rochester of his generosity, and he drops the dishes he's drying. Dishes continue to drop each time the incident is mentioned. That night Benny dreams about his magnanimity. Frank Nelson announces that dignitaries have gathered at a banquet to honor "the most generous man in the world." A variety of notables are impersonated by Fontaine and Dennis Day, including Winston Churchill, James Cagney, Cary Grant, and semiregular Ronald Colman, who greets the guests with "Good health to all from the Taj Mahal!" As the dream unfolds it turns out that Sivoney used the fifty cents to buy a sweepstakes ticket and won $150,000. Benny wakes up screaming, "It's mine! It's mine!"

Lucky Strike Program *OCTOBER 22, 1950*

The program revolves around Benny's preparations for his first television show. Mary is surprised by how little Benny is packing for a twelve-day trip to New York. Benny explains that the airline charges extra if your luggage weighs more than forty pounds. Benny's wearing five suits since they don't weigh the passengers. Mary is aghast at the old tuxedo he plans to wear. "If you do, it'll be awfully confusing," she says, "*You'll* be on live, and that tuxedo looks like a kinescope." Phil Harris arrives to lend Benny his suitcase, which is adorned with labels from such places as Empty Jug, Texas, Rack 'em Up, Arkansas, and Mishmash, Arizona, all of which he has purportedly played with his band. The balance of the program is an updating of Benny's previous train trips, now using an airport setting. Mel Blanc is heard making the announcements, including one for a flight arriving from "Fort Worth, Galveston, and Empty Jug" and another, "Loading at Gate Five for Anaheim, Azusa, and Cucamonga." On his way to buy fruit, Benny meets Mr. Kitzel. He is waiting for his wife, who was visiting their son in college. Benny asks what college he's attending. "The same one I attended, Southern Methodist," Kitzel responds. At the fruit stand, Benny encounters the race track tout, played by Sheldon Leonard, who advises Benny, "Lay off the bananas. I've been watchin' 'em for three days and have yet to see one of 'em get out of the bunch."

Benny meets Frank Nelson behind the ticket counter. "Are you the validating clerk?" Benny asks. "Well, who do you think I am behind these bars, your agent?" sneers Nelson. Benny says he has had enough and is going to have Nelson fired. Nelson wails that his wife and five children will starve. Benny backs down, even though he is certain Nelson's making the whole thing up. "Ooooooooooooohhhhhh, am I!" squeals Nelson. "I'd punch you right in the nose if I didn't have to take off five coats," counters Benny. Before he boards his flight, he asks Mary for a kiss. "Look, Mister, don't get fresh with me," she says. "Mary, it's me, the propeller blew it off," he replies, employing another toupee gag. Once aboard, Benny and Don Wilson mention the guest star for his television show, Dinah Shore, and next Sunday's radio show, Mr. and Mrs. Ronald Colman.

MARCH 2, 1952

Lucky Strike Program

Don Wilson introduces Benny by reciting a poem honoring the program's Palm Springs locale. It concludes, "and there, out by the pool / far from strife and toil / is our blue-eyed star / selling suntan oil." Benny reacts by calling Wilson "Henry Wadsworth Fatfellow." Benny jokes about his golfing partner, Eddie Cantor, complaining, "He put down a dime to mark his ball. He divided my point of interest." Phil Harris interrupts the conversation with "Does this dull twosome mind if a funny man plays through?" In an overtly campy manner, Harris delivers a poem on the weather that alludes to a current hit record: "I was getting some sun / Then I went inside / 'Cause the little white cloud sat down and cried." "Isn't that cute!" responds Benny. An exhausted Dennis Day enters. He went to a drive-in the night before, but didn't have a car. "I was carrying an umbrella and they thought I was a convertible," he explains. "What's that on your nose?" asks Benny. "A windshield wiper," explains Day, prompting a "Now cut that out!" from Benny, the favorite phrase of his exasperation. Mr. Kitzel visits, telling Benny he has rented a bicycle built for two for his wife's exclusive use. "Believe me," Kitzel explains, "she can use it!" Rochester phones from Pomona to explain he's been delayed by a flat tire. "Oh, that's too bad," Benny empathizes. "No, that's good," counters Rochester, "It was laying on the road, and it's better than the one we had on!" Don Wilson introduces Danny Kaye, who tells Benny he's formed a quartet to sing Benny's song "When You Say 'I Beg Your Pardon,' Then I'll Come Back to You," which he "wrote" on the September 30, 1951 program. The rest of the quartet enters: George Burns, Frank Sinatra, and Groucho Marx. In honor of Groucho, Benny paraphrases his *You Bet Your Life* line, "If you say the magic word you get a bottle of suntan oil." Benny goes on to express his gratitude. "No one but real friends, real pals, would give up a Sunday

afternoon just to come over here and do this wonderful song—" Burns interrupts, "Jack." "What?" asks Benny. "Shut up," responds Burns, and the crowd roars. The performance that follows is extremely loose and embraces both hillbilly and klezmer rhythms. It concludes with a "wow finish" from Sinatra, "So my darling, though we've parted, come back to whence we've started." The others join in, "And sweetheart, I'll come back to you!"

Lucky Strike Program

DECEMBER 14, 1952

The annual Christmas shopping episode begins with the harried department store salesman, played by Mel Blanc, on the psychiatrist's couch rehashing past holiday encounters with Benny. He begins with his 1946 battle with the "kindly looking blue-eyed old gent," who came back six times to exchange shoe laces. In 1951 the gent was equally indecisive about the purchase of cuff links. This year the salesman plans to avoid Benny entirely by working in the Gardening Tools Department. The scene switches to Benny's arrival at the store, and the inevitable fight with the floorwalker, portrayed by Frank Nelson. "Ask me anything. I'm a talking horse." When Benny tells him he doesn't look like one, he responds with an allusion to transsexual Christine Jorgensen. "There's a veterinarian in Denmark who does wonders!" an unusually topical remark. Since Don Wilson has just bought a little ranch in the San Fernando Valley, Benny decides that a gopher trap would be the perfect gift; Nelson sends him to the Gardening Tools Department and another collision with Mel Blanc. Benny learns that Wilson's wife faints at the sight of dead gophers, so he exchanges the trap for one that captures rather than kills. On his way to the lingerie counter to buy a gift for his sister, he meets Sheldon Leonard as the race track tout, who advises against nylon because "silk will give you a run for the money." Benny asks about a sheer negligee. "A great show bet." Benny wonders why Leonard never touts horses. "Floorwalker in the second" he touts. "I saw him," Benny counters, "and he's carrying too much weight." Bob Crosby, who succeeded Phil Harris at the beginning of the season, convinces Benny that gopher traps that kill are the best choice, sending Benny back to the Gardening Tools Department. Blanc has been relieved at his position by his psychiatrist, and Benny drives *him* crazy too.

NOVEMBER 1, 1953

Lucky Strike Program

Don Wilson opens the show in a whisper, since the program is set in Benny's home at 4 A.M. Benny's sleep is disturbed by an inane call from Hank, an all-night deejay. Unable to fall back asleep, Benny decides to take a nice long walk. Like nearly all of the radio plots, this bit was done on Benny's television show on February 6, 1955 (see page 194). He invites Mary Livingstone to to join him, but she assumes that he must be calling from jail, "Jack, let me talk to the man." Out on the street, Benny greets the street cleaner, portrayed by Mel Blanc, who warns him, "Hey, wait a minute, Mac! You can't take nothing out of that barrel!" Benny explains, "But he's a friend of mine—Remley!" Spotting a movie theater, Benny observes, "I've never seen a theater so empty. Yes I have, but I don't want to think about it." Bob Crosby drives by with members of the band. They're going duck hunting, but first "we've got to go to the City Dump and pick up Remley!" (Crosby has inherited the Frankie Remley jokes begun with Phil Harris.) Benny returns home and goes to sleep, but is awakened by Mary Livingstone, who has come to take him shopping for new suits. Frank Nelson is the salesman. The suits cost $28.75 and $29.50. "Or would you prefer something cheaper?" Nelson sneers. "I didn't come here for anything cheap," Benny huffs, "I'll take the $29.50." Asks Nelson, "Would you like me to measure your chest or would you rather not know?" Nelson asks Benny if he'd heard about the store through their newspaper ad or on the radio. He informs him, "We sponsor Hank, the all-night disc jockey!" Benny is furious and starts to choke Nelson. "Nobody's gonna wake me up at four o'clock in the morning and get away with it!" The program concludes with Benny back in bed. He has slept for ten hours. "It's four o'clock in the morning again," says Benny wistfully. "Well, I guess I'll just have to take another walk."

Lucky Strike Program *SEPTEMBER 26, 1954*

This is the first program of Benny's final radio season. Bob Crosby enters boasting about his daily television show and the fact that he gets paid every week. "Money isn't everything," says Benny, who explains he has a new writer who "hasn't grasped my character yet." Responds Crosby, "When he gets his first check he will." Benny kids Crosby about his brother, Bing. He bets that Bing's home will become a state before Hawaii. There are also jokes regarding Bing's investment in the Pittsburgh Pirates. Dennis Day announces that he's quitting the show, explaining, "I grasped your character twelve years ago!" Don Wilson is upset because everyone gets applause but him. When he does receive his ovation, Benny snipes, "Never has so little made so much so happy so fast!" Rochester phones to let Benny know that the program isn't on the air. Instead, there's organ music playing. Benny goes to see the chief engineer, George Foster, first meeting his assistant, played by Mel Blanc. "It aren't my fault," says Blanc. "I'm not saying it am," Benny responds. Foster is portrayed by Frank Nelson, who sneers, "May I shake your hand? I've already *grasped* your character." He refuses to put Benny back on the air, claiming it was the sponsor's idea. The routine concludes with an exasperated Benny declaring, "This is ridiculous! I'm going home and listen to *Sam 'n' Henry*"—an arcane reference by 1954 to the characters better known as Amos 'n' Andy.

APRIL 3, 1955

Lucky Strike Program

This episode is built around the first time Ed, who guards Benny's subterranean vault, is allowed out for a vacation. Don Wilson begins the show by reminding Benny's radio audience, "Tonight, Jack Benny does another television program," then switches the scene to Benny's home, where Rochester is filling out his income tax return. Under the "occupation" heading, he lists "butler, chauffeur, cook, gardener, valet, masseur, window washer, and author of *What to Do in Your Spare Time.*" He enters his salary in red ink, "I want them to know I'm blushing." Ten years after Benny's first trip to the vault, the visits have become extremely elaborate. "Here come my alligators!" Benny exclaims, "Gee, I don't see Irving." After the usual round of rattling chains and creaky doors, Benny observes, "You *can* take it with you!" Benny withdraws ten dollars he owes Frankie Remley and an extravagant six dollars for dinner with Mary, "I might want dinner, too." Ed (played by Joe Kearns) tells Benny he's been stationed in the basement for so many years he's lost track of how long: "It was your birthday. You were 38." After removing Ed's chains, Benny takes him upstairs, where he has to explain a light bulb to him. "Is Ben still flying that kite?" Ed asks. Following a visit by Don Wilson and the Sportsmen for their weekly Lucky Strike commercial, Benny panics when Rochester tells him that Ed is missing. He goes to the police station, where the sergeant (Mel Blanc) refers him to the Missing Persons Bureau, which is administered by Frank Nelson, who greets Benny with a typically elongated "Yeeeeeesss!" While there, Rochester phones to tell Benny that Ed has been hiding in the closet. He'd mistook a bus for a dragon. Back home, Ed tells Benny he wants to return to the vault. "So long, Ed," says Rochester. "Goodbye . . . man," says Ed, showing that he had picked up some of Rochester's lingo in his short sojourn in the real world.

Lucky Strike Program *MAY 22, 1955*

On the final Benny radio program, Don Wilson introduces "a man I thought wouldn't last, Jack Benny!" Benny responds with an updated "fat" joke, characterizing Wilson as "Cinemascope stomach." Benny is lauded as a pioneer in the broadcasting business. When he started there were hardly any radios. "And darn few people!" says Mary Livingstone. Benny's response is Gleason-like: "Pow! Back to the May Company!" (Sadie Marks really was a hoisery salesgirl in that department store in 1926 before she married Benny.) Dennis Day interrupts his litany of praise for Benny. "I can't keep reading this stuff! It's making me sick!" Mel Blanc as sound effects man George Twombly tells Benny that his relatives are listening in and they would like him to demonstrate his artistry. (The real name of the program's sound effects man at this time was Eugene Twombly.) After Dennis Day's song, music director Mahlon Merrick is thanked for the discipline he brought to the band. Sammy, the band's drummer, presents Benny with a monogrammed ice cube, and Mr. Kitzel drops by to announce his vacation plans. He's going to Europe to "visit my relations" in Ireland. He's getting there by way of Anaheim, Azusa, and Cucamonga. The Sportsmen sing their farewell. Benny has a few words with the telephone operators. Rochester calls to tell Benny he is packed for his trip. Benny pads the conversation with extra "goodbyes" because Twombly won't provide the sound effect of a phone hanging up. Bob Crosby is credited but not heard on the broadcast. Benny tells the audience that the program's success "is due to the competent people I have working with me."

The Jack Benny-Fred Allen "Feud" Shows

No account of the radio career of Jack Benny would be complete without his legendary feud with fellow comedian Fred Allen. This is the tale as it has come to be known through the years: *On the last* Fred Allen Show *of the 1936 radio season, Stewart Canin, a brilliant ten-year-old violinist, played Rimsky-Korsakov's "The Flight of the Bumble Bee." Allen was so impressed by the young man's virtuosity that the dour comedian quipped, "A certain alleged violinist should hang his head in shame!" This was the first volley in the Jack Benny–Fred Allen feud that convulsed radio audiences for over six months before the participants ever had occasion to discuss it. When the two comedians finally faced off on Allen's Sunday night broadcast, which aired thirty minutes after* The Jack Benny Show, *Benny exclaimed, "You wouldn't dare talk to me that way if my writers were here!"*

It's a terrific story told countless times, and little of it is accurate.

The real tale of the Benny–Allen feud, like so much else in early radio, begins in vaudeville. Although Jack and Fred's battles were played strictly for laughs, both were acquainted with the genuine article. Before becoming "Jack Benny," Benjamin Kubelsky was known as Ben K. Benny, a billing that resulted in a rebuke from another comic fiddler (and future radio personality), Ben Bernie, who accused Benny of cashing in on his fame. Similarly, in 1917 Fred Allen, then "Freddy James," feuded with Harry LaToy, who had purloined Allen's billing as the "World's Worst Juggler." These and other quarrels, both real and fanciful, were generally limited to written exchanges in trade papers. It took radio and the inspired Benny and Allen to bring such feuding before the public.

While the feud did explicitly ignite in 1936, Benny and Allen were far from strangers. They claimed their paths crossed in vaudeville (which seems likely enough), and they were certainly friends by the time they were living in New York City in 1930. Benny was starring in Earl Carroll's Vanities, *and Allen, who had recently come off the road tour of* The Little Show, *was preparing for another revue,* Three's a Crowd. *The Bennys and the Allens lived within blocks of each other and frequently socialized with other show business couples, such as Ida and Eddie Cantor, Flo and Jack Haley, and Gracie Allen and George Burns.*

It was in the fall of 1929 that Fred Allen made his earliest known radio appearance, as the guest of Alexander Woollcott on The Town Crier *on WOR. Over the next three years Allen made a handful of other appearances, and on Sunday, October 23, 1932, three days before the end of Jack Benny's first season on the* Canada Dry Program, *Allen's first network radio show, the* Linit Bath Club Revue, *premiered on*

CBS. In his 1989 biography Fred Allen: His Life and Wit, *Robert Taylor theorized that the Benny–Allen feud sprang from Allen's habit of inserting his friends' names into his broadcasts. Perhaps it was to just such a mention that Jack Benny was responding in June 1933, when he worked an impression of Allen into his* Chevrolet Program.

Chevrolet Program *JUNE 23, 1933*

Benny's opening monologue includes a dispatch from Detroit. "Big industries raise employees' salaries 10 percent," he says. Mary Livingstone asks, "When do I get a raise, Jack?" "When we're in Detroit, Mary." The majority of the program is devoted to an end-of-season banquet, which includes impressions, most by Johnny Woods, of Clark Gable, Greta Garbo, Maurice Chevalier, Ed Wynn, Walter Winchell, Mae West, Eddie Cantor, Al Smith, Rudy Vallee, and Marlene Dietrich. One impersonated guest is introduced by Benny as "that great artist, Freddy Allen." Commenting on the evening's one-course dinner, the ersatz Allen says, "All I have at night is coffee, anyway, but as you have no coffee, we're all even." At the time, Allen was temporarily between radio programs. His *Linit Bath Club Revue* concluded on April 16, and he would not be back on the air until August 1933.

Benny and Allen's first joint on-air performance was still two years away when Allen's Salad Bowl Revue, *sponsored by Hellman's Mayonnaise, premiered on Friday, August 4, 1933. His Wednesday evening* Sal Hepatica Revue, *later dubbed* Hour of Smiles *and then* Town Hall Tonight, *premiered in January 1934. With his friend back on the air, Benny mentioned Allen on his February 18* Chevrolet Program. *Each time Benny began a joke, another cast member would cite the radio program that was its source. Again, Allen is referred to as "Freddy," which most likely alludes to one of his vaudeville monikers, "Freddy James." However friendly in person, Benny and Allen were considered competitors by the media observers of the day. In its review of Benny's first* General Tire *program,* Variety *opined, "As a smooth working aggregation of mirth specialists the Benny ménage can give the Fred Allen troupe a tight run for top position." Actually, the top spot was held by former vaudevillian and musical-comedy star Eddie Cantor, whose Sunday night NBC broadcast was the most popular program on the air. Cantor left radio for a year at the end of the 1934 season, creating a vacuum that allowed Benny and Allen to gain in popularity.*

Fred Allen and Jack Benny's first radio encounter took place when Allen appeared as a guest on Benny's Jell-O

Program *on July 14, 1935, the last show of the first season. Allen's radio shows were based in New York, but he and Portland Hoffa, his wife and radio costar, were in Hollywood for what would be Allen's most successful motion picture,* Thanks a Million. *On February 12, 1936, Mary Livingstone made a rare solo appearance on* Town Hall Tonight. *Two weeks later, Benny joined her in his first appearance on Fred Allen's NBC program.*

FEBRUARY 26, 1936

Town Hall Tonight

In an interesting departure from the conventions set on Benny's own show, Mary is introduced as Benny's wife, rather than as his quasi-girlfriend. She refers to Benny as "some stooge who works on my program," in one of her many acerbic remarks to Benny that give her the upper hand. In this pre-feud encounter, it is the men versus the women, as Allen *defends* Benny: "Jack is my guest here tonight, and I'm not going to see him insulted." Allen suggests that they play "Love in Bloom," which was just beginning to be associated with Benny, as a violin-clarinet duet. The program's weekly dramatic farce, "The Mighty Allen Art Players," is replaced by a sketch purportedly written by Mary and Portland Hoffa. Benny plays a wolfhound, and Allen provides a dog's bark. Benny concludes the piece with "something Fred and I wanted to do for a long time." They "shoot" Mary and Portland, then return to their duet for a "wow finish," a vaudeville term referring to a spectacular ending.

In reaction to their joint Town Hall Tonight *appearance, a reader of the weekly* Radio Guide *suggested a regular hour show featuring "Jack Benny, Mary, Fred Allen and Portland, all together." A* Guide *columnist added, "I say the idea has merit, but I refuse to vote for the merger unless Kenny Baker and Don Wilson are thrown in." Jack Benny had another idea.*

Jell-O Program *APRIL 5, 1936*

Eight months prior to the acknowledged start of the feud, Benny, "with the aid of a clothespin on my nose," presents "a vest pocket edition of Mr. Allen's program, *Clown Hall Tonight.* Are you listening, Freddy?" The parody opens with Allen's familiar theme, "Smile, Darn Ya, Smile," with Don Wilson paraphrasing Allen's opening announcement with "Jell-O, for the smile of satisfaction." Fred Allen is one of the few people Benny seriously attempted to impersonate, although the effort apparently made him self-conscious. He breaks himself up and ad-libs, "Am I awful!" Benny poses the question: who is the better comedian, Fred Allen or Jack Benny? This is the same question that will be replayed in various skits for the next eleven years! Mary Livingstone impersonates the high-pitched squeal of Portland Hoffa. Benny refers to her, variously, as "Seattle" and "Tacoma." Johnny Green is called Peter Van Green, a takeoff on Peter Van Steeden, Allen's orchestra leader. Benny satirizes "The Mighty Allen Art Players" and Allen's segment with amateurs, "Town Hall Varieties" (which is the segment that will feature the young violinist who is at the root of the feud).

Town Hall Tonight *DECEMBER 30, 1936*

This is the program that officially ignited the Benny-Allen feud; it was the last show of the year, not the 1936 season. It begins with an innocuous, offhand remark. During a special children's edition of "Town Hall Varieties," Allen presents ten-and-a-half-year-old violinist Stuart Canin, who performs Franz Schubert's "The Bee," not the more commonly known "Flight of the Bumble Bee," which had actually been performed by a harmonica player the previous Wednesday. (To add more confusion to the particulars of the event, the Schubert is not the well-known Austrian-born Franz Peter, but a similarly named, Dresden composer who was himself a violinist and whose piece "Die Biene" was once popular!) Allen characterizes Canin as "the most remarkable child violinist I have ever heard." He marvels at the fifth-grader who "already plays better than Jack Benny." On this broadcast there is no remark resembling "a certain alleged violinist should hang his head in shame." (However, as each program was done twice—once for the West Coast—it is possible that Allen may have made a different remark during the second show.)

Also part of the "Varieties" that evening was the harmony trio, the DeMarcos, who, as a quintet, would become Allen regulars in the next decade. Allen observes, "When these little girls grow up, you realize that television will be here?" By this time, experimental television programs were originating from NBC's Studio 3H in Radio City.

The "feuding" got off to a slow start. Benny acknowledged Allen's remark at the conclusion of his January 3, 1937 Jell-O program. "Oh, Mary," he said, "Take a wire to Fred Allen. Dear Fred: I am not *ashamed of myself, (evidence that Allen may have made a different remark on the second broadcast of his December 30 program). When I was ten years old I could play "Flight of the Bumble Bee" on my violin, too. (Even Benny confused the two compositions!) Nyah!" Allen responded on his January 6 broadcast by ridiculing Benny's claim of prepubescent virtuosity.*

Benny and Allen's radio exchanges were preceded by a series of publicized clashes between columnist and NBC commentator (and, not incidentally, former vaudevillian) Walter Winchell and bandleader Ben Bernie. The principal accomplishment of this farcical feuding was to elevate maestro Bernie from relative radio obscurity to national prominence. Although clever, their mock battles lacked the spontaneity and wit of Benny and Allen's efforts, but they did result in a 1937 motion picture, Wake Up and Live, *another precedent Benny and Allen followed when they made the 1940 film* Love Thy Neighbor.

JANUARY 10, 1937

Jell-O Program

Benny is introduced as "America's boyfriend who can't get a date." Throughout the program he is exasperated as members of his own cast enter one by one and ask if he heard Fred Allen's barbs on the previous *Town Hall Tonight.* Benny dismisses Allen as a "reformed juggler." Benny demands that Allen "apologize, or send me a watch," a reference to the platinum wristwatch Phil Harris had given to Benny on December 20 to placate him following their "fight" of December 6. Buckingham Benny, a window dresser from Pomona effeminately played by Benny Baker, protests the Western serial "Buck Benny Rides Again." Chapter 10 follows anyway, with Jack Benny as the sheriff in pursuit of the notorious outlaw Cactus Face. The segment concludes with recurring cast member Andy Devine asking Sheriff Benny if *he'd* heard Fred Allen on Wednesday night. Devine was heard regularly with Benny through 1940 and periodically thereafter; his last appearance was in 1949.

Jell-O Program *FEBRUARY 7, 1937*

Benny declares his intention to put that "Town Hall ghost in his place" by playing Schubert's "The Bee." In fact, he claims he can play "The Bee" with one hand and "Love in Bloom" with the other. "Buck Benny" regular Andy Devine drops by to hear Benny play and to inquire when they will continue tracking down Cactus Face. Instead, Benny says they will be hitting the trail for New York in pursuit of "Rattlesnake Allen." Devine, with his trademark cracking voice, says that Allen's voice "gets on my nerves." When the moment arrives for Benny to vindicate himself, his violin is gone. He theorizes that Fred Allen himself hired somebody to steal it. The show suddenly turns thriller. There is a gunshot, a scream, and a Mysterious Stranger is heard, sounding much like the character in Benny's 1934 "Stooge Murder Case."

FEBRUARY 10, 1937 Town Hall Tonight

In their opening exchange Fred Allen and Portland Hoffa discuss the case of the man who chained himself to his girlfriend's radiator until she accepted his marriage proposal. Allen likens it to Jack Benny's "breach of promise case" by failing to play "The Bee." "If he chained himself to his violin last week, it wouldn't have been stolen," says Allen. The weekly "Mighty Allen Art Players" is devoted to Benny. "Down through the ages, ladies and gentlemen, the Bennys have been a sixteen-bar rest in the development and progress of music as we know it today." To the accompaniment of a poorly executed "Love in Bloom," Allen presents "Cavalcade of Benny House." It begins with Beelzebub Benny with Adam and Eve, then Nero Benny in A.D. 64, Mendelssohn Benny in 1850, and Old Black Joe Benny with Stephen Foster in 1863. Benny is also credited with the invention of radio. According to Marconi, "I must invent a device to enable him to play his violin and still be safe from the violence of music lovers." In 1935, the story goes, Benny found sanctuary in a radio studio. When a gunshot is heard, Allen explains that it is the composers of "Love in Bloom" shooting themselves. Later, Benny is characterized as a "wolf in Kreisler's clothing" (an allusion to one of the great violinists of the time, Fritz Kreisler). When announcer Harry Von Zell asks Allen if he had heard Andy Devine's remarks on Benny's February 7 program, Allen responds that Devine sounds like "a man with false teeth eating slate pencils."

The feud was not limited to the principal antagonists' programs. On the February 15, 1937 Lux Radio Theatre, *on which Benny and Mary Livingstone starred in* Brewster's Millions, *host Cecil B. DeMille joked about Benny's skill on the violin. When Benny offered to play "The Bee," DeMille claimed it was "an obsession that's gone to your head." Benny responded with an apparent ad-lib, "Is that DeMille or Fred Allen?" On the February 28* Jell-O Program, *Benny read a letter from Mary Livingstone, who was vacationing in New York. "I ran into Fred Allen," according to the letter, "He spoke about you, and, believe me, that's no way to talk in front of a lady!" Benny's violin was returned on this program, so he was able to play "The Bee," an event he characterized as "the moment when I will erase all verbal stains and oral blemishes from the once-illustrious name of Jack Benny!" Benny punctuated his quavery performance with periodic buzzing, and, in the middle, he segued into a movie tune, "With Plenty of Money and You," before concluding. Greeted by thunderous applause, Benny remarked, "Well, what now, Mister Allen?"*

By now the feud was beginning to pick up speed and publicity, fueled in part by the fact that the two comedians shared a common network (NBC) and advertising agency (Young & Rubicam). Fred Allen had more to gain from the feud than Jack Benny, since his audience, though substantial, was only two-thirds the size of Benny's. Listeners to one show, it was hoped, would tune in to the other in anticipation of the response. Although radio was an entirely live medium, its programs were scripted, and off-the-cuff remarks were prohibited by the networks. No doubt radio audiences were captivated by the ad-libbing inherent in the Benny–Allen phenomenon, particularly during their highly publicized face-to-face encounters. For the first one, Benny took his program from Hollywood to Allen's turf, New York City.

Jell-O Program

MARCH 7, 1937

This program, broadcast from the Grand Ballroom of the Waldorf Astoria, fueled the publicity for the big face-to-face encounter set for the following week. Benny is introduced as the man who made "The Bee" "public insect number one." Phil Harris is in Hollywood making a movie, so Abe Lyman leads the orchestra. Their encounter is reminiscent of Benny's earlier bandleader battles with George Olsen and Frank Black. When they meet, Benny lays down the law. "Whatever I say goes. Do you understand?" Lyman barks, "You might be Buck Benny, but don't try to ride me!" and "I can handle you and Fred Allen!" Benny discusses "The Bee" controversy. Although he played the piece on the previous program, he still does not feel completely vindicated. Benny suspects that Stuart Canin is older than ten. If so, then "Mr. Allen has deceived his listeners, thereby misinforming over four hundred people around the country." Finally, Stuart Canin arrives. "If it's about the violin," he says to Benny, "I don't give lessons." As he starts to leave, Benny orders him restrained, searched, and disarmed. Don Wilson takes over the interrogation. As the program ends, Benny thanks Stuart Canin for his performance of "The Bee," "which kept us going for weeks." The Benny character and his cast were always conscious of the artifice of the radio show and its conventions of scripts, writers, rehearsals, and so forth. Benny in his feud role readily acknowledged it was a gimmick to get laughs.

MARCH 14, 1937

Jell-O Program

This program, which garnered one of the largest audiences in radio history, climaxes the first feud cycle. It originates from the Grand Ballroom of the Hotel Pierre. Benny is pleased with the setting. "Not every entertainer would be granted" the privilege of broadcasting from the Pierre, "particularly *one* that I know of," a reference to Fred Allen. Mary Livingstone reads a telegram from Kenny Baker, who is in Hollywood. "Right now I am listening to the program and I certainly miss me," she reads. Benny and Mary sing a special version of "You Do the Darndest Things, Baby," which is interrupted by Fred Allen, who says that Benny makes "Andy Devine sound like Lawrence Tibbett," a well-known operatic baritone. Benny calls Allen "a fugitive from a Ripley cartoon." The two depart from the script long enough for Allen to remark, "Anything we say accidentally will be better than the script." They decide to step outside. "I'll knock you flatter than the first eight minutes of this program," says Allen. Allen, like Benny a veteran of stage experience, also ad-libbed lines that show a real consciousness of how the show is going. In vaudeville, a performer learned to be extremely sensitive to the audience reaction to the material. After the "fight," they return laughing about their days in vaudeville. They sing another special version of "You Do the Darndest Things, Baby," which concludes with the line "And now we're friends!" Benny comes back with what was thought to be the last word on the feud. "Now I won't have to listen to his program to hear what he's saying about me. Good night, folks."

Town Hall Tonight

DECEMBER 22, 1937

Nine months after the alleged end of their feud, the two stars could not resist exchanging insults when Benny appeared as a guest on Allen's show, which was being broadcast from Hollywood. The opening seems innocent enough. Fred Allen introduces Benny as an old friend from his days of vaudeville. Benny assures him that he does not expect to get paid for this guest shot, since he hasn't "any more right to take money working on this program than you have." For Allen's drive back East, Benny tries to sell him his newly acquired old Maxwell. The price, Benny explains, is ninety-five dollars F.O.B.—"for old Benny." Allen slanders the car, claiming the "engine is so dead, the front tires are rubber pallbearers." Benny resents this and other criticisms. "That's libel, Allen! And if I had my writers here, what we'd call you!"

Fred Allen was Benny's guest on the January 2, 1938 Jell-O Program, *and a new round of insults took off. On the March 23* Town Hall Tonight, *Allen warned his cast not to mention Benny. Nonetheless,* he *commented on Benny's baldness and joked about his cheapness: "When Benny buys an orange out there, one orange, mind you, he drinks the juice, uses the two halves for Jell-O molds, and makes cuff links out of the seeds." He announces that Benny is coming to New York to find furnishings for his new house in Beverly Hills.*

MARCH 27, 1938

Jell-O Program

The broadcast originates from New York's Radio City. *Town Hall Tonight* announcer Harry Von Zell substitutes for Don Wilson. Abe Lyman and His Orchestra replace Phil Harris. Von Zell tells Benny, "I hope I can fill Don Wilson's shoes." "Oh, you can, Harry," Benny assures him, "but don't ever get into his pants without a compass." Robert Ripley, the creator of *Believe It or Not,* an NBC radio series sponsored like Benny's, by General Foods, visits the show with a few questions. "Is it true," Ripley asks, "that when you make a picture you wear a silver fox toupee?" At the end of their exchange, Benny asks, "Would you like a picture of me?" "Not unless you've got three arms," replies Ripley, a reference to his sideshow subject matter. Kate Smith enters. (Her Thursday night CBS series was sponsored by General Foods's Calumet Baking Soda). After her song, a phone call comes from Kenny Baker. Benny assures him, "No! No! She's not taking your place." Rochester arrives, explaining, "I've been weekending up in Harlem. We had a gin barbecue." Benny orders his valet to "go right over to the Waldorf Astoria and straighten up my suite!" Cracks Rochester, "Did you move from the YMCA?" The arrival of Fred Allen concludes the program. "I'm not going to open my mouth on this program, except to yawn, until you give me what you promised me," says Allen. It turns out to be a Boy Scout knife. "My mood changes here," ad-libs Allen. "The script can go from now on," adds Benny. Benny tells Allen, "I saw your picture . . . well!" Allen says the film, which was *Sally, Irene, and Mary,* is "funnier than Don Wilson thinks you are!" Benny calls Allen a "weather-beaten gargoyle!" Allen counters with "Waukegan whippersnapper!"

Town Hall Tonight *MARCH 30, 1938*

Three days following his appearance on the *Jell-O Program*, Allen spends most of the second half of his sixty-minute program griping about Benny. Portland Hoffa says her mother's radio is all mixed-up, since she heard Fred Allen on a Sunday. Announcer Harry Von Zell enters reciting the flavors of Jell-O. He had forgotten them on Benny's show, but had the last laugh, he claims. "Jack forgot to pay me! Boy, is that guy absentminded!" Allen's orchestra leader, Peter Van Steeden, complains about guest bandleader Abe Lyman's performance on Benny's show. Finally a series of people arrive at Allen's "door." First the house detective from the "Naldorf Pastoria" claims that Benny stole the twin beds from his hotel room. "All he left was a due bill and a second-hand toupee." A floorwalker from the "Feinway" Piano Company says Benny swiped a piano. Next an employee of Dolan's Glassware Shop declares that Benny took a two-gallon fish tank. A representative of the Aquarium says two goldfish are missing. Allen claims Benny's motive for this thievery is to furnish his new Beverly Hills home. When Allen finds that his matches are missing, he erupts, "With my matches, Benny's housewarming will be on me!" As Allen's voice fades, he is heard fretting about the fate of his slingshot and pogo stick.

Town Hall Tonight *MAY 18, 1938*

On the day Benny was scheduled to move into his new Beverly Hills home, the program features what Fred Allen describes as "a musical tableau," "This Is the House that Jack Built." The skit revolves around the premise that "a Benny has yet to cross the threshold of a dwelling and say to himself, 'This Is Home, Sweet Home.' " As with "Cavalcade of Benny House," a variety of Bennys are profiled, beginning in 200,000 B.C. with Gog, a stonecutter. "This first Benny was a chiseler," says Allen. Michelangelo is heard escorting Stradivarius Benny to his newly erected home in Pisa. When Benny complains that the tower is leaning, Michelangelo explains it is because he used Jell-O for the foundation. The march of time continues through the exploits of Jock MacBenny, Truman Benny, and Snagtooth Benny, who arrived in Waukegan in 1849. "Other Bennys came to Waukegan later," Allen explains, "but they lived in parking spaces and formed little communities in pool halls behind the eight ball." The presentation concludes with a "last minute flash from Beverly Hills." A poorly impersonated Benny balks at paying two dollars for a doorknob. He opts to live in a barn instead, adding, "My horse will have to move over."

The barbs continued to fly furiously during the 1938–39 and 1939–40 radio seasons. On September 26, 1938, the Monday before the first Jell-O Program *of the new season, Benny and Mary Livingstone starred in "Seven Keys to Baldpate," the duo's second appearance on CBS's* Lux Radio Theatre. *As before, the feud followed Benny. At intermission, violin virtuoso Efrem Zimbalist played "The Bee," extending a gag nearly two years old. Allen's name came up on two Jell-O shows originating from Radio City on December 4 and 11. On the first show Benny complained about the meal he was served at Allen's home, saying, "You think he could have had sardines some other night!" Benny, in turn, was discussed on the December 14* Town Hall Tonight. *Benny claimed to have saved Allen's life on the January 22* Jell-O Program. *On January 29 Benny was in training to box with Allen, and he challenged Allen to a fight on his February 5 broadcast. The following Sunday, Benny commented on Allen's poor circulation, saying, "He hasn't got any more pulse than a snowman." On February 19 Benny barked, "I'll never understand why Universal Studios spends thousands of dollars to make up Boris Karloff when they can use Allen in the raw!" It is important to realize that lines such as this come across far more harshly on paper than they did in their original on-air context. The good-natured humor of the feud was apparent to the legions of radio listeners who followed it.*

The March 19, 1939 Radio Guide *captured the spirit of the feud, asserting that Benny was "out to settle that old score with the Mighty Allen." Allen had revitalized the feud on his March 15 broadcast when he claimed that the star of the* Jell-O Program *was not Jack Benny, but a man named Maxwell Stroud. On March 22 Allen presented his Benny, expertly impersonated, who introduced "Old Dad Talcott," the hansom cab driver at the Waukegan depot. (Mancel Talcott was in fact the mayor of Waukegan and had appeared on Benny's show.) Inside humor is evidenced again when Allen presented a notary public, "Sam Lyons," who verified that Allen's Benny was genuine. (Sam Lyons was the name of one of Benny's agents.) Allen's motive for his exposé was to "let Carmichael know the company he's keeping." Carmichael, Benny's pet polar bear, was first heard on February 12. At that time Benny speculated that the beast had been sent by Allen.*

Although Benny and Allen did not meet on the air again until June 1940, feud jokes continued. On his March 24, 1940 appearance on the Campbell Playhouse *adaptation of* June Moon, *Benny, as Frederick D. Stevens, would rather see a radio show than go to a nightclub, explaining, "One guy I never miss. Gee, he's a scream. Fellow by the name of Jack*

Benny." Another character responded, "Jack Benny? Sure, I hear about him all the time on the Fred Allen program."

Benny reprised his Fred Allen impression and "Clown Hall Tonight" for his April 28, 1940 broadcast, which originated in New York to correspond with the opening of Paramount's Buck Benny Rides Again. *The movie starred the entire Jell-O cast save Mary Livingstone (who was only heard) and included an audio cameo by Allen. On June 9, the next-to-last* Jell-O Program *of the season, the cast discussed their vacation plans. Benny was due back in July for* Love Thy Neighbor, *a feud-inspired Paramount picture he was making with Allen. He claimed the characteristic bags under Allen's eyes looked at Phil Harris's and said, "My son! My son!" Later in the program Benny fined Harris five dollars for admitting he had listened to Allen. Harris said he didn't mind the fine, "but I hate to see all that dough go out of circulation."*

Fred Allen Show

JUNE 19, 1940

Town Hall Tonight became *The Fred Allen Show* on October 4, 1939. Benny is the guest on this 1940 program originating from Hollywood shortly before the start of production of *Love Thy Neighbor.* Allen gripes to Harry Von Zell that "the announcers have the fun and the comedians have the worry." Allen does a Don Wilson "fat" joke, saying Benny's announcer looks like "the Hollywood Bowl with a vest." In a parody of Allen's segments with "real people," Benny portrays a second violinist formerly with the Waukegan symphony, who says, "Our first violinist only had one finger on his left hand." Allen adds, "And after he had given the violin part the finger . . ." "I would follow through," Benny concludes. Benny goes on to say that after the symphony job he went into vaudeville, but "I left vaudeville because a certain juggler *killed* it," a shot at Allen that gets a big reaction from the audience. Benny says he moved on to film work, but has become typecast in he-man roles. Commenting on Benny's equestrian skills in *Buck Benny Rides Again,* Allen inquires, "Have you ever turned around, looked down, and had the illusion you were looking into a mirror?" Benny takes nearly fifteen seconds to respond. (Nearly twice as long as the oft-cited "Your money or your life" pause!) "No, Mr. Allen. I'd say the view was about the same as the one I'm enjoying right now." They discuss their joint film project, which Benny refers to as *All This and Benny Too.* (*All This and Heaven Too* was a Bette Davis film then in release.) Allen asks Benny about his costar. Benny huffs, "If you must know, they are trying to palm off a certain louse on me." "Good luck to me in your new picture, Mr. Benny," says Allen. The conversation concludes with Benny saying, "Good night, punk." "Good night, rat," counters Allen.

When The Fred Allen Show *changed sponsors and moved to CBS on October 2, 1940 the sniping was heard less frequently but not abandoned. Mary Martin, Benny and Allen's* Love Thy Neighbor *costar, was the guest on the November 17, 1940* Jell-O Program. *Two December programs concern Benny's trip to New York for the film's premiere. On his December 15 program Benny hired a bodyguard to shield him from a possible attack by Allen. On the same show Benny asserted that Allen was so money mad, "not only is he on the air for Texaco every Wednesday night, but he pumps gas the rest of the week!" Mutual Broadcasting, a "neutral" network, provided coverage of the film's New York premiere on Tuesday, December 17. Don Wilson characterized the film as "the comic climax of the greatest laugh feud of the century." Among the guests for the premiere were Tommy Dorsey, Ed Sullivan, the Ink Spots, and Stuart Canin, now fourteen-and-a-half, who played "The Bee." During their exchange, Allen said that Benny was "as funny as a leak in an oxygen tent."*

A new round of mutual irritation began on Benny's February 8, 1942 broadcast that would be played out continually through the decades (with some interruption during the war years). In March 1942 Benny presented "The Life of Jack Benny" in response to a radio autobiography Allen had presented.

MARCH 15, 1942

Jell-O Program

Rather than making his "usual hackneyed introduction," Don Wilson presents Dennis Day. Wilson tells Benny he might not be with him next season, since he has gotten an offer from the fictitious *Baxter Beauty Clay Program.* Mary Livingstone has been offered a job too. Benny is outraged. "Who started you out in vaudeville?" "I started in vaudeville with my sister Babe," responds Mary. They were tumblers called "The Bouncing Livingstones." "A lot of us helped to kill vaudeville," remarks Benny, "but you and your sister jumped on it!" (Acrobats were a vaudeville staple, but Mrs. Benny's vaudeville experience was limited to working with her husband.) Phil Harris is sticking by his boss, saying, "Next season we'll have just you, me, and a one-hundred-piece symphony orchestra!"—in this comment Harris's vanity depicts what he thinks the show should be. Don Wilson concedes that he "couldn't leave you or Jell-O." Finally, Benny turns his attention to Fred Allen and the "soggy saga of his miserable life" he had presented the previous week. Benny intends to set the record straight about Allen by presenting "The Life of Jack Benny." It begins in the farmhouse of Mr. and Mrs. Zeke Benny, progresses through his childhood to "somewhere in France" in

1917, then shifts to 1922, when Benny starts his career "as a concert violinist." Mary Livingstone wants to know, "What's all this got to do with Fred Allen?" "We're coming to that," Benny assures her. It is a cold winter day in 1927, and a "ragged unkempt stranger with icicles on his adenoids" asks Benny for five cents for coffee. Since it is Benny's fantasy, he gives him ten dollars. "Three years later" Benny approaches vaudeville juggler Fred Sullivan (Allen's real surname) and asks him for money for "a cup of instant Postum." "Get out of my way, you derelict," says Sullivan, impersonated by Peter Lind Hayes. A fight erupts, and Sullivan is left blubbering. "I knocked him *silly,* folks," Benny concludes, "and that's how Fred Allen became a comedian!"

Benny's commentaries on Allen were usually far less elaborate than the one heard on March 15. On the May 3, 1942 Jell-O Program, *set at the Warner Bros. studio where Benny was filming* George Washington Slept Here *with Ann Sheridan, Benny claims he is an ad-lib comedian. "Then why don't you answer Fred Allen once in a while?" cracks Sheridan. "Because in order to answer him I'd have to listen to his program!" was Benny's response. The two comedians met again in December 1942, when their facetious hostilities took a backseat to genuine enemies.*

Command Performance USA *DECEMBER 24, 1942*

Bob Hope, the "Commanding Officer of *Command Performance,*" is the master of ceremonies for this Armed Forces Radio Service "request" broadcast. Originating in Hollywood, this was the first time the show was heard in the United States. Hope's monologue is peppered with wartime references: "My aunt gave her girdle to the scrap drive. Now she's dreaming of a wide Christmas." The Andrews Sisters start the entertainment, then Red Skelton performs with Harriet Hilliard. Hope brings on "the old Groaner himself," Bing Crosby, who is referred to as "short, squat, and melodic." Crosby tweaks Hope regarding the show's worldwide audience. "Brother, when you lay an egg tonight, it's an international omelet."

Benny and Fred Allen conclude the entertainment portion of the program. "For a long time, Jack Benny has been a-feuding with Fred Allen. But thousands of you guys in the AEF [American Expeditionary Forces] have commanded that on this Christmas Eve the feud should be patched up," says Hope, who then turns things over to the "peace conference" in New York. Benny and Allen, who are introduced as an old vaudeville team, begin by battling over who should get top billing. Then Allen repeats a joke

Hope told in the first half of the program. "There's a three-hour difference in time," he reasons, "that joke didn't even get here yet." Their dialogue concludes with Benny declaring, "The greatest thing in the world today is friendship," the cue for the pair to sing their version of Cole Porter's "Friendship." As they finish, Allen says, "On the advice of our lawyers, we return you to Hollywood."

Allen's final CBS program was heard on June 25, 1944. He would not return to the air with his own NBC program until October 1945, but was heard four times with Benny during his first season for Lucky Strike. On the October 1, 1944 premiere, Allen attacked Benny in a conversation with actor-impersonated American Tobacco president G. W. Hill. [See page 105 for summary of this program.] "Benny wasn't delivered by the stork, he was brought by a leech!" he said. Later, Benny tells "Hill" that Allen looks "like a hen trying to lay a square egg."

OCTOBER 29, 1944

Lucky Strike Program

Benny has invited his gang over for a late Sunday breakfast. He decides to serve them sliced oranges, and the sound of slicing is heard for eleven seconds until Benny concludes, "Well, there's no use stopping now. I might as well slice the other half." On his bus ride into work, Benny encounters Fred Allen, whose first line is, "Here, old man, take my seat." He tells Benny, "You'll say anything for a laugh, and someday you may get one." Benny responds with a dig at Allen's upcoming film, *It's in the Bag,* "You're advertising it under each eye." Allen remarks that their listeners "think our feud is on the level," which cues a retrospective of their exchanges. Says Benny, "The way Allen talks through his nose, he's the only comedian in radio who tells 'em and smells 'em at the same time." He tells Allen he's "willing to pay as high as thirty-five dollars a week" for a singer to replace Dennis Day. Allen suggests they take a poll to determine the replacement, "I know just the place we can get a cross section of public opinion"—"Allen's Alley." This segment was probably Allen's best-known feature, though it was not formally established until December 1942, more than a decade into Allen's radio career. The usual routine consisted of Allen "walking" down the alley to ask the inhabitants a topical question.

In this episode John Doe complains about Phil Harris, the "jelly head" who is always singing "That's What I Like About the South." Mrs. Nussbaum is not a Benny fan, listening instead to "the other droop, Droop Pearson." Drew Pearsons's commentaries were heard Sundays at 7:00 on ABC. Socrates Mulligan is a Bing

Crosby admirer. "I always eat his cheese," he says, a reference to the *Kraft Music Hall.* Finally they arrive at the home of poet Falstaff Openshaw, who offers some "new odes," including, "The Siamese twins are going screwy / One's voting for Roosevelt / The other's for Dewey." Benny is shocked to find Rochester (not heard until now) working as Openshaw's butler. When Rochester offers a sample of his verse, Benny shrieks, "Now cut that out and come home right now!"

Allen joined Benny for a broadcast from the Grand Ballroom of the Hotel Astor on January 14, 1945. He even did the Lucky Strike commercial. He and Portland Hoffa joined Benny for his February 4 broadcast from Saint Albans Naval Hospital. These guest appearances anticipated Benny's cameo in Allen's film, It's in the Bag, *which opened on April 21, one week before Benny's final feature film,* The Horn Blows at Midnight.

On Benny's first show of the 1945–46 season, one month prior to Allen's return to NBC, he was told that Allen had appeared as a guest with Edgar Bergen. "What's the matter," asked Benny, "is Charlie McCarthy sick?" "It isn't that I dislike the stinker personally," Benny added, "I can't understand why people laugh at his kind of jokes." "Me neither, boss," said Rochester supportively. Benny continued, "It's a mystery to me why a sponsor would give him a job." "Maybe it's just that our vines have sour grapes," concluded Rochester.

Allen was declared the Supreme Judge of the "I Can't Stand Jack Benny Because . . ." contest on December 2, 1945 and was next heard with Benny on January 27, 1946 for the announcement of the winners. Clearly Allen's return to NBC gave the feud new life.

MARCH 17, 1946 **Lucky Strike Program**

Mary Livingstone is wearing something green for Saint Patrick's Day—the gold bracelet Benny gave her for Christmas. When a couple of lines are fumbled, Benny ad-libs a remark about the lack of rehearsals. Mabel Flapsaddle and Gertrude Gearshift, the telephone operators played by Bea Benaderet and Sara Berner (first heard at the beginning of the 1945 season), come on the air. Gertrude remarks that the contest has been over for six weeks and she still cannot stand Benny. (The "I Can't Stand Jack Benny Because . . ." contest began on the December 2 program, offering ten thousand dollars in Victory Bonds as prizes.) Dennis Day returns from the Navy on this program. When he arrives, the sound of kissing is heard. "Oh, boy! I never expected this. Are you going to kiss me, too, Miss Livingstone?" The cast presents its version of "Allen's Alley," "Benny's Boulevard." The question: is Fred Allen or Jack Benny the better comedian? (This is the same question posed on Benny's April 1936 Allen satire.) Mary Livingstone portrays "Cleveland," based on Portland Hoffa. Dennis Day plays "Titus Day," based on Allen's New England farmer, Titus Moody. The stentorian Senator Claghorn is parodied as "Senator Harris." Mr. Kitzel is the Mrs. Nussbaum equivalent, another Yiddish-American character. Rochester plays the poet, Openshaw, who recites an ode on the Benny-Allen feud: "And I often wonder just what it means as they hurl their epitaphs / For while they're knocking each other out / Cass Daley gets all the laughs." Comedienne Daley was the star of the *Fitch Bandwagon,* whose program was heard on NBC between Benny and Allen.

Fred Allen Show *MAY 26, 1946*

Announcer Kenny Delmar, who doubles as Senator Claghorn, bills Benny as "Mary Livingstone's husband." Allen's age comes up in his weekly dialogue with Portland Hoffa. "I was born before the Decca company started, so there weren't any records in those days." Following a visit to "Allen's Alley," the program is interrupted by the arrival of a stowaway on the "Radio City 60-cent tour"—Benny. "Go ahead, be like other comedians," says Benny, "tell some cheap jokes. Say I'm tighter than the skin on Sidney Greenstreet's hip!" Allen tries to convince Benny his program may have run its course, "You with that 'Hmmm' and 'Yipe!' Fourteen years is a long time." This leads to a boastful exchange about their vaudeville careers. "I stopped every show," says Benny. "Except this one," responds Allen. "This one stopped five minutes before I got on it!" counters Benny. Allen tells Benny that radio has changed, "People don't want entertainment today. A radio show has to give away things." Benny is aghast, "I'll die first!" Allen presents "King for a Day," a parody of the Mutual Broadcasting network's *Queen for a Day.* Benny is Myron Proudfoot, "a chaplain in a bakery," who announces, "Start giving things away, brother!" "Proudfoot" wins a canoe paddle, a chromium pitchfork, and other absurd prizes. Plus, says Allen, "We're going to start right now to make you look like a king!" Benny is given a shine, hat blocking, and, finally, gets his pants pressed. Chaos reigns as his trousers are removed. "Now wait a minute!" pleads Benny, and "Allen, you haven't seen the end of me!" "It won't be long now!" says Allen menacingly. The roars of the audience continue through Delmar's attempt to get in a final plug for Tenderleaf Tea as the program ends.

On June 9 Benny was the guest on ABC's Chicago-based Quiz Kids. *He was accompanied by a six-year-old pianist for "Flight of the Bumble Bee." Instead, Benny plays "The Bee." When the error is pointed out, Benny dismisses it, "A bee is a bee! Benny isn't my right name, either!" Dennis Day was Fred Allen's guest in New York that same evening. Eddie Anderson was with Allen the following Sunday.*

MAY 25, 1947

Lucky Strike Program

Benny presents another version of "Allen's Alley," "Benny's Boulevard." As before, he impersonates Allen supposedly with a clothespin on his nose. Again, Mary Livingstone is "Cleveland." The question, too, is unchanged: "is Fred Allen or Jack Benny the better comedian?" Mr. Kitzel (Artie Auerbach) portrays Mr. Nussbaum, who says he prefers "Duffy's Temple," a play on *Duffy's Tavern.* Dennis Day, spoofing Ajax Cassidy, likes "A Day in the Life of an Irish Lad," a plug for Day's own Wednesday night show, *A Day in the Life of Dennis Day,* but his choice is Benny, "because this is the last program of the season and I want to be back next year." Benny visits "a new house at the end of the Alley," one occupied by Fred Allen himself. "If you were thirty years younger, I'd punch you right in the eye," says Allen. Benny is shocked. "What! You'd hit a kid of 7!" Following a commercial, Benny introduces Jack Paar. The two had met in the South Pacific, where comedian Paar was entertaining fellow GIs. Benny and Allen fret that Paar may get too many laughs on his summer show, which replaces Benny the following Sunday. Benny concludes by thanking Allen "for lousing up my show, and I'll do my best to do the same thing for him next week." He adds, "I know you'll enjoy Jack Paar very much during the summer." On June 15, 1947 Benny appeared on Paar's program, which featured Benny regular Frank Nelson as his wisecracking announcer.

Allen's sponsor changed again, from Standard Brands to the Ford Motor Company, on January 4, 1948. On his April 11 broadcast Allen asked his cast if they had heard Benny's show that evening. "His show was cut off again tonight. Cut off last week, too." Benny's April 4 program featured an encore of the now-legendary "Your money or your life" routine and ran long. Allen concludes, "There's a new saying in radio: You'll never hear the end of Jack Benny."

Fred Allen Show *JUNE 27, 1948*

Benny is the guest on the last program of Fred Allen's penultimate radio season. In the course of his dialogue with Portland Hoffa, Allen savages quiz shows. He claims their slogan is "If you can't entertain people, give them something." At the time Allen's audience was being eroded by *Stop the Music,* an ABC game show. The "only one who listens to our program is Edgar Bergen," Allen's CBS competitor. Allen visits "Allen's Alley." After chatting with Senator Claghorn, Titus Moody, Mrs. Nussbaum, and Ajax Cassidy, Allen introduces the Five DeMarco Sisters, three of whom were on Allen's December 30, 1936 *Town Hall Tonight* broadcast that launched the Benny–Allen feud. Following the DeMarcos, Allen excuses himself. "Jack Benny's sailing for England," he explains, "I promised to see Jack off." Allen visits Benny's hotel room, where Benny reveals he swam to New Jersey to save twenty-four cents on a carton of Lucky Strike cigarettes. For his British stay, the Colmans have recommended "His Majesty's Trailer Camp," which is operated by the "Howard Johnson of England." When Benny learns his hotel bill is $43.80, he collapses. The clerk instructs Allen to go through his pockets, but they are locked. He orders the bellboy to put Benny in the safe until he comes to, but Allen agrees to pay. The scene switches to the ship. Benny is not allowed on board, since he bears no resemblance to the "shrunken up old bloke with no hair and no teeth" in his passport photo. "Where was the picture taken?" Allen asks. "Warner Bros. They do it to me every time." (Warner Bros. was the studio that released *The Horn Blows at Midnight.*) On board Benny and Allen descend several flights of stairs. When they wind up amidst a herd of cows, Benny confesses he does not have a ticket. "I knew you were cheap," says Allen, "but going to Europe as a stowaway! The Captain'll find you down here with all these cows, and then what are you going to say?" "Moo!" Benny replies.

On his November 7, 1948 Lucky Strike Program, *Benny griped about Allen. Phil Harris was also heard bragging about his own radio show, which was heard between the two. Even if Benny does a bad show, Harris boasts, "I come on right after you!" That changed for both Harris and Allen on January 2, 1949 when Benny moved to CBS; after the switch Benny's show was heard before* Amos 'n' Andy *and* The Edgar Bergen-Charlie McCarthy Show. *Allen commented on the impending change on his December 19, 1948 program, "The networks ran out of refrigerators, and somebody gave Jack Benny away!" Allen even took a swipe at Benny's replacement, bandleader Horace Heidt's* Youth Opportunity Program. *"In the number one position, I hear," said Allen, who realized that was entirely due to Benny occupying the time slot. Heidt's audience dropped to one-third the size of Benny's, further eroding Allen's following.*

"Stop the Music," *said Harriet Van Horne of the* World Telegram, *"tumbled Fred Allen from the plush pew reserved for Hooper's Top Ten to a camp stool in back of* Lum and Abner," *which was another long-running broadcast suffering from declining popularity. In spite of the network switch and the downturn in Fred Allen's radio fortunes, Benny continued taking amusing shots. On Benny's first television broadcast on May 8, 1949, he speculated that Allen would have problems with the new medium, saying that the baggy-eyed Allen "looks like a short butcher peeping over two pounds of liver."*

During the 1948–49 radio season, an executive of J. Walter Thompson, the advertising agency that produced the Ford program, asked Allen to give up his radio show and turn his talents to television. Allen resented the suggestion, and if it were not for his concern about his cast and crew, he would have walked off the show immediately, but he played out the season.

JUNE 26, 1949

Fred Allen Show

This is Fred Allen's final radio program. Near the top of the show, Portland Hoffa congratulates herself on her jokes, "If I can keep up this pace, I'll wind up with my own program." "The way radio is going," Allen observes wryly, "that is quite possible." Allen directs a bitter barb at "Mr. Television," Milton Berle, "the only comedian I know who uses an Airwick as a straight man." Allen takes a walk down Main Street to discuss summer vacation plans with Senator Claghorn, Titus Moody, Mrs. Nussbaum, and Ajax Cassidy. He stops by Main Street's Ford dealer to say goodbye, then encounters protégé Henry Morgan in front of a pawn shop. "When I'm working," says Morgan, "I'm in front of the cigar store." Morgan owes three hundred dollars to the Mohawk Loan Company, so Allen takes him to the Chase National Bank to ask a certain "Mr. X" for a loan. Getting to Mr. X's vault is not unlike a trip to Benny's. Benny is, in fact, the mystery man who spends his summer in the vault. "It's cool down here and it's so nice and green," he says. Benny gives Allen and Morgan a tour of the facility, pointing out a pile of Confederate money and commenting, "If the South ever comes back, brother, I'll be the John D. Rockefeller of Atlanta!" Perhaps because of Morgan's presence, Benny seems ill at ease. His delivery is clipped and his only apparent departure from the script is to complain, "Nobody ever made me this cheap on my own program!"

During the season following the demise of his own show, Allen visited Benny on January 15, 1950, where the two reminisced about their vaudeville days and accused each other of stealing material. Broadcasting from New York the next month, Benny reassembled the "Allen's Alley" cast in a satire of a program that no longer existed!

The end of The Fred Allen Show *was not the end of Fred Allen on radio. In spite of a minor stroke and a heart attack, Allen made dozens of guest appearances through December 1955. He was a writer on NBC's* Big Show *from November 1950 to April 1952 and was heard on the program every other week beginning on February 4, 1951. He joined Benny for the last time in April 1953.*

Lucky Strike Program *APRIL 26, 1953*

One week after their only joint television appearance, (see page 244 for summary) Fred Allen performs on Benny's radio show. The setting is the dressing room of a San Francisco theater, where Benny is appearing. Don Wilson calls from Hollywood with a Lucky Strike–related idea for a 3D picture with the Sportmen set in a tobacco field. When Fred Allen arrives, he tells Benny he has been in town since the previous evening. Benny asks why he didn't call. Allen is amazed, "You mean, you're staying at one that has phones?" "Well, no," replies Benny, "but there's a candy store in the lobby that takes messages." Rochester suggests the pair go on stage that evening, but Allen says he has no material, not even old vaudeville routines. "If I did, I'd be on television." Besides, says Allen, he is working on a new motion picture shot in "No dimension." "When it comes out, you don't dimension the whole thing." This is apparently an Allen ad-lib, since Benny comments, "So far, that's better than what we've got written here." The pair reminisce about their fictitious vaudeville act. The scene switches to those days, where the duo is heard in the office of theatrical agent Mickey Rockford. Benny asks Rockford's secretary, played by Bea Benaderet, "Don't you recognize us?" "Why," she asks, "is there a reward?" Benny and Allen present their "violin, clarinet and snappy patter" act to Rockford, played by Mel Blanc. They play alternating choruses of "Tea for Two," punctuated by bad gags. Says Benny, "Music once saved my uncle's life." Asks Allen, "Well, how did music save your uncle's life?" "They played the 'Star Spangled Banner' just as he was sitting in the electric chair." Rockford isn't interested in the team, but quips, "I've got an opening for a single in Scranton for fifteen dollars a week." The two bid each other down to nothing. "Well," says Rockford, "at that price I can afford the both of you." The pair is joyous. Allen says, "Did you hear that? We're working!"

Fred Allen died on March 17, 1956, a little less than a year after Jack Benny's last original radio broadcast, and a significant chapter in the history of early radio had ended.

Violinist Stuart Canin, nearly forty, was invited to play "The Bee" on Benny's television program in 1965, the show's last season. According to Irving Fein, following a light-hearted conversation with Canin, Benny proceeded to prove to the audience, once and for all, that he really could *play the piece. Benny continued to perform "The Bee" in concert for the rest of his life.*

FEBRUARY 8, 1937

A British Broadcast

One day after a regular *Jell-O Program,* Benny and his cast contribute a segment to a transatlantic broadcast that explains the program to an audience unfamiliar with it. Don Wilson bills it as "fifteen minutes of our typical American comedy." He presents Benny as "not only a comedian, but a suave, debonair, lover type." Benny introduces himself with "Hello, everybody, are you there?" then presents his cast. He characterizes Phil Harris as "Tall, fair, except in business matters" and says "I wish I were as handsome as he thinks he is." Mary Livingstone arrives with an umbrella, since it is raining in London, where the show is being heard. She presents a poem, "Dear Old England," which concludes with a salute to "that good old Palladium Theatre where Jack lasted just one week." Benny describes Kenny Baker as "a little dumb, but cute." "Yeah," Baker giggles agreeably, then sings an English hit, "When the Poppies Bloom Again." The balance of the program is a reprise of "The Bennys of Wimpole Street," a movie parody originally presented on October 28, 1934. Benny takes the role played by Charles Laughton, prompting another giggle from Baker, who explains, "I was just thinking how much better Charles Laughton played the part than you do."

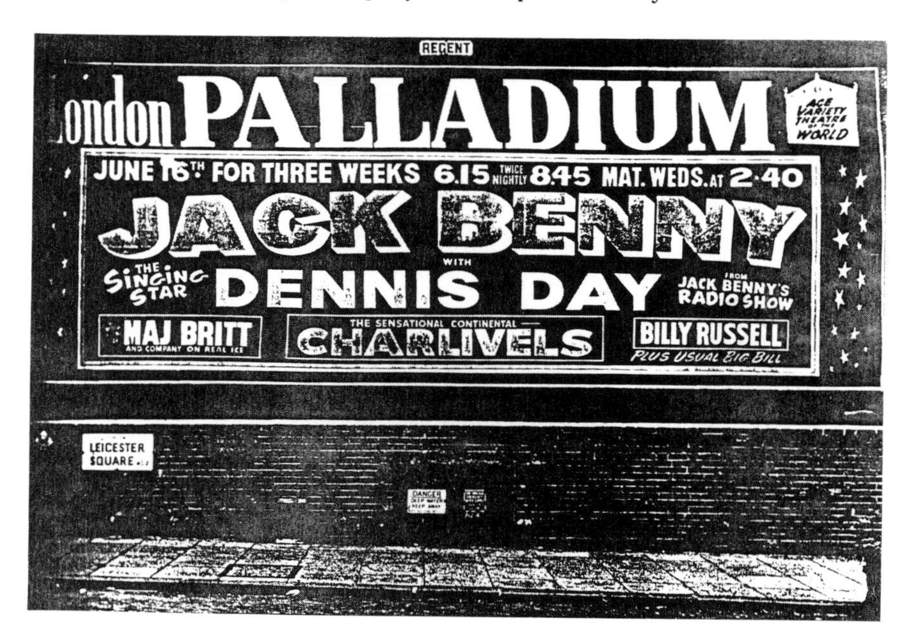

Lux Radio Theatre

FEBRUARY 15, 1937

Benny and Mary Livingstone star in *Brewster's Millions* on this prestigious CBS Monday evening broadcast. As was the case with their *Town Hall Tonight* performances, Mary Livingstone is billed as Benny's wife. Host Cecil B. DeMille even tells the story of how the pair was introduced by one of the Marx Brothers. Benny portrays Jack Benjamin Brewster, "who claims to be a musician." At one point he is practicing "Love in Bloom." His fiancée, Mary Gray, is played by Mary Livingstone, her girlish giggle resurfacing. Brewster inherits $1 million from his Uncle Ned. His grandfather has bequeathed him $6 million, provided he can spend the smaller amount, stay single, and keep the terms of the will secret for one year. Despite a couple of close calls, Brewster manages to spend himself broke by the end of the hour. After the performance DeMille introduces Mary Livingstone and her "assistant." When Benny offers to play "The Bee," DeMille claims it is "an obsession that's gone to your head." The February 16 *New York World Telegram* described the program as a "very amusing version of the play rewritten along Jack Benny lines." Mary Livingstone, the critic stated, "actually plays a role instead of merely passing acid digs."

MARCH 24, 1940

Campbell Playhouse

Benny stars in this radio adaptation of George S. Kaufman and Ring Lardner's *June Moon*. From the outset, producer Orson Welles makes it plain that "our offering is our guest star, Mr. Jack Benny." Benny portrays a small-town, small-time lyricist who is corrupted by life in the big city. Although he interrupts Welles during the introduction and at the intermission, Benny plays it much straighter than in his previous "dramatic" efforts. At one point, however, Benny, as Frederick D. Stevens, wants to see a radio show rather than go to a nightclub: "One guy I never miss. Gee, he's a scream. Fellow by the name of Jack Benny." Another character responds, "Jack Benny? Sure, I hear about him all the time on the Fred Allen program." The closing of the broadcast restates the gag that had been running since the previous Sunday, when Benny complains that his role "still doesn't have the dramatic quality that will get me an Academy Award."

MARCH 31, 1945

Jubilee

Benny and Rochester are the guests on this Armed Forces Radio series produced for black GIs that generally featured jazz artists. Rochester made more guest appearances on this program than any other, both with and without his "boss." Announcer Wendell Niles introduces the duo as the audience's "Consensus combination for convulsin' comedy." Ernest "Bubbles" Whitman is introduced as "Your massive of ceremonies." He bills Benny, who had previously appeared on a program recorded in January 1944, as "one of the finest instrumentalists of today." When Benny meets Whitman, he comments, "You look a little like Don Wilson around the stern." Benny is annoyed that Rochester hasn't arrived with his violin. The week before he didn't show up to help Benny get dressed for a dinner party at Ann Sheridan's house. "It's not easy," Benny explains, "those laces are behind me, you know." When the crowd reacts, Benny adds, "What are you laughing at?" Rochester phones. He doesn't have the violin anymore and suggests a trombone as an alternate, or even tissue paper and a comb. "No. No," Rochester realizes, "You wouldn't have a comb." Benny accuses Rochester of pawning the instrument. Rochester corrects him, "Around Central Avenue we prefer to call it three-ball Social Security." Besides, says Rochester, the violin was full of baby termites. "Maybe when you played "Love in Bloom" they took you serious," says Rochester. Later, when Rochester arrives with the violin, Benny learns that he used the Maxwell to get it out of hock. "My! It almost fills up the whole store window!" explains Rochester. After an elaborate warm-up and several false starts, Benny plays "Ida," including a fews words of praise for himself, "Boy! Am I hot!"

The Quiz Kids *JUNE 9, 1946*

Two weeks after the conclusion of the *Lucky Strike Program*'s 1945–46 season, Benny appears on this Chicago-based ABC broadcast. "Chief Quizzer" Joe Kelly tells the audience that he is going turn his cap and gown over to "the visiting professor from Waukegan." Benny refers to Kelly as "Don" (as in Wilson), and following the introduction of the kids, he announces, "I'm Jackie Benny. I'm 37 years old. And I was born in Waukegan in 1894. I went to the Waukegan High School for twelve years." These and other remarks throughout the program are punctuated by the giggles of the children. Benny clearly enjoys himself and appears to be ad-libbing through much of the show. During an answer about uranium, he interrupts with "I'll see you later" and "I gotta get a haircut!" The kids are asked to identify two famous love songs. First Benny is heard tuning up, then he plays "Love in Bloom" and "Intermezzo." When the latter is guessed, Benny quips, "Is that what that was?" When Benny is accompanied by a six-year-old pianist for "Flight of the Bumble Bee," he plays "The Bee," the same composition that ignited the Benny and Fred Allen "feud." When his error is pointed out, Benny fumes, "A bee is a bee! Benny isn't my right name, either!" For the balance of the program, Benny moves over to the Teacher's Desk. When sounds are the clues to movie titles and the answer is Benny's *The Horn Blows at Midnight,* he says "that sound effect was better than my whole picture!" The program ends on a sweet note. "I know a fond uncle never goes visiting without a present in his pocket. So here's a monogrammed ring for each of you from your Uncle Jackson."

Possibly Quiz Kid Joan Bishop.

Eddie Cantor–Pabst Blue Ribbon Show

JANUARY 30, 1947

Announcer Harry Von Zell leads the audience in a chorus of "Happy Birthday" in celebration of Eddie Cantor's fifty-fifth, only two years older than Benny's real age. Cantor jokes with Von Zell about the event, saying, "The product may be as good as ever, but the package is a little frayed around the edges." Cantor expresses the desire to buy a radio network, NBC, which will stand for "Nothing but Cantor!" All Cantor needs is half a million dollars. "I know just the man who'll give it to me, Jack Benny!" he enthuses, to a big reaction from the audience. Von Zell is amazed. "You expect to get *jack* from Benny?" Although Cantor claims the real Jack Benny is not cheap, he concedes that Benny parks his car in Glendale, miles from the studio, to save a quarter on parking. Benny's arrival is typically low-key, simply, "Hello, boys." He explains that the reason he parks so far away is not to save money, it is just that "it's such a bother making out a check each time." When Benny's age comes up, he explains, "Well, officially, I tell everyone I'm 37, but listen, I can't lie to you, Eddie, I'm 32." The mention of the half-million-dollar loan is greeted by silence. Cantor exclaims, "His toupee turned white! Jack, say something!" "Look, Dennis . . ." is Benny's response when he comes around. Benny thinks that Cantor should start smaller than an entire network, suggesting a few tubes and some wire. Microphones aren't necessary, either, "Not if you have a loud voice." The conversation ends with Benny explaining to Cantor, "I can't say 'no' to you," and suggests that Cantor call his business manager (and Benny's brother-in-law), Myrt Blum. "He'll say 'no' to you. I haven't got the heart. So long, Eddie."

Philco Radio Time

MARCH 26, 1947

Ten days after Bing Crosby guest starred on Benny's program, Benny and Mary Livingstone visit Crosby's ABC program. Announcer Ken Carpenter introduces Crosby as "The slip cover that walks like a man." Jokes about Crosby's taste in clothes, large family, and horse-racing ventures parallel the jibes directed at Benny's vanity and parsimony. "The calendar says spring is upon us," says Crosby, who believes that "Love in Bloom" "seems indicated." It was Crosby who introduced the song in 1934. The orchestra plays an introduction, and the unmistakably clumsy sound of Benny's violin is heard. "Let me alone, I'll get it!" yells Benny, "I can't understand it. I've never played so poorly." "Oh, cheer up, Jack," Crosby comforts him, "sure you have." Benny is bewildered that he's not getting enough laughs, saying in disbelief, "Bill Morrow used to write for me." Morrow and his partner, Ed Beloin wrote for Benny from 1936 through the end of the 1942 season. Benny tries to convince Crosby to do an act, "Jack Benny and Company," with Crosby on the cymbals and Mary on vocals. He wants to rehearse "Margie," which Crosby scoffs "was on the *Hit Parade* when 'men who know tobacco best' were Indians," a Lucky Strike allusion. They rehearse the tune, then Ken Carpenter returns for a Philco commercial. "Say, Ken, what are you talking about?" inquires Benny, "some new kind of gramophone?" Carpenter explains that the gramophone went out with button shoes. "And when did button shoes go out, may I ask?" huffs Benny.

At the closing, Mary asks, "Who's on your show next week, *Bing?*" incorrectly putting the interrogative emphasis on the last word. "Read that right, Mary!" says Benny, "Oh! These short rehearsals!" The upcoming guests are John Charles Thomas and Al Jolson. "I'd rather hear those guys sing than eat," Benny says. "How do you know, you've never heard them eat," counters Mary. Benny tells Crosby he's pleased, "We didn't do one joke about my toupee and your horses." "That reminds me," says Crosby. "You owe me twenty dollars. Your last toupee was made out of the tail of one of my horses."

NOVEMBER 9, 1948

Bob Hope Show

Bob Hope opens his Tuesday night NBC broadcast with a topical monologue that begins with Harry Truman's upset win over Thomas E. Dewey the previous week. According to Hope, pollster Dr. Gallop "was still peeking in the White House window singing 'Maybe You'll Be There!' " There's also a surprisingly early reference to car telephones, "A guy's driving along. His wife calls up and says, 'Honey, bring home a head of lettuce, some carrots, a cucumber . . . and get that tomato out of your car!' " Following a song by Doris Day, there's a behind-the-scenes look at Paramount studios, where Hope is nursing a torn leg muscle. In his dressing room, Hope discusses his injury with Day, "Now I'll never be able to wear my pedal pushers with the split up the side." Benny is first heard playing with Les Brown's orchestra. "Well," Benny explains, "Just once I wanted to sit in a band and not worry about the leader's breath taking the varnish off my violin." As he did when appearing with Bing Crosby, Benny complains about his lines. Hope explains that they had planned on giving him something he could sink his teeth into, "but we weren't sure if you'd have them with you tonight." "You wouldn't dare say that if you were still with Pepsodent, brother," exclaims Benny, a reference to Hope's previous toothpaste sponsor, which earns a audience roar of more than ten seconds. It's so big that Hope ad-libs, "Standby, Fibber," as if to warn the succeeding program *(Fibber McGee and Molly)* that they would be getting off late. In their sketch, Hope and Benny portray a team of disc jockeys, "Be-Bop Bob" and "Jazzy Jack Benny," who greet the "Make

Believe Washroom" listeners with "Hotcha! Vo-De-o-Do!" Hope announces a new release by "that brilliant young Waukegan violinist, Benny Kubelsky" and, Benny adds, "That new Cleveland singing discovery, The Velvet Smog," a reference to Mel Torme. Accompanied by Benny, Hope sings "Buttons and Bows," but Benny segues into "Love in Bloom," causing Hope to yell over the closing announcements, "Jack! Wait a minute! Wait a minute!"

Phil Harris–Alice Faye Show

DECEMBER 19, 1948

Two weeks before Benny moved to CBS, he plays Santa Claus on this Rexall-sponsored NBC program heard between Benny and Fred Allen. Harris has promised his daughters that they will see Santa Claus on Christmas Eve. Elliot Lewis portrays guitarist Frankie Remley, who assures Harris, "The real guy will show up." Not taking chances, Harris tries to hire Don Wilson, who can't make it; Wilson, however, finds an actor willing to portray Santa. When Santa Benny arrives, applause precedes his first lines, "Ho! Ho! Ho! Merry Christmas and where's my ten dollars?" After Benny learns he has been hired to entertain the Harris children, he lowers his price, "Seven fifty is plenty! What kind of heel do you think I am?" To make sure he can fool his daughters, Harris tries Benny's Santa out on Julius, a wise-guy neighborhood kid. "What would I find if I lifted up that white wig?" Julius asks. "A brown one!" says Benny. Benny greets the children with "Hello again, this is Santa Claus talking," a line that echoes his radio greeting. He tells them, "I've lived for hundreds and hundreds of years!" "How old are you?" one asks. "Thirty-nine," deadpans Santa Benny.

MARCH 4, 1949

The Ford Theatre

Benny stars with Claude Rains in "The Horn Blows at Midnight" on this CBS program. Warner Bros.'s *The Horn Blows at Midnight,* released in 1945, was Benny's last starring vehicle, and its alleged putrescence was a long-running gag. Benny portrays a minor angel named Athanael, who plays 455th trumpet in the Ethereal Philharmonic. Athanael is assigned to destroy the earth by going to the roof of the Waldorf Biltmore Hotel and blowing his horn at midnight exactly. As adapted for radio by Hugh Wedlock, Jr., and Howard Snyder, two of Benny's Lucky Strike writers, Benny essentially plays his radio character. When he is given money before coming to earth, he asks, "What are these, gilders?" Told they are dollar bills, he gets a big laugh when he replies, "Oh. Well, I wouldn't know about that." Later he explains to a policeman he's 355 years old, but "I tell everyone up there I'm 339." There are also gags about television and the proliferation of radio game shows. Benny encounters a *Sing It Again* winner in the hotel lobby. When a "Jack Benny" is paged, she declares, "I listen to him every Sunday, even though I can't win anything." Following a touching encounter with a pair of French refugees, Athanael decides against destroying the earth. "Maybe most people are good. Maybe the war has been a lesson." At the conclusion of the program, Benny tells the show's director, Fletcher Markle, "If I ever make another bad picture, you can have the first crack at it."

DECEMBER 25, 1949

Hotpoint Holiday Hour

Benny gives the best acting performance of his radio career in George S. Kaufman and Moss Hart's *The Man Who Came to Dinner.* He portrays Sheridan Whiteside, a character said to have been inspired by Alexander Woollcott and portrayed on the stage and screen by Monty Woolley. The program is introduced by John Garfield, narrated by Henry Fonda, and directed by Mel Ferrer. The cast is outstanding and includes Charles Boyer, Gene Kelly, Gregory Peck, and Rosalind Russell, actors not generally associated with radio. Although the adaptation was done by Hugh Wedlock, Jr., and Howard Snyder, two Lucky Strike writers, there is virtually no accommodation made for Benny's radio persona. References to such contemporary personalities as Errol Flynn, Margaret Truman, and Gorgeous George (the professional wrestler) are the only apparent alterations to the original.

A Salute to Jack Benny

NOVEMBER 9, 1951

CBS presents a celebration of Benny's twentieth anniversary in radio written by Benny regulars Hugh Wedlock, Jr., Howard Snyder, and Al Schwartz. It is directed and produced by Irving Mansfield and features Milton Berle as the host. He tells a story about renting a house near Benny's. During one visit to Berle's home, Benny spots a photo of Dagmar, the buxom star of network television's first regular late-night program, *Broadway Open House,* in an issue of *Look.* "Gee, it's a big picture," Benny says, earning a big laugh. "Continued on page 40." Another laugh. Finally, he puts on his glasses and discovers he was actually looking at a photograph of a B-29. Berle receives a call from the secretary of the president of CBS, William S. Paley, regarding the gift Paley should buy for Benny's testimonial dinner. Berle suggests money. Paley's secretary suggests something that will last. Berle counters, "I guarantee you, when Benny gets his hand on a buck that's the last of it." Benny phones Ronald Colman to ask him to care for his parrot, Polly, while he is in New York. Colman turns him down. He can't stand the idea of having to listen to the bird singing "When You Say 'I Beg Your Pardon' Then I'll Come Back to You," the song Benny wrote on his September 30 program. Colman's refusal nets an elongated "Well!" from Benny. Benny calls again and shames Colman into caring for the bird. When Colman gets off the phone, he is in tears. "Who was that you were talking to?" asks Benita Colman. "Bette Davis," he explains, who was closely associated with her tearjerker roles.

The scene switches to Broadway, where Benny meets Ethel Merman. He invites Merman to his dinner, suggesting undiplomatically that she might get a job out of it. Merman explains that she has been in *Call Me Madame* the last two years. Benny tells her the last show he saw was *Peg O' My Heart.* The locale changes to the dinner. Merman sings "There's No Business Like Show Business." William S. Paley's speech includes a reference to a "fine and generous humanitarian." Berle interjects, "Who's he talking about now?" When Paley presents his gift to Benny, a scroll, Benny faints. Paley notes, "We at CBS love Jack Benny" and hope that he continues "at least until he's 59, another twenty years." Benny gets the last word, griping "Twenty years on radio and they give me a scroll. Well, maybe on my fortieth anniversary they'll give me a frame for it."

A Radio Script for

NBC

the *Jell-O Program*

SUNDAY, APRIL 20, 1941

The General Foods Company Jell-O Program

RED NETWORK (7:00–7:30 P.M. E.S.T)
(8:30–9:00 P.M. P.S.T)

This is Jack Benny's twenty-ninth program of his sixth season sponsored by Jell-O. The broadcast originated from NBC's Sunset & Vine studio, (which he had been using since 1938) and was heard on 105 radio stations affiliated with the Red Network. The program was performed twice: at 4:00 P.M. Pacific Standard Time for East Coast and Central time zone listeners and again at 8:30 P.M. (Pacific time) for the Western and Mountain areas. This is Mary Livingstone's script for the afternoon "feed." The revisions made for the "night" or West Coast broadcast would often tailor the humor for the West Coast listeners.

The program starts cold, with no Jell-O introduction.

The script is divided into four "routines" with musical numbers between them that give the half-hour show its structure.

The program begins before the "radio show" that they are going to do starts.

(First routine starts before the signature)

(FIRST ROUTINE)

JACK: No . . No Mary, I've made up my mind., I am *not* going into that studio and broadcast tonight.

MARY: Oh Jack, let's not stand out here in the hall arguing . . Everybody's looking at us.

Benny was the guest star on this NBC Blue Network program on Wednesday, April 16. The Kids: Richard Williams, Gerard Darrow, and Claude Brenner had been on the Jell-O Program on April 6 and 13.

JACK: Let 'em look . . . If you think I can do a show tonight after making a monkey out of myself on the Quiz Kids Program, you're crazy.

MARY: That was Wednesday . . . People have forgotten all about it.

JACK: Oh they have, eh.

MARY: And besides, you're a comedian, you're not supposed to have any brains.

Benny started joking about his age on his 1932 appearance with Ed Sullivan. He didn't settle on age 39 until 1948, seven years after claiming to be 34!

JACK: Oh, you're just trying to make me feel good . . . Hm! . . There I was with those little kids, and I couldn't answer one question . . . And me thirty-four years old . . . I couldn't even answer a simple question like, where's the Taj Mahal?

MARY: You coulda *built* the Taj Mahal since *you* were thirty-four.

JACK: Go ahead, rub it in . . . What a blunder! After all the years I've spent in show business, I had to stick my neck out and ruin everything . . . oh well . . That's life for you.

Reproduction of actual radio script belonging to Mary Livingstone.

JOAN: Pardon me, Mr. Benny, may I have your autograph?

JACK: You don't want my autograph, girlie, I'm washed up . . . Thanks just the same.

MARY: Oh Jack, you have to dramatize everything.

JACK: I do, eh?

MARY: Supposing you did miss on a few questions . . you're not supposed to be Einstein.

JACK: I'm not supposed to be Phil Harris, either . . . My cousin Booboo would have been as good as I was on that program . . and all he knows is (*STRUMS LIPS*). . . . I tell you Mary, I'm not going on the air tonight.

MARY: Oh for Heaven's sake, if you're so ashamed of yourself, why don't you go out and join the Foreign Legion.

JACK: You might think that's a gag, Mary . . but the Foreign Legion isn't such a bad idea . . I can't get over it. Imagine, not getting that one about the Taj Mahal . . I knew the answer, but I opened my mouth and nothing came out . . . Not only that, a fly came in . . . Oh well, there's nothing I can do about it now. *(DOOR OPENS)*

WILSON: Jack . . Jack, hurry up . . the program starts in thirty seconds!

JACK: Well I won't be on it.

MARY: *Now Jack Benny, stop acting like a big baby* . . . He'll be right in, Don.
(DOOR SLAMS)

JACK: Mary, I'm not going to. . . . STOP PULLING ME! *(DOOR OPENS) MARY, LET GO OF MY ARM!*

MARY: COME ON JACK, Remember—you're a trouper!

In fact, Benny was not a believer in this show biz axiom, and he and Mary missed programs over the years rather than perform when ill.

JACK: A what? Oh yes, that's right . . . ONCE A TROUPER, ALWAYS A TROUPER . . . THE SHOW *MUST* GO ON!

WILSON: Quiet Jack, we're on the air.

JACK: Okay . . . Gee, I hope I'm good tonight.
(SIGNATURE - JELL-O)

The show's signature was the voices of the Jell-O "cheerleaders" spelling out the word harmoniously (J-E-L-L-O!).

WILSON: THE JELL-O PROGRAM STARRING JACK BENNY . .

WITH MARY LIVINGSTONE, PHIL HARRIS, DENNIS DAY AND "YOURS TRULY" DON WILSON . . . THE ORCHESTRA OPENS

Mention of Eddie "Rochester" Anderson in the opening announcement did not begin until the next season.

THE PROGRAM WITH "THE VINE STREET VIGGLE".
(SEGUE INTO NUMBER
1. PHIL HARRIS #6—ORCHESTRA)

"Vine Street Valtz" was indicated for the second show, which is for the West Coast.

OPENING COMMERCIAL

WILSON: Friends . . . every housewife knows that in cooling and baking, you'll get the best results if you follow *specific* recipes . . . instead of just *guessing* at the measurements and ingredients! And it certainly pays to be *very specific* when you're *ordering the foods* that go *into* those recipes! That's why it's always a wise thing to ask for *Jell-O* whenever you're buying *a gelatin dessert.* If you ask for this swell dessert *by name,* you can be sure of getting

. . . *every single time!* all those good things that Jell-O has come to stand for! You'll get Jell-O's brilliant *colors* that always look so gay and inviting! And you'll get Jell-O's *grand, distinctive flavor!* . . . a flavor as *refreshing* as the juicy-ripe fruit itself! . . . the *very ultimate* in *rich dessert enjoyment!* So when you ask for any of those famous *six delicious flavors,* remember . . . ladies and gentlemen . . . to specify the name *Jell-O!* Jell-O is a trademark . . . the property of General Foods. And those big red letters on the box tell you that here's a *mighty delightful treat!* . . . America's favorite gelatin dessert! . . *Jell-O!*

(SECOND ROUTINE)

The La Brea Tar Pits of Los Angeles is substituted in the script for the Empire State Building on the second show, to give the comedy a regional slant.

WILSON: That was "The Vine Street Viggle" played by the Orchestra . . AND NOW LADIES AND GENTLEMAN, AT THIS TIME WE BRING YOU ONE OF THE MOST BRILLIANT MINDS IN AMERICA TODAY . . A MAN WHOSE MEEK AND HUMBLE APPEARANCE CONCEALS THE BRAIN OF A GENIUS. . . . A MAN WHO APPEARED ON THE QUIZ KIDS PROGRAM WEDNESDAY NIGHT. AND DIDN'T KNOW THE TAJ MAHAL FROM THE EMPIRE STATE BUILDING . . . JACK BENNY!
(APPLAUSE)

JACK: Jello again, this is Jack Benny talking . . . And Don, I can't blame you for ribbing me tonight . . Those Quiz Kids really gave me the old one-two . . . I was never so humiliated in my life.

WILSON: Well I wouldn't take it so hard . . After all Jack, it's nothing to be ashamed of.

Barney Dean was a Hollywood character employed as a "gag man" by several radio comedians. He "punched up" the script of The Road to Singapore *starring Bing Crosby and Bob Hope and was the subject of gags on Crosby's* Kraft Music Hall.

JACK: Oh it isn't eh? . . Well let me tell you something, Don . . Everybody's snubbing me. I met Barney Dean on the street the other day, and he wouldn't even speak to me.

WILSON: Barney Dean, who's he?

JACK: Just throw a cigar away in front of the Regent Hotel, *you'll* find out. . . . I can't understand it, we've always been such good friends.

WILSON: Well . . that's the way it goes!

JACK: But I'm not complaining, Don . . I had it coming to me after that showing I made Wednesday night . . I can take it, though.

MARY: You can take it?

JACK: Yes.

MARY: Then why did you try to hang yourself Thursday morning?

JACK: Oh for Heaven's sake! I was hanging up a little laundry, fell off the ladder, and got tangled in the clothes-lines. . That's all.

MARY: Then explain that note you left, *"Farewell, cruel world."*

JACK: Oh that must have fallen out of my scrap book . . That's an old note I wrote one time when Clara Bow wouldn't go out with me . . . She got mad at me because my garter got caught in her wrist-watch during a Charleston Contest . . We were disqualified . . Anyway Don, when Mary saw me, I was just hanging up a few socks.

Clara Bow was a famous actress from silent films known for her wild behavior: she was the girl who had "It." The "Charleston" gag got a big laugh, which shows how Benny set himself up as the butt of age jokes.

MARY: *On Thursday?* . . I thought you always did your washing on Monday.

JACK: I couldn't do it Monday, I gave a reception for Lady Mendl . . . What do you want me to do, ask her to run the wringer? .

Lady Mendl was Elsie de Wolfe, the renowned interior decorator and international hostess of the twenties and thirties.

. . . She came over to my house to meet the Quiz Kids.

The "night revision" deletes the whole allusion to Lady Mendl and substitutes "Rochester was making matzah [sic] pancakes with the wringer . . . They were delicious, too." Perhaps the writers felt the international hostess was an East Coast personality, not a West Coast one.

MARY: Then why didn't you do your laundry Tuesday?

JACK: You know darn well that Tuesday is my day to go out and catch dogs in Beverly Hills. . . . I was elected to the office, and it's my duty . . . And on Wednesday . . . Oh Hello, Dennis.

DENNIS: Hello Mr. Benny . . . I heard you on the Quiz Kids program last week.

Benny's exchange with Day drew lots of laughs from the audience and off-microphone chuckles from Wilson and Livingstone.

JACK: Oh, did you?

DENNIS: Yeah, you sure were smart.

JACK: Smart? . . Why I didn't even open my mouth.

DENNIS: That's what I mean, don't talk Brother, unless you got a lawyer with you.

JACK: Hm! . . . You're a little mixed up Dennis, but thanks anyway.

DENNIS: You know Mr. Benny, when I was eight years old, I was just as bright as any of those Quiz Kids.

JACK: You were?

DENNIS: Yeah . . . WHAT *HAPPENED* TO ME?

JACK: I'm sure I don't know.

DENNIS: Some say one thing and some say another.

JACK: Well don't worry about it . . . You've got a good voice, what more do you want? . . . . You know Don, as a rule, I'm pretty hard-boiled . . . but even tho those Quiz Kids made me look like a nickel, I can't help liking 'em . . . they're so sweet and unspoiled.

WILSON: By the way Jack, are they still living at your house?

JACK: Yes Don, but they're leaving tonight.

According to Mary Livingstone, this was Day's actual response when called upon to sing at his audition for Benny, and it became his stock, self-effacing phrase.

MARY: They better check out before six o'clock or they'll be hooked for another day.

JACK: Listen Mary, at a lot of hotels the guests have to be out by noon . . . so don't run down the Beverly Hills Tourist Haven . . . . . . Rotary Club Every Wednesday.

MARY: I thought the Camp Fire Girls met on Wednesday.

JACK: Only in the Winter. . . . But honestly, fellows, those kids really made a hit with me . . . Gosh, they were wonderful company . . I may be a bit sentimental . . but I don't know . . I'm gonna miss that patter of little feet, running around the house . . . It'll be so quiet.

MARY: Why don't you put shoes on the mice?

JACK: Oh, stop . . there's no use being sentimental around here . . . Say Dennis.

DENNIS: Yes, please?

JACK: As long as Phil isn't here yet, how about your song . . What's it going to be.

DENNIS: I'm gonna sing a brand new number called "Once Upon a Summertime," and this is the first time it's ever been done on the air.

JACK: Well . . a newie, eh? . . Let's hear it, Dennis.

DENNIS: Okay.
(KNOCK ON DOOR)

JACK: Hold it a minute . . Come in.
(DOOR OPENS)

BALDWIN: Telegram for Jack Benny.

Benny substitutes "dime," for "nickel." Harry Baldwin was described on a May 1941 Benny tribute as "Jack's faithful secretary, who's been with him ever since his early days in radio." The bald-headed Baldwin made numerous appearances in similar black-out bits. Both his remark, "Now I can get my curls out of hock" and Benny's response, "That's all that zombie needs is curls!" were not indicated in the script, but were heard on the air.

JACK: Take it, Mary. . . . Wait a minute Buddy, here's a nickle for you.

BALDWIN: Oh goody, now I can go to Ciro's, and make a phone call.
(DOOR SLAMS)

JACK: Hm! Every time I see his head. I get hungry for egg plant.

MARY: Say Jack, this wire's from Waukegan.

JACK: Oh, from home, eh?

Benny frequently mixed fact and fantasy in describing his hometown. Actual friends and family were combined with imaginary ones.

MARY: Yeah . . it says ". . YOU CERTAINLY DISGRACED THE FAMILY ON THE QUIZ KIDS PROGRAM . . . PERSONALLY, I'M DISGUSTED WITH YOU."

JACK: Disgusted with me? Who's that from?

MARY: Cousin Booboo.

JACK: Well how did Booboo ever find out about telegrams . . He must have seen the picture "Western Union" . . Sing, Dennis.
(INTO NUMBER
2. ONCE UPON A SUMMERTIME DENNIS DAY)

(THIRD ROUTINE)

JACK: That was "Once Upon a Summertime" written by Jack Brooks and Norman Berens, and sung by Dennis Day . . . And Dennis, that was not only a great number, but your voice was really Heavenly. It was positively ethereal. . . . Allright Don, *ethereal.*

WILSON: Oh Jack, it's so ridiculous.

Benny often violated Wilson's sense of propriety; Wilson was particularly protective of his commercial spots. One running gag was that Benny would fire Wilson or embarrass him to the point that he walked off the show.

JACK: *Don . . . Dennis'es voice was positively ethereal . . .* Now go ahead.

WILSON: Oh, allright . . . LADIES AND GENTLEMEN . . THE NEXT TIME YOU'RE IN THE MARKET FOR A REAL TREAT, BE SURE AND BUY A PACKAGE OF JELLO.

JACK: Keep going.

WILSON: REMEMBER, FOLKS, . JELLO IS NOT A THEREAL . . IT'S A DESSERT.

JACK: There!

WILSON: But what does it mean? I don't get it.

JACK: Don . . *thereal* is a pun on the word *cereal* . . . Jello is not a thereal . . . Now continue, this is the cute part.

WILSON: O.K. . . WHY DON'T YOU RUN DOWN TO YOUR NEIGHBORHOOD GROTHER, AND ATHK HIM FOR ANY ONE OF THE THIX DELITHITH FLAVORS.

JACK: Keep going, Don.

WILSON: Oh, thith ith tho thilly.

A huge, ten-second laugh.

JACK: *Don!*

WILSON: *(VERY FAST)* THO LOOK FOR THE BIG RED LETHERS ON THE BOCKTH, *DARN YOU JACK BENNY, I'M GOING HOME.*
(TERRIFIC DOOR SLAM)

JACK: What? . . . Well I'll be darned, he left . . . I must have wounded his big fat vanity. . . . He's so temperamental lately.

MARY: Well I don't blame him, Jack . . did you write that commercial?

JACK: Yes.

MARY: Well it thertainly thunk.

Harris's rapid-fire delivery is unlike his earliest efforts on the program, when his slower, almost lazy style prompted one critic to remark that he could be confused with Benny.

JACK: Mary, those are all clever ideas and should be tried out . . . You know I've got a marvelous one for next week . . Look, as soon as Dennis finishes his song . . Oh hello, Phil.

PHIL: Hya Jackson, what's the matter with Don? . . I just seen him walking down the hall.

JACK: Oh, he's mad at me.

PHIL: The guy's screwy . . . I said "Hello" to him . . and he said, "I'm *thick* of you, too!"

JACK: He did, oh?

PHIL: Yeah . . you know, he was lipsing.

JACK: That's *lisping* . . . not lipsing.

PHIL: Well he did it with his lips.

JACK: I don't care what he did it with . . . the word is lisping.

PHIL: Allright, have it your way . . . Hy ya, Mary.

MARY: Hello, Phil. . . . Say Phil, how are you and the boys going over at the Paramount Theatre?

PHIL: Mary, we're a riot . . . You oughta hear the laughs I get with my gags.

JACK: I can imagine.

PHIL: Get this one, Jackson . . . When I first walk out on the stage, I say to my guitar player . . "HEY FRANKIE, WHO WAS THAT LADY I SEEN YOU WITH LAST NIGHT"?

JACK: A-huh.

Another fact and fantasy mix. Harris was doing a theater appearance at the time, but it is extremely unlikely that the act included a pie toss. Frankie Remley was the band's guitarist as early as 1937 and through Benny's television years.

PHIL: And before he can answer, I hit him in the kisser with a blueberry pie.

JACK: Hm! . . . Why Phil Harris, you oughta be ashamed of yourself . . Throwing a pie in a guy's face, is the oldest comedy bit in Show Business.

PHIL: *With blueberry?.* . . . You're thinking of custard.

JACK: Oh. I see you modernized it.

MARY: You know I can't imagine people laughing at that kind of stuff nowadays.

JACK: Neither can I.

PHIL: You can't, eh? . . . Why after the first show, the Manager came backstage and told me I was terrific . . . He said, "HARRIS, YOU OUGHTA HAVE YOUR OWN RADIO PROGRAM".

JACK: He did, eh?

PHIL: Yeah, but don't worry Jackson . . *I'm loyal* . . I'll be with *you* for years.

In fact, before Harris joined the program in 1936, Benny had used six different bandleaders in four years. The night version includes a Benny aside, "I don't know what Alice sees in him," which might be more suited to the West Coast audience. At the time, Alice Faye was engaged to Harris. They married on May 12, 1941.

JACK: Well thanks . . . Now if *I* was loyal, you'd be all set . . . Let me tell you something, Phil . . I used to be in Vaudeville . . . but I never stooped so low as to throw a pie at anybody . . That's real hokum.

MARY: What about that corney piece of business you used to do in your violin act?

JACK: Corney piece of business?

PHIL: What was it, Mary?

MARY: *(GIGGLE)* Jack used to play "By The Waters of the Minnetonka" . . and for a finish, Barney Dean would squirt him in the face with a bottle of Seltzer.

Mary's giggle is actually indicated in the script. On the night revision of the script, the Barney Dean gags are deleted. In their place, Mary says, "Jack used to play Mendelssohn's Spring song . . . and for a finish, Mendelssohn would come out and break his fiddle."

JACK: Yeah . . And now the guy won't even speak to me. . . . . But Mary, that was a very clever tie-in. . . . You see the song I was playing was about water . . so Barney Dean squirted water on me . . . That was the idea.

MARY: Remember the time you played "Among My Souvenirs" and he took your watch?

JACK: Well that was just for a gag, I got it back later . . Anyway, I'll never forget one day when he— *(KNOCK ON DOOR)*

JACK: Come in. *(DOOR OPENS)*

ROCHESTER: Hello, Boss!

JACK: Oh hello, Rochester.

ROCHESTER: I got the Quiz Kids out in the car . . They're all set to go to the Station.

JACK: Already? . . . I didn't know it was that late . . . Say Phil, the kids are going back to Chicago tonight, and I promised to take 'em down to the train . . . so you carry on with the show, will yuh?

Benny "leaves" the show to take care of some imaginary "real life" business.

PHIL: Okay . . . HEY FRANKIE, GO OUT AND GET A BLUEBERRY PIE.

JACK: You don't have to do that here. . . . Just play some numbers . . Come on Mary, you ride down with us . . . So long, Phil . . See you later, Dennis.

DENNIS: So long, Mr. Benny.
(DOOR SLAMS—WE HEAR THE THREE OF THEM WALKING)

JACK: The kids are in the car, eh Rochester?

The car is not identified, but by 1941 Benny's association with the Maxwell was so strong that everyone knew it to be the infamous automobile.

ROCHESTER: Yes sir . . . And Boss, listenin' to those kids talk, is really an education.

JACK: It certainly is.

ROCHESTER: You know I told 'em the salary you were payin' me . . . and they took my weekly earnings, multiplied it by fifty-two, and gave me the *square root* of my annual income.

JACK: The square root, eh? What was it?

ROCHESTER: Believe me Boss, it ain't worth rootin'.

JACK: That's too bad . . . Now listen, Rochester—

Frank Nelson was first heard with Benny in June 1934. At this time he was beginning to be heard with greater frequency, but his parts were not as yet clearly defined (such as the floorwalker) or as broadly played as they would be in the mid to late forties.

NELSON: Oh there you are, Mr. Benny.

JACK: *(FOOTSTEPS STOP)* Yes?

NELSON: I've got your papers ready to sign . . You leave in ten days.

JACK: What?. . . . Oh, I meant to get in touch with you about that . . I'm not going!

NELSON: Well it's pretty late for that, Mr. Benny.

JACK: I'm sorry, you'll have to forget the whole thing . . . Come on, Mary.
(A FEW MORE FOOTSTEPS)

JACK: *(MUMBLING)* Darn it, I meant to write him a letter.

MARY: Who was that, Jack?

JACK: The Recruiting Officer for the Foreign Legion . . . You know how depressed I was . . . It's all off now, though.

Although scratched out of the script, the following lines are heard. Rochester: I'm sure disappointed Boss, I got a girl in Morocco. Jack: Well you weren't going!

JACK: *(DOOR OPENS)* WELL . . THERE ARE THE KIDS NOW . . . COME ON MARY.

MARY: Okay, Beau Geste.

JACK: HELLO KIDS, HERE'S UNCLE JACKIE TO TAKE YOU TO THE TRAIN!
(START THE NUMBER)

JACK: Now I'll sit up front with Rochester . . . And Mary, you get back there with the kids . . . Move over, Gerard.
(MUSIC UP—
3. BLUES MY NAUGHTY SWEETIE TAUGHT ME—ORCHESTRA)

At one minute and thirty seconds, this was long for a band number. Perhaps the show was running short at this point.

The automotive sounds are not yet impersonated by Mel Blanc, who will later "become" the Maxwell.

(FOURTH ROUTINE) (SOUND: LOUSY MOTOR - BEEP-BEEP . . . BEEP-BEEP)

JACK: You know Rochester, I don't like that horn, it sounds too cheap and tinny.

ROCHESTER: A-huh.

JACK: That didn't come with the car . . . Where did we get that bulb horn, Rochester?

ROCHESTER: That ain't no horn, it's an old atomizer.

JACK: An atomizer?

ROCHESTER: Yeah, don't you smell that "Toujours Lamour" every time I squeeze it?

The night (West Coast) version substitutes "Moment Supreme."

JACK: Well that's one on me . . . An atomizer for a horn.

ROCHESTER: That's nothin', our spare tire is a life preserver from the Albany Night Boat.

The night version switches S.S. Avalon for Albany Night Boat.

JACK: Oh yes, I fell overboard one night . . It's lucky I had that on. . . . Everything comfortable in the back seat, kids?

GERARD, CLAUD & RICHARD:
(AD LIB: YES, MR. BENNY, ETC.)

JACK: Good. . . . You know Uncle Jackie is going to miss you little rascals . . but you certainly had me on the ropes last Wednesday night.

GERARD: We sure did.

JACK: Yes sir!

Benny alternates between arrogance and ignorance, punctuating his dialogue with giggles of insecurity and "Yes, sir!"

RICHARD: Do you still feel like hanging yourself, Mr. Benny?

JACK: No no, I'm allright now. . . . But you kids certainly made a monkey out of me. . . . Gosh, I didn't know anything.

MARY: Cousin Booboo is sick about it.

JACK: Never mind . . . Well Claud, are you going to miss California?

CLAUDE: I certainly am, Mr. Benny . . . I believe that Horace Greeley put it very succintly when he said, "Go West, Young Man!"

JACK: Oh he did . . . He put it very . . *Yes sir!*. . . . You know Horace Greeley was a great inventor.

CLAUDE: Why Mr. Benny, Horace Greeley wasn't an inventor.

JACK: Hm!

CLAUDE: He was a *newspaper editor.*

JACK: Oh he was, eh?. . . . Well if you're so smart, what paper?

CLAUDE: The New York Tribune, from 1841 to 1872.

JACK: Hm! . . I'd give a thousand dollars if I could learn to keep my mouth shut . . . Anyway, I wouldn't be surprised if Horace Greeley *did* invent something.

The first part of the remark is addressed directly to the audience.

GERARD: Would you like to make a little bet on that? Ask Don Ameche, he'll know!

In 1939 Don Ameche played the inventor of the telephone in The Story of Alexander Graham Bell, *which was an enormously popular picture.*

JACK: Never mind. Allright, Gerard. . . . 1841, I'll check on that!

ROCHESTER: Hey Boss, there's Mr. Wilson walkin' down the street.

JACK: Oh yes . . Pull up alongside of him.

ROCHESTER: Okay.
(MOTOR SLOWS DOWN - PULLS OVER)

JACK: OH DON . . DON! WOULD YOU LIKE TO RIDE DOWN TO THE STATION WITH US?

WILSON: I'M NOT THPEAKING TO YOU! *[off mike]*

JACK: OKAY, OKAY. . . . Keep going, Rochester . . Poor guy, his tongue is still twisted . . . Well Richard, you're rather quiet back there . . Did you enjoy your visit with Uncle Jackie?

RICHARD: Yes, Mr. Benny . . . But I'm sure sorry I didn't get to see Carmichael.

Benny's pet polar bear was introduced in February 1939. Carmichael was believed to have eaten the gas man on a recent episode, prompting an eleven-second laugh of delightful recognition to Rochester's line.

CLAUDE: Oh yes, I was quite anxious to see your Polar Bear, too.

GERARD: Me too.

JACK: Well kids, you certainly missed a treat . . . Carmichael is just about the cutest thing you ever saw . . . soft, white, silky fur . . . loves to play . . . and he's just as gentle as a lamb.

ROCHESTER: *THEN WHAT HAPPENED TO THE GAS MAN?*

JACK: You just drive the car . . . And Rochester, watch out for that bump up ahead.

ROCHESTER: The what?

JACK: That bump. . . . Oh-oh, hang on, everybody.
(TERRIFIC CRASH)

JACK: Rochester, will you please watch where you're driving.

ROCHESTER: YOU'RE AT THE WHEEL NOW!

JACK: Oh my goodness, get over here . . . Mary, are the kids allright?

MARY: You better call the roll.

JACK: Okay . . . Claude.

CLAUDE: Here.

JACK: Richard.

RICHARD: Here.

JACK: Gerard.

GERARD: I am Gerard Darrow, seven years old and I go to the Bradwell School.

JACK: Don't give your billing, just answer . . . Well thank Heaven, you kids are allright . . . Be careful now, Rochester.

ROCHESTER: Yes sir.
(SOUND: BEEP-BEEP. . . . BEEP-BEEP)

JACK: I still don't like that horn . . . I'd like to get something unusual . . . something that sounds different.

MARY: Why don't you get your Cousin Booboo to go. *(STRUMS LIPS)*

JACK: Just keep my relatives out of this, will you?. . . . Well kids, it won't be long now before you'll be on that choo-choo.

RICHARD: Choo-choo, what's that?

CLAUDE: That's baby talk for locomotive.

JACK: Baby talk, eh? . . *I* said choo-choo 'till I was twenty-nine years old . . . Hm!

MARY: You didn't stop drooling 'till you were thirty.

JACK: Oh, quiet . . . Hey Rochester, we're near the Station, aren't we?

ROCHESTER: Pretty soon, Boss.

CLAUDE: Oh Gerard, I think we oughta straighten things out with Mr. Benny now, don't you?

GERARD: Let Richard do it.

JACK: Do what? . . What is it, Richard?

RICHARD: Well, Mr, Benny . . . we've been living at your house and we haven't paid our bill yet.

JACK: Your bill? . . . Oh, *forget* it kids . . I don't want your money.

RICHARD: But Mr. Benny, we ought to pay you . . . we lived at your house two weeks.

JACK: Two weeks and a day . . . But *forget* it, kids . . . It's allright with me, I enjoyed having you . . . Really!

CLAUDE: But Mr. Benny, if we went to a Hotel, it would have cost us money . . so why shouldn't you get it.

JACK: Yeah, why shouldn't I . . . Oh, *forget* it, *forget* it . . . You kids were my guests, let it go at that.

CLAUDE: But Mr. Benny—

MARY: Watch out Claude, this can't last forever.

JACK: Mary, you know very well I wouldn't accept any rent from these lovable children . . . *But* . . . when they get to Chicago and they feel like sending me a little gift . . that's entirely up to them. . . . Well kids, here we are at the Station . . Pull up by the entrance, Rochester.

(SOUND: WE HEAR CAR COMING TO A STOP—SQUEAKY BRAKES—RECORD OF STATION NOISES)

JACK: Well, we haven't got much time . . so pile out, kids. *(SOUND: RATTLE OF CAR AS KIDS GET OUT)*

CLAUDE RICHARD & GERARD: *(A LITTLE TALKING AS THEY GET OUT)*

JACK: Watch your step, kids, watch out there. . . . Take it easy.

ROCHESTER: Say Boss, should I put my Red Cap on and take the bags in?

JACK: Not so loud, there are a lot of 'em standing around . . . Come on kids . . . Come on, Mary. *(START THE TRANSITION MUSIC SOFTLY)* This way kids, you've just got time to make the train.

CLAUDE: Oh look, there's Mr. Kelly, our Quiz Master.

RICHARD: Yes, and there are the other kids.

GERARD: And there's Aunt Bessie.

JACK: Wait for us, Gerard, don't run ahead . . . Everybody stick together . . Come on, come on.
(TRANSITION MUSIC UP)
(WHICH BLENDS INTO TRAIN EFFECT—TRAIN WHISTLE—FADES)

CLAUDE: . . . . . Well . . . here we are on the choo-choo, as Mr. Benny puts it.

RICHARD: Gee, he's a nice man . . And he didn't even charge us for those two weeks.

GERARD: He certainly fooled *me.*
(AT CUE: TRAIN WHISTLE TWICE)
(TRANSITION MUSIC—WHICH FADES DOWN—)

ROCHESTER: Ready to go, Boss?

JACK: Yes . . . *(THEN CRYING)* Gee . . . I hated to see those kids leave . . You know Mary, they got to be just like my own children . . . No kidding, I was crazy about 'em.

MARY: Oh, stop blubbering . . you'll see 'em again.

JACK: Yeah, but I was so used to playing with 'em and everything, what'll I do now? . . . What'll I do when I come home evenings? . . . What'll I do in my spare time?

ROCHESTER: LET'S LOOK FOR THE GAS MAN!

JACK: Oh, quiet . . . Let's go!
(INTO NUMBER—#1 POOR MOON—ORCHESTRA)
CLOSING COMMERCIAL

WILSON: Here's a dessert, folks, that is just "as pretty as a picture!" And you'll be so proud of how *good* it looks that you'll probably want to put a frame around it and hang it on the kitchen wall, for family and friends to admire! But put it on the dining-room table *instead!* . . . and you'll find it *tastes* just as good as it *looks!* The name of this dessert masterpiece is *Banana and Raspberry Mold* . . . a really different dessert that's not only *easy* to *eat,* but *easy* to *make!* Simply dissolve one package of Raspberry Jell-O in two cups of hot water . . . and chill until slightly thickened. Next, fold in two medium bananas, sliced! Mold and chill until firm. Then garnish with sliced bananas and serve. And *what a treat!* . . . a dessert that's as *different* as it is *delicious!* Incidentally, *Raspberry* Jell-O like Strawberry and Cherry Jell-O . . . has a *new improved flavor,* obtained by using a natural flavor base, artificially enhanced! And that means it's *better than ever!* Discover its new goodness for *yourself* by making this swell dessert combination of luscious sliced bananas and rich red *Raspberry Jell-O!*
(JELL-O PUDDING CREDIT)
(MUSIC UP AFTER CLOSING JELL-O COMMERCIAL)

Occasionally announcers other than Wilson would be on to promote a General Foods product other than Jell-O gelatin.

BINGMAN: *(ALMOST A WHISPER)* Folks, the next time you buy Jell-O, get Jell-O puddings too! You'll find that. . . .

WILSON: Hey! . . . why all the whispering, Frank?

BINGMAN: *(VOICE STILL LOW)* I'm not really whispering, Don. I'm just holding myself in. Because if I let myself go when I talk about Jell-O Puddings *(GETTING LOUDER EVERY WORD)* I get so excited *(LOUDER YET)* I *just can't talk straight!*

WILSON: *(SOOTHINGLY)* Oh, now . . . try it again! Go ahead!

BINGMAN: *(NORMAL VOICE)* All right . . . Jell-O Puddings, ladies and gentlemen, are made by the same folks who make Jell-O . . . and like Jell-O, they're downright swell! For smooth, creamy goodness, Jell-O puddings are simply unrivalled! They're easy to prepare . . . just as Jell-O is! And they sell for the same low Jell-O price! So try these rich, mellow puddings . . . in all three flavors . . . Chocolate, Vanilla, and Butterscotch!

WILSON: THERE! I told you you could do it . . .

BINGMAN: *Get Jell-O Puddings tomorrow!*
(MUSIC) (TAG)

JACK: Remember, next Sunday, April 27th . . this program will come to you on Daylight Saving Time. See your local newspaper, or Movie and Radio Guide for the current time in your community . . . (And once more, ladies and gentlemen . . *(STARTS CRYING)* I want to thank the Quiz Kids and Alka Seltzer . . for making these past three weeks the happiest ones of my life . . . Goodnight, folks.)
(JELLO SIGNATURE)

In a departure from the script, Benny returns following the pudding commercial to mimic Frank Bingman's last line and add, "Oh, we're a little late, Good night folks." Following the Jell-O signature, Wilson—not Benny—reminds listeners about the time change for daylight savings. The Alka-Seltzer plug is not heard.

Telecast Overview

The Jack Benny Program began as a series of live specials broadcast from New York for the first two seasons beginning in 1950. In the fall of 1952, the program moved to Los Angeles, first as monthly specials and then as alternate week episodes. *The Jack Benny Program* finally became a weekly series on October 16, 1960. Throughout the first ten years, the creative team strove for a feeling of a live telecast whether it was actually aired live or recorded on videotape for later transmission. There were occasional experiments on film, most notably the four programs produced in Europe in 1956. In 1959 Irving Fein and Jack Benny agreed that the series had syndication potential and a decision was made to preserve all future episodes on film. The entire run of the show, from 1950 to 1965, was produced in black and white.

The television series was modeled on the radio format, though there was less emphasis on a cast of regulars. Announcer and companion Don Wilson and valet Eddie "Rochester" Anderson were with Benny throughout the run. Also appearing on a more irregular basis were Dennis Day, Mary Livingstone, Mel Blanc, Artie Auerbach, and Frank Nelson.

From 1950 through 1959 *The Jack Benny Program* was sponsored by Lucky Strike, a product of the American Tobacco Company. The Sportsmen Quartet often made an appearance to perform the commercials. After 1959 the major sponsors included Lever Brothers, State Farm Insurance, and General Foods.

CBS October 28, 1950
Saturday 8:00–8:45 P.M.
Premiere Show

CBS January 28, 1951–June 14, 1959
Sunday 7:30–8:00 P.M.
Series of Specials October 1950–June 1952
Monthly Specials October 1952–May 1953
Alternate Week Episodes September 1953–June 1959

CBS October 4, 1959–June 26, 1960
Sunday 10:00–10:30 P.M.
Alternate Week Episodes

CBS October 16, 1960–June 17, 1962
Sunday 9:30–10:00 P.M.
Weekly Episodes

CBS September 25, 1962–April 28, 1964
Tuesday 9:30–10:00 P.M.
Weekly Episodes

NBC September 25, 1964–September 10, 1965
Friday 9:30–10:00 P.M.
Weekly Episodes

The Jack Benny Program 1950–1965

Executive Producers . . . . . . Ralph Levy
Irving Fein

Producers . . . . Norman Abbott
Seymour Berns
Fred de Cordova
Ralph Levy
Hilliard Marks

Directors . . . . Norman Abbott
Seymour Berns
Fred de Cordova
Ralph Levy
Dick Linkroum

Writers . . . . George Balzer
Hal Goldman
Al Gordon
Milt Josefsberg
Sam Perrin
John Tackaberry

The Television Work

OCTOBER 28, 1950

Premiere

In his starring television debut, Benny transfers intact to the new medium the format he perfected for twenty years on radio. He combines elements of vaudeville (for instance, Benny as host and monologuist in front of a curtain) with situation comedy revolving around his family of radio regulars. The cheapskate aspect of Benny's character, so strongly established on radio, is emphasized in the opening moments of this show as the ever-frugal star is seen emerging from a bus in front of the theater; his stinginess is further played upon to convey Benny's apprehensions about television with his opening line, "I'd give a million dollars to know how I look." Regulars from the radio cast who appear in this first program for television include Don Wilson, Eddie "Rochester" Anderson, Mel Blanc, and Artie Auerbach as Mr. Kitzel.

In this episode's loosely structured plot, Benny stands on the stage in front of a closed curtain and welcomes the audience. He jokes that *he* was not nervous about appearing on television, it was his sponsor, a joke that was sustained throughout Benny's career. He talks about working in television, then recounts via flashback how television personality Dinah Shore came to be his first guest star. The action switches to the Benny living room in Beverly Hills, where the television adaptations of several running gags from radio are established. One example is a wise-guy talking parrot who tattles to Benny on Rochester's activities (the parrot was originally heard in a 1945 radio broadcast with Mel Blanc supplying the voice). When Benny calls Dinah Shore on his pay telephone to ask her to be on the show, she establishes the television side of an aspect of his persona that was developed in radio: Benny the outsider who is mocked yet tolerated by other celebrities. This outsider status contributed to an insecurity in the Benny character, as he always questioned his worth and appeal to an audience and his sponsor. The show's action returns to the present as Benny, back in front of a curtain, introduces Miss Shore, who sings two songs. The program ends as Benny plays the violin, inciting the studio audience to get up and leave; this gag will be used many times on future episodes and specials. The forty-five-minute premiere episode was cited by critics for presenting a faithful visual interpretation of the characters and conventions created by Benny in radio.

The Faye Emerson and Frank Sinatra Show

JANUARY 28, 1951

Benny's second television show remains set in the theater, integrating extended sketches into the variety format. With the show in progress, viewers see Benny in his dressing room telephoning Mary Livingstone at home to ask how he looks on television (she confuses him with Frank Sinatra). Benny's relationship with the character Mary has always been ambiguous. Her picture is given a prominent place on Benny's desk, and it is assumed she is his girlfriend. However, the Benny character would date others without compunction. Carrying over an old gag from radio, Benny answers a telephone call from nemesis Fred Allen (whose voice is not heard) who claims he misdialed. Appearing on the program are Sinatra, who mentions his CBS musical-variety series as well as his sponsor, and Faye Emerson, the popular blond hostess of several series in the early fifties and a frequent guest star on many quiz, dramatic, and variety programs. Benny, Emerson, and Sinatra perform a sketch in which Benny, as a means of inveigling a kiss from Emerson, complains that he never gets cast as a romantic lead. His kiss is, of course, foiled by the sexy know-how of Sinatra. This same sketch is repeated in a 1956 show with Frances Bergen and William Holden. If a sketch worked, the writers would invariably recast and use it again.

APRIL 1, 1951

The Claudette Colbert and Basil Rathbone Show

This program revolves around one sketch stretched out to the entire show: Jack Benny's attempts to win a serious dramatic role on TV's *Lucky Strike Playhouse* (more commonly known as *Robert Montgomery Presents*), an acclaimed live anthology drama series of the era. Both the Benny program and *Robert Montgomery Presents* were sponsored by the American Tobacco Company. Benny's thwarted dramatic aspirations began to be parodied in radio during the late thirties. In this episode he shows up in the sponsor's office to plead his case and beseeches the program's producer, Robert Montgomery, as well; the program he has in mind is set to star Basil Rathbone and Claudette Colbert. Benny refuses to take no for an answer and proceeds to hound Claudette Colbert (in her television debut) to persuade Montgomery to unload Rathbone in favor of himself. He goes on to invade a rehearsal for the program in Colbert's apartment; Montgomery appeases him by giving him a small role to read, but Benny's characteristic petulance and disruptive behavior make it impossible to rehearse. The actors leave the apartment in disgust, after Rathbone calls Benny a "schlemiel." None of Benny's regulars appear on this program, which draws heavily on various aspects of the Benny persona (stinginess, vanity, boorishness) to create the comic situation. The writers reworked this premise of Jack trying to get dramatic roles in a 1953 filmed episode with Irene Dunne and Vincent Price. Arguments with the sponsor are incorporated into many future episodes. Usually it is someone like Fred Allen or Phil Silvers who tries to convince Benny's sponsor that they should take over as the show's host.

Gracie Bit *MARCH 9, 1952*

Benny is visited by his old friends, George Burns and Gracie Allen. The duo were seen "rehearsing" for this appearance a week earlier on their own television series. This episode opens backstage with Benny frantic because Gracie hasn't shown up. George persuades Jack to dress as Gracie and take on her role in the scheduled Burns and Allen routine. Benny reluctantly agrees to appear in drag as Gracie, though he is furious. Dressed as Gracie, Benny uncannily imitates, rather than parodies, her role in a classic routine, complete with Allen's signature charming delivery. This is an interesting contrast to the standard drag routines practiced at the time, most notably by Milton Berle on his *Texaco Star Theater.* This episode generated so much interest that it was re-done in 1954 and performed at many charity dinners.

Buck Benny Rides Again

NOVEMBER 2, 1952

In 1940 one of Jack Benny's radio characters, Buck Benny, was translated into a motion picture, *Buck Benny Rides Again.* In search of material for the visual medium of television, the writers harkened back to the movie and the conventions of the radio program, but with some substantial changes. They decided not to employ Buck's sidekick Andy Devine (who was then a regular on the syndicated series *The Adventures of Wild Bill Hickok*), but to feature Dinah Shore instead. Benny explains this odd casting choice with his characteristic affection for free gifts. He says that it is customary for a guest star to receive a sample of the sponsor's product: hence Dinah Shore will receive a carton of Lucky Strikes, and in return Benny hopes to appear on her Chevrolet series so he can get a car.

The live sketch takes place in a noisy Western saloon. Dinah Shore is the saloon's entertainer and belts out "Blues in the Night." Buck Benny must save her from the evil machinations of Tombstone Harry, played villainously by Sheldon Leonard. In a filmed sequence Buck must compete with Tombstone in a rodeo. The mixing of live performance and film inserts was not uncommon in early television (*Captain Video* intercut between old Western movies and space fantasy to keep down costs). Buck's cockeyed pistol eventually kills the villain. At the close Jack Benny marvels that his program utilized a cast of thirty-five—a far cry from the four or five players and the all-powerful sound effects machine that would re-create a Western on radio.

DECEMBER 28, 1952

Cafe Skit

Although married to Mary Livingstone in real life, Jack Benny remained a bachelor on television. The character Benny never wore a wedding ring, and rarely was there any discussion of marriage. Whenever a situation called for him to bring a date to an event, she would invariably be a garish and flamboyant floozy. The comic convention would be that Jack would show up for evenings with dignified couples from the Hollywood community (for instance, the Ronald Colmans or, in this case, the Jimmy Stewarts in their television debuts) with one of these women on his arm. The woman's crude demeanor, combined with Benny's cheapness, would inevitably ruin the evening for the others.

In this program the Stewarts' planned-for quiet New Year's Eve at a club is ruined by the invasion of Benny and his date, Mabel Flapsaddle, a CBS telephone operator. Mabel is portrayed by Bea Benaderet, re-creating her role from the radio program. She was a regular on *The George Burns and Gracie Allen Show* and later starred in her own series, *Petticoat Junction.*

APRIL 19, 1953

Fred Allen Show

See page 242 for the complete script with annotations by Ron Simon.

MAY 17, 1953

Gisele MacKenzie and Bob Crosby Go Down to the Vault

Jack Benny's subterranean vault, a popular running gag on radio beginning in 1945, makes its first television appearance on this program. The vault is guarded by an ingenious series of devices, guaranteed to thwart the hardiest burglar, and by Ed, a sentry who seemingly hasn't seen the light of day in decades. Joe Kearns, who portrayed Ed on radio, re-creates his characterization.

In this live broadcast, the season finale, Jack takes Gisele down to the vault with him as he retrieves her salary for joining him in a concert engagement. (Bob Crosby declines because he has seen Bing's vault and "when you've seen one, you've seen them all.") Among the deterrents in use are a moat with a live alligator, a flash camera that records all who enter, and sirens when the vault is opened. The vault is seen again in a 1961 filmed episode in which U. S. Treasury agents request a tour to get ideas for beefing up security at Fort Knox.

The Humphrey Bogart Show *OCTOBER 25, 1953*

Humphrey Bogart joins the ranks of film stars who chose *The Jack Benny Program* as the vehicle for their television debuts. Bogart joins Benny and regulars Don Wilson and Bob Crosby in "Baby Face," a comedy sketch satirizing the era's newest hit police drama, *Dragnet,* which had debuted in 1952.

Benny provides voice-over narration to the sketch with a straight-faced Bogart portraying vicious killer Baby Face Bogart, in a caricature of the criminal toughs he portrayed in such films as *The Petrified Forest* and *High Sierra.* Semiregular Sara Berner (Gertrude Gearshift on radio) appears as a shrill-voiced petty thief. The sketch cleverly works in a plug for sponsor Lucky Strike, saving the trouble of breaking for a commercial. At the end of the program, Benny thanks Bogart for appearing and works in a plug for Bogart's recently completed film, *Beat the Devil.* Humphrey Bogart's only other acting appearance on television was in 1955 when he starred in a live version of *The Petrified Forest,* in which he re-created his role as killer Duke Mantee.

DECEMBER 27, 1953

New Year's Eve Party

This episode underscores the implicit affection between Jack Benny and his raspy-voiced valet Rochester. On television Rochester became Benny's confidant, to whom the character could express his worries and concerns. It was this emotional bond that allowed Rochester to transcend his stereotyped origins.

It is noteworthy that this program begins with a gag that tacitly establishes Benny's control over Rochester: Benny in his monologue states that Rochester had to come down the chimney on Christmas Eve . . . because when he is not in by ten o'clock, Jack locks all the doors. The program concludes with Benny and his servant as equals, both attired in white tie, singing "Auld Lang Syne" and ringing in the New Year together. The sketch explains what happened in between. Jack's hot date for New Year's Eve cancelled at the last minute. As Benny wanders the streets seeking solace, there are moments that evoke Chaplin's Little Tramp and Gleason's Lost Soul. Unlike the other two characters, Benny does not find comfort in solitude. Instead his identity comes from his place within a larger family. Thus, this story, more sentimental than most other episodes, would have to end with Benny together with a member of his cast.

Benny's identity becomes more clearly in focus on television when he is paired with Rochester than with any other of the regulars. It began as a matter of plot convenience. Numerous programs commence with Benny and Rochester at home, sharing secrets and bickering like any other situation comedy couple. Soon, it was just as important and just as funny to see Rochester's reaction to a Benny scheme as to witness the scheme itself. In radio, Rochester was a harsh (but funny) voice, rich with wise-cracks aimed at his boss. There was a gentler side to him and the relationship, for example when Rochester *talks* about nursing Benny from a cold. In television, however, we actually *see* Rochester physically take care of his boss, and this visual dimension engenders for the viewer a deeper meaning to the relationship. In one episode (November 30, 1952) we see Rochester rock Jack to sleep in a giant cradle. Rochester provided the emotional foundation to the series. It is only natural for the two to celebrate the New Year together. (This moving episode was later filmed and broadcast on December 31, 1963.)

The Jam Session Show *OCTOBER 17, 1954*

Jack hosts a jam session at his home in this episode featuring some of the era's most popular motion picture stars. The program opens in the studio, where Benny insists that Don Wilson jump rope while singing the Lucky Strike jingle. A call from Rochester comes, asking Benny when he will be home for the jam session. After they hang up, Rochester moves the hands of the clock ahead to read the time Benny gave him, and Benny walks in. Such disruptions of "real time" continuity are among the creative games played by the Benny writers to find visual equivalents for the verbal gags that worked on radio. Participating in the convivial jam session are Dick Powell (flügelhorn), Tony Martin (clarinet), Fred MacMurray (saxophone), Dan Dailey (drums), and Kirk Douglas (banjo), with help from Benny's studio orchestra, and Jack, of course, on violin. (The plot is reminiscent of a radio broadcast with Tommy Dorsey and Dick Powell.) The stars make use of the various vending machines in the Benny living room that dispense Coke, cigarettes (Lucky Strike), and fruit. Benny remains in character, but the guests are given the opportunity to banter in an informal setting. There is such a conviviality during the sketch that it is surprising the show features three actors known for their tough, hardboiled images. Dick Powell was the cynical detective in *Murder My Sweet* and *Cornered.* Kirk Douglas was cited for his cocky bravado in *Champion, The Bad and the Beautiful,* and *Detective Story* and Fred MacMurray was the coldblooded murderer in *Double Indemnity.* For these actors, the Benny program was an opportunity to humanize their tough screen images.

FEBRUARY 6, 1955

Four O'Clock in the Morning Show

The comic agility of the Benny writers is evident in this entertaining episode adapted from a 1953 radio bit (see page 124), which takes a simple concept—Jack is exhausted from being awakened at 4 A.M. and not able to fall asleep again—and builds an episode around it. Jack is awakened from a sound sleep by an all-night disc jockey asking a trivia question; when he can't fall back asleep, he decides to dress and go for a brisk morning walk. Later that day Mary insists on taking him shopping for a new suit; in the store the cranky Benny continually dozes off and is several times mistaken for a mannequin. Worked into this plot are amusing turns by former radio regulars Rochester, Don, Mary, and Frank Nelson as an unctuous sales clerk, as well as a commercial by the Sportsmen Quartet. The episode also employs several sight gags that demonstrate the writers' growing affinity for the visual medium. For example, as Jack steps outside for his morning stroll, he comments on how far he can see in the clear, smog-free dawn, and an image of the Statue of Liberty is cut in; when an unbelieving Benny puts on his glasses for a better look, the viewer sees an image of the Eiffel Tower.

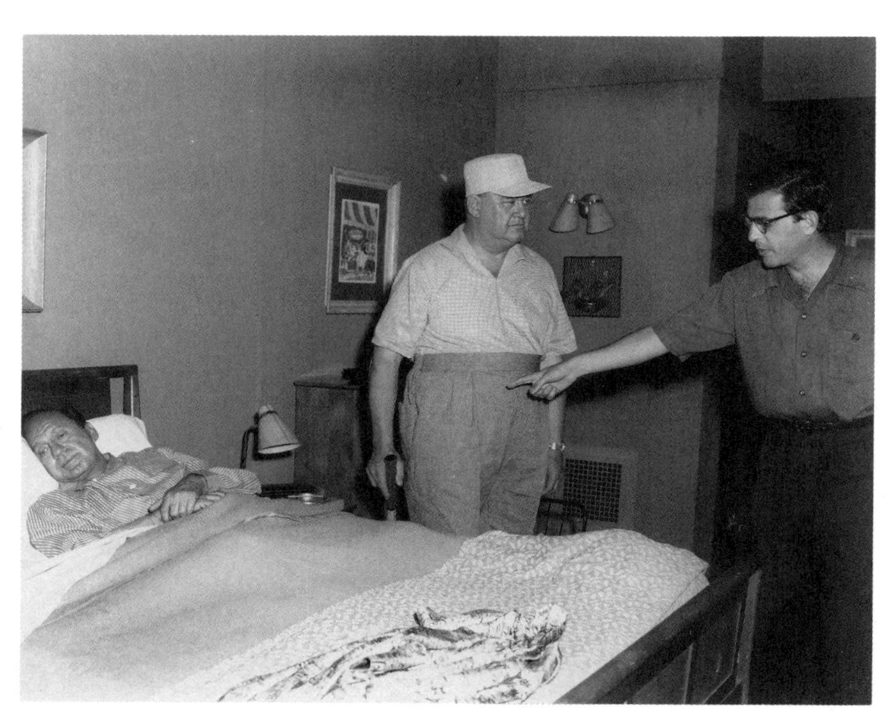

You Bet Your Life APRIL 3, 1955

This live program is an inventive comedy of disguises. Jack prepares to go to a costume party to which he is has not been invited. While getting dressed as Little Boy Blue, he notices in the newspaper that Groucho Marx is giving away three thousand dollars on his quiz program. Groucho was the host of one of television's most successful game shows, *You Bet Your Life,* a series noted for witty repartee and a secret word. Jack forgoes the party and masquerades as a musician with a false moustache and flamboyant hair to win the quiz money.

During the main sketch the set of *You Bet Your Life* is re-created with Groucho as host. In an improvised exchange Jack identifies his character as "Ronald Forsythe." Groucho retorts that in the rehearsal it was Rodney; the change of names is "a cheap way of sucking around Colman" (a reference to romantic actor Ronald Colman, who frequently appeared on radio to be taken advantage of by Benny). Benny gamely tries to guess the secret word to win extra money. The question to win all the money is "What is the real age of Jack Benny?" There is a classic pause as Benny stares into the camera and ponders whether to win the money or keep the myth of his character intact. He answers 39—his vanity wins out over his cheapness.

JANUARY 15, 1956

Don Invites Gang to Dinner

Jack's never-ending exasperation with announcer Don Wilson is spotlighted in this filmed episode that also includes a reworking of the classic "Your money or your life" sketch from the 1948 radio program. The action opens with Jack, laid up with a bad cold, being tended to by Rochester and Mary Livingstone. When his lawyer arrives, Jack orders him to break Don Wilson's contract; his reasons are explained via flashback. Don had invited the entire gang over for dinner (Jack, Mary, Dennis Day, Bob Crosby) without consulting his wife. He asks them to wait in his bushes, and brings them in one by one. Jack, of course, is last, and during his lonesome wait is held up by a burglar played by Benny Rubin. Together they re-create Benny's most popular routine from radio, the "Your money or your life" skit. It is unusual that the writers decided to play the scene in the pouring rain, thus diminishing Benny's manipulation of silence; but the raison d'être of the sketch is different, namely, to explain how Jack got a cold.

JANUARY 29, 1956

How Jack Met Rochester

Flashbacks of Jack's initial encounters with members of his cast of regulars are a favorite plot device of the series. In this episode Jack relates to his guest Sarah Churchill (actress and daughter of Winston who was a frequent television performer in the 1950s) the story of his first encounter with his valet, Rochester Van Jones. This tale of how they met was originally concocted on radio in 1950 (thirteen years after Rochester assumed the role). In a flashback, Jack is seen traveling cross-country by train with Don Wilson, dressed as a child to avoid paying full fare. On television Benny frequently demeans Don Wilson by requiring him to wear silly costumes, all the more ridiculous because of Wilson's portly frame. Rochester, working as a porter, catches on to the ruse, and Jack persuades him not to turn them in. When Rochester is subsequently caught and fired, Jack hires him.

Jack Runs for President of Beavers

OCTOBER 21, 1956

The action in this episode is focused away from the back stage of *The Jack Benny Program* as Jack runs for president of the Beverly Hills Beavers, a local boys' troop. (It is similar to a 1949 radio program in which Jack ran against a twelve-year-old Beaver up for re-election.) Running against him is guest star George Gobel, the uncle of one of the boys. Red Skelton makes a cameo appearance at the end as a surprise third candidate. "Lonesome George" Gobel was the host of his own successful comedy-variety series, as was Red Skelton. Gobel's low-key humor contained many of the same elements as Benny's, but was more "down-home" in nature, reflecting a rural comic tradition. It is interesting that both Benny and Gobel were born around Chicago and developed two distinct comic styles.

DECEMBER 2, 1956

Jack Locked in the Tower of London

The Jack Benny Program filmed four episodes on location in Europe in the summer of 1956; this was the first to be broadcast. These films were among the first productions of Benny's new company J & M Productions, which was organized in 1956 by Benny to produce programs for CBS. Previously, the network supervised production. The show opens with Jack being tutored privately on the British currency system and its American equivalent. He and Mary then set out to tour London with a group led by a professional guide. (Being characters of 1950s morality, Jack and Mary are staying at separate hotels.) When the group reaches the Tower of London, Jack is particularly mesmerized by the collection of Crown Jewels. The group inadvertently leaves the Tower without Jack, who is locked in the torture chamber when the gates close for the evening. In an imaginative fantasy sequence, Jack dreams himself back to the sixteenth century as the man accused of alienating Anne Boleyn from her husband, King Henry VIII. He single-handedly fights off a team of guards sent in to torture him; inventive visual gags are used in sequences involving the rack and a swordfight. Jack is finally startled back to the present by Mary and the guard, who have returned to retrieve him. While this program does make passing reference to Benny's cheapness and vanity, the humor in this episode is derived more from the situation itself than from Benny's reactions. Jack, usually a passive character, was rarely presented as the swashbuckling hero.

Jack Falls into a Canal in Venice

MARCH 10, 1957

One of four episodes filmed on location in the summer of 1956, this was the third to be broadcast. (Surprisingly, it was previously performed on radio in 1950.) The Venice sequences are seen in flashback, as Benny, back in Beverly Hills, reminisces about the trip with Rochester. Jack is at his most overbearing when he and Mary join a gondola sight-seeing excursion, first holding up the group to buy a hat, then falling into the canal as he climbs into the gondola. As the ride proceeds he complains constantly, falls in again, and causes a fellow American tourist to fall in as well. Benny ribs his own celebrity status several times, introducing himself to oblivious Europeans and Americans alike with his signature, "Jack Benny, star of stage, screen, and television." His pompousness echoes an earlier movie role in *To Be or Not to Be* in which he plays a vain Shakespearean actor.

Mary Has May Company Reunion

APRIL 7, 1957

This episode, an example of *The Jack Benny Program* at its most inventive, relates the story of why the Jack Benny and Mary Livingstone characters never married. The sexuality of the Jack Benny character had always been ambiguous. It takes two flashbacks, one to the previous year and one to the 1920s, to reveal that Jack did indeed propose but had second thoughts when it came time to buy an engagement ring. After Mary tells the story to the old friends attending her annual reunion luncheon, Jack takes offense, saying that at the time he couldn't afford the ring. Now, however, he owns the jewelry store, and if she still likes the ring he will sell it to her wholesale. The episode takes place in the characters' homes instead of the studio, and it was filmed without a live audience.

DECEMBER 1, 1957

Filming Jack's Life Story

The production head of the Twentieth Century-Fox motion picture studio, Buddy Adler, appears as himself in this episode depicting the studio's interest in producing a film on Jack's life as an entertainer. The vainglorious Jack (who is seen at home taking on all the pretentious trappings befitting a movie star) expects to produce, write, direct, and star in the epic. In a meeting with Jack and Mary, Adler reveals that the studio wants Jack to portray his own father and they want the star power of Van Johnson (who appears in this episode) in the role of Jack, with Mary portraying Jack/Van's sweetheart. Jack has a tantrum in the office, and the project is canceled.

Several mentions are made of Benny's infamous film *The Horn Blows at Midnight* (1945), whose lackluster success was a running joke on both the Benny radio and television programs for years. Mel Blanc portrays a studio parking-lot attendant whose last job was directing that film. There were many comic permutations to the plot of filming Jack's life story including a 1944 *Lucky Strike Program* where Danny Kaye was to play Jack and a 1949 version when Benny tried to convince Tyrone Power to play the lead.

Imitating Jackie Gleason

JANUARY 26, 1958

Benny's underutilized talent for caricaturing other personalities (seen earlier in his portrayal of Gracie Allen) is showcased here with a lively interpretation of Jackie Gleason's hapless bus driver, Ralph Kramden. In this parody of *The Honeymooners,* guest star Audrey Meadows re-creates her role as Alice and Dennis Day contributes a commendable Ed Norton (the role played by Art Carney). The plot of the sketch is worthy of a real *Honeymooners* episode: Ralph thinks Alice has bought herself some new dresses, when in fact she has bought him a new bowling ball. Benny evokes Gleason in every aspect, from his timing and delivery to the visual humor in his swaggering á la Kramden. Although Benny's voice does not adapt easily to the bellowing braggadocio characterized by Gleason, he manages to capture its essence. Interestingly this sketch was done two seasons after the "classic thirty-nine" filmed *Honeymooners* episodes were broadcast, which was one of the two only seasons during the fifties when there were no Jackie Gleason programs on the air at all.

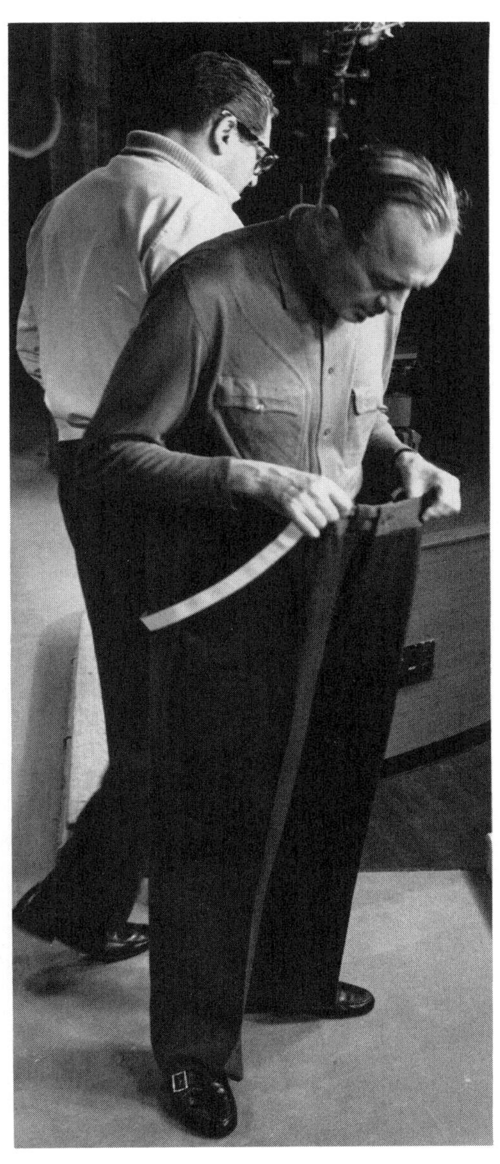

SEPTEMBER 21, 1958

The Gary Cooper Show

Benny opens his ninth season by remarking to the audience, "Since I first went on television, all the rest of you are nine years older." Legendary movie star Gary Cooper marks his television debut on this program, gamely participating in the requisite put-downs of Benny's acting. Cooper, winner of two Oscars for his performances in the films *Sergeant York* and *High Noon,* had recently completed the film *Man of the West* when this program was broadcast. He had previously worked with Jack in 1942 on radio. The sketch revolves around casting the sequel to *Man of the West;* Jack wants the only available role, that of Cooper's twin brother, but Cooper says he's too short (Cooper was over six feet; Benny appreciably shorter). Benny enters the auditions clad in cowboy garb identical to Cooper's, with high-heeled boots that make him Cooper's height. When Jack sees the physical violence necessary for the role, he starts walking on his knees, saying he would rather portray Toulouse Lautrec in a movie.

DECEMBER 14, 1958

Gisele MacKenzie Show

The singer and violinist Gisele MacKenzie is the guest on this variety program. Formerly a *Your Hit Parade* cast member, MacKenzie was starring in her own half-hour variety series at the time of this broadcast. She was a frequent Benny guest star, appearing first on a 1953 show. In this program she and Benny play a duet on the violin, and comedian Red Skelton, popular host of his own comedy-variety series, makes a cameo appearance as a piano tuner. Dale White appears as Don Wilson's "son" Harlow, in one of the recurring sketches in which Don wants him to become an announcer. Harlow was a character created for the television show whose identity was not developed.

The Ernie Kovacs Show *JANUARY 25, 1959*

Comedian Ernie Kovacs, who personified a new generation of television comedy, joins Benny on this show. Kovacs, unlike Benny, had no training in vaudeville or network radio. The opening exchange between the two, in which Kovacs shows off his false moustache collection to Benny, exemplifies the gentle, absurd humor both often used. The program continues with a sketch featuring the two as inmates in a country-club-type prison of the future. Kovacs was newly based in Los Angeles at the time of this appearance, pursuing a career in feature films while continuing to create unique television specials.

FEBRUARY 22, 1959

Airport Sketch

Jack's flight to Los Angeles on ultrathrifty I.O.U. Airlines is late (they don't land until they run out of gas), so Don and Dennis take over the show. Scenes of Rochester helping Jack to locate his luggage in the airline's dilapidated hangar alternate with Dennis and Don's attempts to fill airtime. Howard McNear, who would later become Floyd the barber on *The Andy Griffith Show,* appears as one of the airline's pilots. This program is particularly funny because Jack's stinginess causes the character to become anxious over missing his own show. In a surreal ending, as the pilot flies the boom camera across the stage, Benny stands in front of the curtain and says this is one of the craziest shows he has ever performed.

APRIL 5, 1959

Ed Sullivan, Genevieve Show

This program is broadcast live from New York. French singer Genevieve, a regular on *The Jack Paar Show,* appears as a guest along with variety-show host Ed Sullivan. Don Wilson hosts a parody of television courtroom dramas, with Benny as the prosecutor, Sullivan as the defense attorney, and Genevieve as the defendant; everyone except the attorney is French. Frank Fontaine appears as John L. C. Sivoney, a character similar to the Crazy Guggenheim character he portrayed in the "Joe the Bartender" sketches on *The Jackie Gleason Show* in 1962. The Sivoney character was first heard on the Benny radio program in 1950.

Opening Show *OCTOBER 4, 1959*

This live premiere of Benny's tenth season on CBS is an excellent example of the unique way the show interacts with its sponsors. Switching to Lever Brothers (Lux Soap) after fourteen years of radio and television work for American Tobacco (Lucky Strike), the greater part of this show is given over to Don Wilson's futile attempts to come up with a Lux Soap commercial that pleases Benny. At one point Don complains that after fourteen years with Lucky Strike, it is difficult to adjust to Lux Soap. Benny retorts, "What adjustment? Stop smoking and start bathing!" Without integrating any actual, separate commercials into the show, the program manages to endorse the product many times. In a sketch, Jack imagines *The Jack Benny Program* thirty years in the future: Don, Dennis, and Rochester are all old men, while Jack remains an ever-youthful 39. Benny was actually 65 at the time of this broadcast.

The Harry Truman Show *OCTOBER 18, 1959*

Former President Harry Truman gives Benny a tour of the Truman Library in this episode, partially taped on location in Independence, Missouri. The sequence, approximately half the show, is incorporated into a flashback as Benny recounts the experience for a fan who comes backstage to ask him about it. In the Truman Library, the former president points out memorabilia from his administration and makes several jokes about Benny's vanity and reputation as a cheapskate. In his Benny biography Irving Fein relates the many production problems that plagued this episode, including trying to record sound in the Truman Library. After the show was successfully received, Benny, in an example of his real-life generosity, donated ten thousand dollars to the library.

NOVEMBER 1, 1959

The Jack Webb Show

This program is a clever depiction of the new personalities created by television. Benny discovers that his guest star, Jack Webb, cannot tell jokes, sing, or dance. Webb was not trained the way Benny's vaudeville contemporaries, such as Bob Hope and George Burns, were trained. Jack Webb's lasting success was the creation of Sergeant Joe Friday in the series *Dragnet,* which typified Webb's desire to inject a no-nonsense realism into television entertainment. But Jack Webb can laugh at his earnestness, which he does in a Charlie Chan skit with Benny.

The sketch, set in a Chinese laundry, parodies many of the late fifties detective series, including *Dragnet, Peter Gunn,* and *77 Sunset Strip.* (Garry Moore also makes an unexpected appearance to promote his new variety show.) The skit prompted a lawsuit by the widow of Charlie Chan's creator alleging copyright infringement, which was later settled out of court.

The Jack Paar Program

NOVEMBER 29, 1959

Benny's opening monologue is surprisingly topical. He speaks about the quiz show investigation, which revealed that many contestants had been given the answers in advance. To conform to CBS's new policy of honesty, Benny admits he is not really 39.

Jack's special guest is an old colleague, Jack Paar, who became host of *Tonight* in 1957. Benny and Paar had met during a USO tour. Paar's situation comedy *The Jack Paar Show* was a summer replacement for Benny's program in 1947. Paar acknowledged that Benny taught him the techniques of performing before a live audience. On this program Paar tries to induce Jack to become a guest host on *Tonight* and leads him to a replica of his set. Benny and Paar spoof the many commercials that appear on the late-night show. Benny says that he will take over the *Tonight* show if he can have Charley Weaver as his sidekick. (Weaver, played by Cliff Arquette, was the homespun philosopher of *Tonight.*) The deal falls through when Dennis Day is caught impersonating Weaver.

Final Show of the Season

MAY 1, 1960

Jack has returned home from Japan and states that the Japanese are watching American kinescopes that are three years old. Continuing his references to the quiz show scandal, Jack says that the Japanese are enthralled by the knowledge of the contestants on *The $64,000 Question.* Benny does not have the heart to tell them that the show was rigged.

The main sketch is a witty spoof on the comedy of Jack Benny. As Dennis Day finishes his song "A Woman in Love," Jack is seen with his sponsors. The executives are reluctant to renew Jack's contract, and they play for him a soundtrack of an earlier show. There are no laughs to accompany Jack's lines; it seems that Dennis is receiving the applause. Jack complains that it is his classic pauses and long takes that prompt the audience's reactions. To prove that they can eliminate him from the show, the sponsors have constructed a dummy that mechanically mimics Jack's slow turn of head. Benny sees a potential rival and tells the dummy the frustrations it will have with his cast.

OCTOBER 16, 1960

The *Nightbeat* Takeoff

This episode inaugurates *The Jack Benny Program* as a weekly series with rotating sponsors, Lipton Tea and State Farm Insurance. Jack misses a golf date with guest stars George Burns, Tony Curtis, and Robert Wagner and overhears a conversation that he does not have the stamina for his new television schedule. Depressed, he imagines he is being grilled by Mike Wallace, who was recognized at the time for his aggressive interviewing on *Nightbeat.* This drama sequence parodies the darkened, smoke-filled intensity of Wallace's program. At the close Jack is consoled that as producer he does not have to pay Wallace because it was only a fantasy.

The Dick Clark Show *OCTOBER 23, 1960*

Jack is still worried about having to perform weekly and wonders how to appeal to a younger generation. He visits Dick Clark, then producing his weekday *American Bandstand* series in Philadelphia. Benny seems bewildered by Dick Clark's employees, who dance the jitterbug across the office floor. Clark recommends a new singing trio, the Sabers. Unwilling to pay the group's fee, Jack forms his own rock 'n' roll band with Don Wilson and Dennis Day.

The Milton Berle Show *OCTOBER 30, 1960*

Ten years before this telecast, Milton Berle had become "Mr. Television." His series the *Texaco Star Theater* was the most popular show on the new medium. Here, Berle tries to teach Jack Benny how to sustain a weekly series. This program becomes a sly commentary on the different styles of television comedy, from the brash burlesque of Berle to the quiet understated humor of Benny. There are references to bowling because *Jackpot Bowling* with Berle had debuted a year earlier. Berle insists that Benny must be funnier because "the thief of bad gags" had stolen a joke from Jack. The finale has Jack dressed similarly to the old Berle, with a baggy vaudevillian suit, crazy hat, and blackened teeth.

NOVEMBER 20, 1960

The John Wayne Show

This program originates from New York City. In an homage to Ed Sullivan, Benny recognizes several guests in the audience, including Betty Furness, former spokeswoman for *Studio One*, and John Wayne, who had recently directed and starred in *The Alamo*. On radio Benny did not interact with the audience, and this program is one of his first television shows to incorporate guests from the studio audience into the show. Benny also confronts a recurrent nemesis, John L. C. Sivoney. Jaye P. Morgan sings "Bill Bailey" and performs a skit with John Wayne in which Jack plays a gypsy violinist. In a commercial integrated into the program Jack recognizes in the audience the gentleman who composed the State Farm Insurance theme song and then speaks in the song's rhythmic manner.

JANUARY 1, 1961

Jack Casting for Television Special

The premise of Jack writing his life story and casting it for television was performed every three years or so. This version is notable for several engaging performances and especially Jack's quintessential reaction shots. Jack is auditioning candidates to play the role of one of his first girlfriends, Mildred. One actress, intentionally evoking Lauren Bacall, seduces Jack for the part and gives him what seems to be his longest television kiss. When caught by his secretary, his reaction of embarrassment and pride is priceless. In a comic reversal, the woman auditioning for the role of Jack's mother turns out to be Benny's Mildred, as incarnated by the familiar character actress Maudie Prickett. Benny also has obvious fun with the penny-pinching youngster, played by Barry Gordon, who is to be cast as the young Jack. The young Gordon will appear in several subsequent episodes.

JANUARY 22, 1961

Jack at Supermarket

This episode brings together the regulars in an extended situation, complete with the cast doing a series of comic turns in drag. Instead of the traditional welcome, the viewer sees Jack Benny in a dress doing the housework. Rochester had tricked his boss in a game of cards, and Jack is now responsible for the daily chores. Jack tricks Don Wilson, who appears in the same dress and tricks Dennis Day in turn. In the final scene Jack has gone to the supermarket to do the grocery shopping, and he exasperates the manager (played by the officious Frank Nelson) as he looks for the best prices. It is interesting that this premise was first used on radio in 1948, when radio audiences had to conjure up their own image of Benny in a dress.

Variety Show

APRIL 2, 1961

Jack Benny overtly returns to his vaudeville roots and presents an old-fashioned variety show with no extended sketches. He welcomes two acts, a newcomer and a juggler, interspersed with comic banter. His new discovery has been appearing in Las Vegas with George Burns, who surprises Benny on stage so that he can take all the credit. The would-be entertainer is a student at Northwestern named Ann-Margret. She belts out two numbers, "I Ain't Got Nobody" and "Have a Good Time." She discusses her upbringing in Wilmette, Illinois, a town Benny mentions is close to his birthplace, Waukegan. Interestingly enough, she does not mention her country of origin, Sweden. Later that year she makes her film debut as Bette Davis's daughter in *Pocketful of Miracles.*

The other act is an energetic juggler, Francis Brunn. Benny dons a tight-fitting outfit and performs several stunts with Brunn. Benny, never noted for his physical dexterity, is in fine form at 67, mimicking the juggler's routine. This program is a creative departure from the formula and does not confine Benny in the stereotypical situations of his established character.

Season Premiere

OCTOBER 15, 1961

A frequent comic routine on the Benny show is a spoof of Jack's negotiations with the network and sponsor. Here, in this opening episode of the 1961–62 season, Jack has returned to New York and says he has not signed his contract yet. In the audience he welcomes Phil Silvers, who is starring on Broadway in *Do-Re-Mi,* and Betty Johnson, a popular singer on *The Jack Paar Show.* The main sketch focuses on Benny and Silvers arguing with a television executive about who is more photogenic and popular with the audience. The argument is interrupted by the special appearances of Alan King, Garry Moore, and Jack Paar, each of whom thinks he should be given Benny's time slot. Underneath the bravado of the Benny character is an insecurity that he has lost touch with the audience. As far back as 1932 the Benny character is convinced that the sponsor is going to fire him.

OCTOBER 22, 1961

Waukegan Show

This show intentionally blurs Benny's character and his own life. Jack returns to his hometown, Waukegan, Illinois, for the dedication of the new Jack Benny Junior High School. The mayor of Waukegan congratulates Jack for being the third individual to be so honored in Waukegan. Jack is impressed that the other two schools were named after Daniel Webster and Thomas Jefferson. The school's glee club performs a special song for the occasion, and a time capsule of Benny artifacts is preserved. The final gag has the character being escorted off the stage by two naval officers because he was never officially discharged from the service. It is obvious that Benny did not want himself so deified that he could not make fun of himself even during the most solemn of occasions. Although the real Jack Benny was proud of this tribute, the show ends with the character dismissed from the proceedings: the character is not worthy of his alter ego's achievements.

DECEMBER 24, 1961

Christmas Show

Before Jack throws a holiday party for his cast, he journeys into the audience for what he says is the first time. Jack never ventured into his audience on radio, and this is a conscious effort to mimic television's roving talk-show host. He engages in several staged routines, including one with the overbearing Frank Nelson, who is accompanied by his purported wife.

The finale features the entire crew celebrating around a Christmas tree. In a touching moment, Jack welcomes back Mel Blanc, who is recovering from a near-fatal automobile accident. Once again, Blanc does the voices of many characters he created for the Benny program, including Professor LeBlanc and the Mexican character Sy. The warmth of the Benny family of regulars radiates throughout this segment. By the end of the show Benny has stepped out of character and is relating to his cast as an equal, not the supercilious character.

The Rock Hudson Show *FEBRUARY 18, 1962*

Jack opens the show by introducing Rock Hudson, who is currently starring in *Lover Come Back.* As he begins his monologue, the audience chants "We want Rock." Benny fails to prove that he also has sex appeal. For the commercial break, Don Wilson introduces his favorite announcer Hugh Downs, recognized at the time for his work with Jack Paar on *The Tonight Show.*

The main sketch spotlights one of Benny's comic skills, his ability to incisively impersonate others. In a takeoff of a late-night talk show, Benny completely captures Jack Paar. He caricatures the emotional tics and heart-on-the-sleeve quality of Paar. With Downs at his side, he welcomes his first guest, "Irving" Hudson, a shy harmonica player and Twist instructor. Benny wants to help the struggling performer and suggests he change his name to Rock, to become Irving Rock. The routine ends with a rousing finish as everyone does the Twist, even the rotund Don Wilson.

OCTOBER 9, 1962

The Phil Silvers Show

Both Benny and Phil Silvers were comic mainstays on CBS. Although longtime friends, they competed for several Emmy Awards during the fifties. By the time of this program, *You'll Never Get Rich* with Silvers as Sgt. Ernie Bilko had been off the air for a few years. In a mischievous opening sketch, Silvers steals Benny's pants so that he can regain the spotlight and deliver the monologue. The main skit shows how the comedians first met and Silvers, á la Bilko, takes over Benny's home and begins to run a poker game. Next season Phil Silvers returns as star of his own series, *The New Phil Silvers Show.* This time his character is named Harry Grafton, a plant foreman always trying to get rich quick.

OCTOBER 30, 1962

My Gang Comedy

What was typical on radio—Benny performing with most of his entire cast of regulars—was unusual on television, especially in the later years. Darla Hood was an actress in *Our Gang,* a series of comedy shorts about a group of mischievous children, and her guest appearance created a reason to round up the crew for a knockabout parody. What roles did the writers imagine for the Benny gang in this geriatric version? Don Wilson was the chubby kid "Spunky"; Rochester in braids was "Oatmeal"; Dennis Day played "Rodney, the Rich Kid"; and Jack was the freckle-faced, devilish "Alfalfa." The gang decides to convert their dog (a Pete look-alike with one circle drawn around the right eye) into a French poodle and wind up being chased by the police in a rousing finale.

Jack Plays Tarzan *NOVEMBER 13, 1962*

Jack dispenses with his usual monologue and immediately welcomes his expensive guest star Carol Burnett so that he can get his money's worth. Burnett had left *The Garry Moore Show* as a regular and had recently starred in the acclaimed special *Julie and Carol at Carnegie Hall.* Burnett sings "The Trolley Song" and is introduced to Don Wilson and his purported son Harlow. As a running gag throughout the show, Burnett performs the bump and grind to "The Stripper," at the time a popular song by David Rose and His Orchestra.

In the main sketch Benny and Burnett play Jane and Tarzan after twenty years of marriage. Burnett performs her trademark yell to startle her meek husband. Benny retaliates by playing his primitive violin, which scatters all the animals in the jungle (in a great use of stock footage). This sketch nicely counterpoints Burnett's aggressive style of comedy with Benny's mild humor.

NOVEMBER 27, 1962

Jack Meets Japanese Agent

After being interrupted by a bored sound man (Mel Blanc), Jack introduces a young Japanese singer, Romi Yamada, who was currently touring in *Flower Drum Song*. From there the show begins a series of comic variations on the meeting of East and West. Jack tries to negotiate another appearance with her agent, played by Jack Soo, a comic actor later known for his portrayal of Detective Nick Yemana on *Barney Miller*. Benny and Soo reminisce about a Japanese variety program modeled on *The Ed Sullivan Show*. Jack tries to win a talent contest over several Japanese teenagers by singing "Long Tall Sally." This program is a conscious effort to appeal to two generations, an older one interested in Broadway musicals and a younger one that likes rock.

DECEMBER 4, 1962

The Bob Hope Show

Bob Hope first guest starred on Benny's television show in 1954. His two appearances in the sixties particularly illustrate how the writers concocted situations for such a familiar personality. In this first one, they imagined what it would be like if Jack and Bob had performed as a team in vaudeville. For the second, on October 23, 1964, they speculate on a form—the comedy record—that the duo had not yet conquered. Journeying into the past and hypothesizing future endeavours were always favorite sketch devices for the writers.

The opening moments of this program underline the clash of comic styles that exemplify Hope and Benny—topical, rapid-fire humor versus the understated comedy of character. Benny suggests that Hope slow down and enjoy his comedy, while Hope races on with a barrage of jokes on the current television scene. In the main sketch, Hope and Benny play struggling vaudevillians specializing in "violin, snappy patter, and soft-shoe." The entire show is marked by an engaging informality with both comedians enjoying each other's miscues and blown lines.

In television, Benny and his writers loved to harken back to the vaudeville days, usually skipping any references to radio. On one episode broadcast on January 7, 1964, George Burns and Jack portray a fledgling vaudeville team and in a 1968 special Benny, George Burns, and Gregory Peck engage in a musical routine, typical of the vaudeville stage.

Johnny Carson Show *OCTOBER 22, 1963*

Johnny Carson had previously appeared on a 1955 episode to receive advice on comedy from Jack. When he returned in 1963 Carson was television's latest celebrity, having taken over as host of *The Tonight Show* a year earlier. Benny questions how much talent is needed to host a talk show, and Carson displays his skills as a magician, drummer, and dancer. Carson also insists he is an actor and proves his point in a parody of his own show. In the sketch Carson welcomes Jack as a guest and his voice-over tells what he is really thinking about the pompous Jack. For the routine, Benny's set designers built an exact replica of the new *Tonight Show* set. The takeoff works well because the setting is so convincing. Jack was a frequent guest on Carson's show and, in fact, was offered the role of guest host, which he turned down.

Jack Directs Film

OCTOBER 29, 1963

This was the sixth television guest appearance by Jimmy and Gloria Stewart. In previous episodes they had encountered Jack in a concert hall, theater, nightclub, and restaurant. For this program the writers concocted a parody of two media, television and film. While having a luxurious breakfast, Jack watches the Stewarts on *This Is Hollywood,* a spoof on a television interview show. Learning his "good friends" are making a film together, Jack rushes to the set to wish them well, hoping it might help his return to the movies. In the melodramatic takeoff depicted on the show, Jimmy Stewart plays a defense attorney, echoing his role in *Anatomy of a Murder* (for which he received an Academy Award). Jack disrupts the same farewell scene several times, offering his advice on how the film should be directed. The vainglorious Jack works nicely with the professional Stewart, and one sees why the writers enjoyed creating comic situations for this pair.

The Peter, Paul, and Mary Show

JANUARY 14, 1964

Peter, Paul, and Mary, the singing trio who popularized acoustic folk music, were presented by Jack Benny to appeal directly to a new generation of television viewers. They perform their popular song "Blowin' in the Wind" on an elaborate backstage set with exposed lights and cables. Jack claims to be their biggest fan, though as a running gag he confuses Peter and Paul. The trio also perform a folk song based on Benny's life:

> *"Waukegan, Waukegan. The son that brought you fame, Jack Benny was his name. Maybe Jackie wasn't very much, he didn't have the skin you would want to touch. But in his grip was a happy thing, a silver dollar was his teething ring. The blue-eyed Jack is really thirty-nine, so is my darling Clementine. He moves from here to Timbuktu, a man whose bills are overdue. He's a cheapskate through and through. Waukegan, Waukegan. . . ."*

In the main sketch, Jack invites the trio back to his home to listen to his own composition, "When You Say 'I Beg Your Pardon,' Then I'll Come Back to You," which he "wrote" in 1951 on radio. He secretly records the group singing his song and plans to make a million by releasing it.

The Nat King Cole Show *JANUARY 21, 1964*

This episode begins at the stage door where Jack Benny is being asked to sign autographs (using the name of motion picture star Tony Curtis). He returns to the studio and welcomes guest star Nat King Cole for two numbers, "Day In, Day Out" and "When I Fall in Love." Entertainer Nat King Cole had hosted his own variety show during the 1956–57 season, the first series hosted by a black star. In a sad reflection of the times, the series was canceled because no major sponsor would advertise on the show for fear of a boycott in the South.

Jack decides that he wants to play "Sweet Sue" on the violin with Cole and rehearses with three of his studio musicians, drummer Sammy Weiss, clarinetist Wayne Songer, and left-handed guitar player Frank Remley, well known to Benny's fans from the radio years. In this program the musicians behave more like the Three Stooges, and drummer Weiss supposedly breaks his hand. Cole saves the number by substituting his purported five-year-old cousin on drums. There is constant joking about Benny's musicianship and he is denied his violin solo on "Sweet Sue."

FEBRUARY 18, 1964

The Final LeBlanc Sketch

One of the most popular sketches on radio and television was Jack's violin lessons with Professor LeBlanc. This final episode, cited as "the definitive Benny-LeBlanc routine" by Mel Blanc in his autobiography, is a conscious effort by the writers to take the joke to its most outrageous extreme and then bring it to conclusion.

In the sketch Jack Benny has finished his television show and receives a call from a psychiatrist seeking information about his patient, who is suffering from a traumatic case of amnesia. When Benny arrives at the doctor's office, he discovers the patient to be his esteemed Professor LeBlanc, now immobilized in a catatonic state. In flashback we see the gradual deterioration of LeBlanc, going out of his mind over Jack's fruitless attempt to learn the violin scales. There are several references to the first lesson that occurred nineteen years ago with the initial performance of the radio sketch on April 29, 1945. Jack's execrable playing has remained constant over the years; the only thing that changed was LeBlanc's first name, from Andre to Pierre. The doctor says that the professor perceives himself a total failure because of Benny's ineptitude and therefore he wants to escape reality. In a tremendous display of uncharacteristic generosity, the Benny character brings LeBlanc back to life by playing a Wieniawski concerto like a professional. As LeBlanc leaves the office in joy, Jack pleads with the doctor: "During my long career as a comedian, I've made a lot of money getting laughs with my violin. So please, *please,* doctor, don't tell anyone that I play that well."

NBC Premiere

SEPTEMBER 25, 1964

When CBS failed to pick up the option on the Benny show, Jack and his executive producer Irving Fein signed a one-year contract with NBC. The opening show was introduced by NBC news anchors Chet Huntley and David Brinkley, who welcome Jack back to the network where he flourished on radio. In perhaps an unconscious updating of his first words on radio in 1932, Jack begins this new venture by saying, "My name is Jack Benny . . . This is my first show for NBC and I can just imagine a lot of people calling in and asking who is that new, young comedian?" Jack introduces his regulars who have been with him in both radio and television. Dennis Day protests being labeled "a silly kid" and brings out his wife and nine children to back his argument.

For the premiere, Jack engages in two sketches. The first centers on two benighted NBC executives who think Jack is returning to his old network to perform on radio. Jack must also bear the slights of an unimpressed NBC secretary. The second sketch brings back several guests who worked well on a Benny special: Jack discusses the affairs of the world with the Marquis Chimps in a spoof of serious interview shows.

Lucille Ball Show

OCTOBER 2, 1964

Lucille Ball had been CBS's most successful star, and it is ironic that her first guest appearance on the Benny program was after the show had moved to NBC. Two years earlier, Ball had started her first solo series, *The Lucy Show,* about the travails of a widow with two children. Jack, resplendent in a white tuxedo, greets "the first lady of television." Lucy shows up in a hillbilly outfit, reminiscent of the premiere episode of *I Love Lucy,* "The Girls Want to Go to a Night Club." Benny praises Ball's acumen as a business woman, and his tribute leads into the main sketch about illustrious women of history. Ball plays the suspicious wife of Paul Revere. Benny arouses her jealousy by singing the tune of the popular 1964 song "Hello Dolly" as a salute to Dolly Madison. After she inadvertently knocks her husband unconscious, Mrs. Revere must make the famous ride herself.

Before Lucy is introduced, Benny does a short routine with a sound man, played by a then struggling comedian, Arte Johnson. Johnson would achieve recognition four years later in *Rowan & Martin's Laugh-In.*

OCTOBER 23, 1964

Jack Makes a Comedy Record

The popularity of comedy records by humorists such as Bob Newhart, Bill Cosby, and Allan Sherman inspired this episode with Bob Hope. Bob and Jack had succeeded in every medium of comedy except this new form. The writers cleverly demarcate the comic differences between the two comedians in the way Benny and Hope attempt to make a recording. Benny prepares for this maiden effort with a well-crafted script that emphasizes the well-known traits of his persona. At the session, Hope casually wings it with a barrage of one-liners. Benny is characteristically exasperated by his inability to ad-lib and is only consoled when he realizes the profit-making possibilities of the record.

DECEMBER 25, 1964

One Man Show

Benny gives his cast the night off, and with the intimate feel of a talk show, he has an engaging dialogue with his studio audience. He begins by displaying several old photographs of himself growing up. One picture, taken when he was six months old, depicts the baby Jack with tightly clenched fists. Benny states that his parents put a dime in each hand. Jack then goes into the audience with the flair of the two most successful talk show hosts of the time, Jack Paar and Johnny Carson. The rapport that Jack Benny had with an audience is clearly evident.

Unlike the 1961 Christmas show, this one is not entirely staged and has a spontaneous atmosphere throughout. The one planned sequence, the discovery of friend Gisele Mackenzie in the audience, even has an improvisational charm to it. Ms. Mackenzie, a versatile performer who began in Canadian radio, has brought her aunt from Toronto. The relative requests that Jack's jokes be translated into French. The program ends with Jack and Gisele in the familiar violin duet of "Getting to Know You."

The Smothers Brothers Show

APRIL 16, 1965

This is the final, original episode of *The Jack Benny Program.* Jack does not invite his regulars back to reminisce, but instead welcomes the Smothers Brothers, who were then known for their comedy albums. After mangling Jack's theme song, "Love in Bloom," the dull-witted Tom Smothers explains that the duo decided to become entertainers when they saw how easy it was: they could easily surpass that guy on television who stares at the audience and does nothing. After his brother takes him aside, Tom apologizes and says to Jack that he looks much younger on television. To the bitter end, Jack was the butt of his guests' jokes.

The main sketch looks back to a ravaged London in 1944 when Jack Benny was abroad entertaining American troops and civilians. A bomb has fallen on Jack, who thought something free was coming out of the sky, and the Smothers Brothers play demolition experts. A lot about the sketch is anachronistic: the London Blitz had occurred several years earlier, and Jack makes a wisecrack about Jack Paar, who was not a widely known personality in the early forties. What makes this episode a memorable ending to the television series is that the Brothers are incompetent defusers and everyone is blown skyward. At the close, all appear dirty and disheveled and Jack gives the familiar farewell: "I'll be seeing you soon." Jack Benny in no way indicated that this would be the very final original broadcast of an extended series that began thirty-three years ago on radio.

Jack Benny's Specials

MARCH 18, 1959 (CBS)

The Jack Benny Hour

In this first of two musical-comedy specials Benny did for CBS during the 1958–59 season, Benny's guests are Mitzi Gaynor, ventriloquist Señor Wences, the Marquis Chimps, and Bob Hope. To distinguish this special from Benny's regular series, producer Bud Yorkin concocted a rousing opening number complete with multiple marching bands. Hope's barbed humor is frequently aimed at Benny, who responds with his characteristic indignation. Highlights include Gaynor singing "I'm in Love with a Wonderful Guy" and "The Third Girl from the End." Benny joins her for "Mr. Wonderful" and Hope joins them both for "Everybody Likes to Take a Bow."

Producer/Director: Bud Yorkin. Writers: Sam Perrin, George Balzer, Hal Goldman, and Al Gordon (with special material by Shirley Henry). Music Director: David Rose. Choreographer: Robert Sidney.

The Jack Benny Hour *NOVEMBER 7, 1959 (CBS)*

In the first of his several specials for CBS during the 1959–60 season, Benny's guests include Danny Thomas, the McGuire Sisters, Benny Rubin (the original radio race track tout), and the Marquis Chimps. Jack had originally worked successfully with the chimps in his first special, and the writers enjoyed creating comic situations for them. Two months after this special Benny would return the favor to Danny Thomas and appear on an episode of *The Danny Thomas Show* entitled "That Old Devil, Jack Benny."

Producer/Director: Ralph Levy. Writers: Sam Perrin, George Balzer, Al Gordon, and Hal Goldman. Music Director: David Rose. Choreographer: Jack Regas.

New York
Philharmonic
Music Director LEONARD BERNSTEIN
PENSION FUND
BENEFIT CONCERT
WED. EVE. APRIL 8 8:30
MUSICAL SURPRISE PARTY!
BERNSTEIN
Conductor and MC
JACK BENNY
Violinist
BRUNO ZIRATO, Managing Director
Steinway Piano
Columbia Records
HALL
FRI. APR.
AT 8:30 P. M.
THE
DUKES
OF
CONCERT
$3.00 - $2.50 - $1.80

Carnegie Hall Salutes Jack Benny

SEPTEMBER 27, 1961 (CBS)

Jack Benny's lifelong dedication to music is honored in this special broadcast from Carnegie Hall. Benny is joined by Eugene Ormandy and the Philharmonic Orchestra, Isaac Stern, Roberta Peters, Van Cliburn, and Benny Goodman and his sextet. Highlights include Peters singing an aria from *Rigoletto* and Stern and Benny performing a movement from Bach's Concerto for Two Violins in D Minor. The evening concludes with Stern presenting Benny with a special plaque. This television special came on the heels of a successful live performance by Benny at Carnegie Hall and was part of a fundraising effort for its preservation.

Executive Producer: Bob Banner. Producer/Directors: Joe Hamilton and Julio Di Benedetto. Writer: Alan Scott.

The Jack Benny Hour

NOVEMBER 3, 1965 (CBS)

Benny's guests are Bob Hope, the Beach Boys, and Elke Sommer in this first special after the demise of the regular series. Walt Disney makes an appearance as himself. Highlights include a comedy sketch that parodies such television shows as *The Addams Family, The Fugitive, My Mother the Car,* and *Peyton Place.* The Beach Boys sing "California Girls" and "Barbara Ann" and act in a comedy skit involving Hope and Benny as surfers. Elke Sommer sings "He's a Clown" and appears with Hope and Benny in a takeoff on Italian movies and *Mary Poppins.*

Executive Director: Irving Fein. Producer/Director: Ralph Levy. Writers: Sam Perrin, George Balzer, Al Gordon, and Hal Goldman. Music Director: Dave Grusin. Choreographer: Paul Godkin.

DECEMBER 1, 1966 (NBC)

The Jack Benny Hour

Benny's guest stars for this musical-variety special are Phyllis Diller, the Smothers Brothers, Trini Lopez, Mel Blanc, and the Tijuana Strings. Also, ten beautiful girls from around the world compete for the title "Miss Northern and Southern Hemisphere." Highlights include the mock beauty pageant (with Benny as emcee and Diller as the girls' chaperon), and Blanc and the Tijuana Strings performing comedy and music (which Benny joins with his violin). Benny and Blanc also reprise their famous "Sy" routine. Irving Fein relates in his biography of Jack Benny that there were many problems in the production of this special; however, this program became the model for the other specials that followed.

Executive Producer: Irving Fein. Writer/Producers: Hal Goldman and Al Gordon. Director: Bob Henry. Music Arranger/Conductor: Jack Elliott. Special Lyrics: Artie Malvin. Choreographer: Jack Regas.

Jack Benny's Carnival Nights

MARCH 20, 1968 (NBC)

This musical-comedy special centers on a carnival theme and features Benny and guests Lucille Ball, Johnny Carson, and vaudeville veteran Ben Blue participating in various midway attractions. Highlights include Carson as a carnival barker and Lucy as an exotic dancer. With Paul Revere and the Raiders and cameos by Bob Hope, Danny Thomas, George Burns, Dean Martin, the Smothers Brothers, and Don Drysdale. This was one of the most highly rated specials of the season.

Executive Producer: Irving Fein. Producer/Director: Fred de Cordova. Writers: Hal Goldman, Al Gordon, and Hilliard Marks. Musical Director: Jack Elliott. Choreographer: Jack Regas.

Jack Benny's Bag

NOVEMBER 16, 1968 (NBC)

Benny's guests are Phyllis Diller, Lou Rawls, Dick Clark, Eddie "Rochester" Anderson, and Eddie Fisher. Walter Matthau, Jack Lemmon, Dick Martin, and Dan Rowan make cameo appearances. Highlights include an extended parody of *The Graduate* with Diller and Benny. Benny obviously relishes his comic role as a young college graduate, adding his penny-pinching characteristics to the mix. Rawls and Fisher sing "Mrs. Robinson."

Executive Producer: Irving Fein. Producer/Director: Norman Abbott. Writers: Bob Fisher, Arthur Marks, Hilliard Marks, Sam Perrin, and Ray Singer. Music Arranger/Conductors: Jack Elliott and Allyn Ferguson. Special Musical Material: Earl Brown.

FEBRUARY 17, 1969 (NBC)

Jack Benny's Birthday Special

Benny's guest stars are Lucille Ball, Dan Blocker (from *Bonanza*), Dennis Day, Don Wilson, and recording artist Rouvaun. Lawrence Welk is the special guest star, with Ann-Margret and Jerry Lewis making cameo appearances. Highlights include a running gag involving penguins; a satire of Westerns starring Ball, Blocker, and Welk; and Ball singing "Big Spender." The entire cast joins in a surprise party for Benny.

Executive Producer: Irving Fein. Producer/Director: Fred de Cordova. Writers: Gerald Gardner, Dee Caruso, Hilliard Marks, Sam Perrin, and George Balzer. Music Arranger/Conductors: Jack Elliott and Allyn Ferguson.

Jack Benny's New Look

DECEMBER 3, 1969 (NBC)

Benny's guests for this special are Gregory Peck (who makes his singing and dancing debut), George Burns, Nancy Sinatra, Gary Puckett and the Union Gap, and Eddie "Rochester" Anderson, with a cameo by Frank Nelson. Highlights include Benny displaying his new "hippy" style and Nancy Sinatra singing "The Best Is Yet to Come." Burns, Benny, and Peck perform a memorable vaudeville act, and Lucille Ball, angry at not being invited on the show, makes a surprise appearance. The special proved extremely successful because of the casting coup of the usually somber Peck as a song-and-dance man.

Executive Producer: Irving Fein. Producer/Director: Norman Abbott. Writers: Al Gordon, Hal Goldman, Hilliard Marks, Sam Perrin, and Hugh Wedlock, Jr. Musical Arranger/Conductors: Jack Elliott and Allyn Ferguson.

NOVEMBER 16, 1970 (NBC)

Jack Benny's Twentieth Anniversary Special

Benny is joined by all his regulars as well as friends Lucille Ball, Bob Hope, Dinah Shore, and Frank Sinatra to celebrate his twentieth year in television. Highlights of past Benny programs are shown, and Rochester, Don Wilson, Dennis Day, and others join Benny to re-create a classic sketch portraying themselves in the future. With Mel Blanc, Frank Nelson, Mary Livingstone, and Benny Rubin. Red Skelton and Dean Martin appear in cameos.

Executive Producer: Irving Fein. Producer/Director: Stan Harris. Writers: Hal Goldman, Al Gordon, Hilliard Marks, and Hugh Wedlock, Jr.

MARCH 10, 1971 (NBC)

Everything You Always Wanted to Know About Jack Benny but Were Afraid to Ask

Loosely based on the best-seller of similar title by Dr. David Reuben, this comedy/variety special spoofs portions of Benny's career. Highlights include Benny and George Burns recreating their first meeting (with a cameo by Bob Hope), and Benny, Burns, Lucille Ball, and John Wayne parodying their early careers. Former Benny radio regular Phil Harris sings his 1937 number "That's What I Like About the South" with Benny attempting to decipher the lyrics (a routine they did together several times on the radio program).

Executive Producer: Irving Fein. Producer/Director: Norman Abbott. Writers: Al Gordon and Hal Goldman.

Jack Benny's First Farewell Special

JANUARY 18, 1973 (NBC)

Jack Benny is joined by Johnny Carson, Issac Hayes, Joey Heatherton, Bob Hope, Lee Trevino, and Flip Wilson in his first farewell to the public. Benny and Flip Wilson perform an *Ironside* parody. George Burns makes a surprise appearance and gives Jack a wheelchair as a retirement gift. Ronald Reagan, the governor of California, presents Benny with a Rolls Royce as an inducement for Benny to retire. Executive producer Irving Fein considers this to be the most successful of all the specials.

Executive Producer: Irving Fein. Producer/Director: Norman Abbott. Writers: Al Gordon, Hal Goldman, Hilliard Marks, Hugh Wedlock, Jr., Stan Daniels, and Tom Tenowich. Musical Arranger/Conductors: Jack Elliott and Allyn Ferguson.

JANUARY 24, 1974 (NBC)

Jack Benny's Second Farewell Special

Taped in Burbank, Jack stars in this musical-comedy special about his retirement deliberation. Benny's guests include George Burns, Johnny Carson, Redd Foxx, and Dinah Shore. Benny and Burns play five-hundred-year-old Roman fountain statues, and Jack forms his own rock group, "Jack Benny's Rolling Pips." Jack Webb and Harry Morgan make cameo appearances as their *Dragnet* characters. An extended sketch features Redd Foxx in a reversal of his *Sanford and Son* character, living the life of luxury.

Executive Producer: Irving Fein. Producer/Director: Norman Abbott. Writers: Al Gordon, Hal Goldman, Hilliard Marks, and Hugh Wedlock, Jr. Musical Arranger/Conductors: Jack Elliott and Allyn Ferguson.

A Love Letter to Jack Benny *FEBRUARY 5, 1981 (NBC)*

This posthumous tribute to Jack Benny and his work is cohosted by two of Benny's longtime colleagues, Bob Hope and George Burns, and one protégé, Johnny Carson. The program features taped and film highlights of Benny's series and specials. Among the performers seen in clips are Lucille Ball, Gregory Peck, Ronald Reagan, Frank Sinatra, and John Wayne.

Executive Producers: Irving Fein and Fred de Cordova. Producer/Director: Norman Abbott. Writers: Hal Goldman and Hugh Wedlock, Jr.

NOVEMBER 15, 1952 (CBS)

Stars in the Eye: Dedication of CBS Television City

The opening of CBS's new production facilities in Los Angeles brings together the stars of the network's programs in this hour of humorous sketches. The loosely constructed plot revolves around Jack Benny's attempts to have absolute control over the show, driving the executives and stars to distraction. Highlights include Benny's repeated intrusion on the *I Love Lucy* set as Lucille Ball and Desi Arnaz attempt to film an episode and Eve Arden of *Our Miss Brooks* accepting a ride to the studio in Jack's Maxwell. With Eddie Anderson as Rochester.

Producer/Director: Ralph Levy. Writers: Hugh Wedlock, Jr., George Balzer, Al Schwartz, Si Rose, and Howard Snyder.

Omnibus: "The Horn Blows at Midnight"

NOVEMBER 29, 1953 (CBS)

Jack Benny stars in this whimsical comedy produced for the acclaimed *Omnibus* series, hosted by Alistair Cooke. He portrays an angel sent down from heaven to destroy the earth, but has second thoughts when he finds the planet not as wicked a place as he was led to believe. Jeff Donnell and Dorothy Malone have the principal supporting roles. This is a restructured version of the 1945 film in which Benny starred. The alleged mediocrity of the film became a running gag on the Benny radio program, and except for several small walk-ons and cameos, Benny never made another film. Benny had also revived *The Horn Blows at Midnight* for radio in 1949.

Director: Ralph Levy. Producer: Fred Rickey. Writers: Hugh Wedlock, Jr. and Howard Snyder.

General Electric Theater: "The Face Is Familiar"

NOVEMBER 21, 1954 (CBS)

In this short comedy for the popular anthology series hosted by Ronald Reagan, Benny portrays an innocent in the center of intrigue based on money. A nondescript citizen working as a waiter, he is inveigled by gangsters into leading a bank robbery, and the take is fifty thousand dollars. Later plagued by guilt, Benny attempts to confess to police; his innocuousness makes it difficult for anyone to believe his guilt. A previous version of this script was performed on the *Suspense* radio series earlier in 1954.

Director: Frank Tashlin. Producer: Z. Wayne Griffin; Writers: Hugh Wedlock, Jr. and Howard Synder. Cast: Otto Kruger, Jesse White, Ken Dibbs, Jean Wills, Joy Lansing, and Benny Rubin.

FEBRUARY 19, 1956 (CBS)

General Electric Theater: "The Honest Man"

Benny once again portrays an innocent who is unwittingly caught in the middle of a robbery in this comedy. Zsa Zsa Gabor costars in a plot about a nightclub owner masterminding a jewel heist. Benny, a mild-mannered piano tuner, is used as a pawn.

Producer/Director/Writer: Frank Tashlin; Cast: Zsa Zsa Gabor, Charles Bronson, Barbara Lawrence, and Mary Lawrence.

Shower of Stars *NOVEMBER 1, 1956 (CBS)*

William Lundigan hosts this live musical-variety series, which for four seasons appears monthly on CBS. Benny appears as the principal guest on almost every program following the first season. The program also features an occasional light play; Benny's first appearance was in the play *Time Out for Ginger,* the 1955 season premiere. The Benny-associated writing team of Hugh Wedlock, Jr., and Howard Snyder wrote the series. The programs with Benny are a combination of comic sketches that could have been performed on his own series and elaborate production numbers.

In this third season premiere, highlights include a comedy sketch between Benny and guest Nanette Fabray and a "smash production number" built around Johnnie Ray's hit recording "Just Walking in the Rain." The sponsor previews the 1957 automobile lines.

Producer/Director: Ralph Levy.

Shower of Stars *JANUARY 10, 1957 (CBS)*

Benny hosts and performs in this installment that features guest stars Liberace, Jayne Mansfield, Vincent Price, and singers Joanie O'Brien and Rod McKuen. In an elaborate musical-comedy sequence, Mansfield defends the Benny character against the accusations of the prosecuting attorney, Vincent Price. Liberace adjudicates.

Producer/Director: Ralph Levy, Writers: Hugh Wedlock, Jr. and Howard Snyder.

MARCH 3, 1957 (CBS)

General Electric Theater: "The Fenton Touch"

Benny portrays an adept and lovable thief who commits a near-perfect crime in this comic outing. About to retire after a long stint working in a department store, Harold Fenton (Benny) steals $50,000 from the store safe—almost undetected.

Director: Don Weis. Producer: William Frye. Writers: Hugh Wedlock, Jr. and Howard Snyder. Cast: Norma Crane, Bill Kendis, Joseph Kearns, Hallene Hill, and Lawrence Dobkin.

MAY 9, 1957 (CBS)

Shower of Stars

Benny and guest stars Yvonne DeCarlo and Van Johnson act in a plantation skit that features the Calypso songs and dances of Jean Durand, a Haitian singer making his television debut. Benny and company are joined by radio regulars Mel Blanc and Artie Auerbach in an elaborate production number of Mr. Kitzel's "Peekle een the meedle" song.

Producer/Director: Ralph Levy. Writers: Hugh Wedlock, Jr., Howard Snyder, Al Gordon, and Hal Goldman.

The Lucy Show

OCTOBER 16, 1967 (CBS)

Bank secretary Lucy Carmichael (Lucille Ball) attempts to persuade Jack Benny to deposit his money in her boss' bank; she demonstrates to him a security system of staggering proportions, including quicksand, a guillotine, and a moat with snapping turtles. The effects rigged for this program were among the most expensive ever done for any single series episode to 1967.

Writers: Milt Josefberg and Ray Singer. Director: Jack Donahue. Producer: Tommy Thompson.

The Kraft Music Hall: "The Friars Club Roasts Jack Benny"

JANUARY 21, 1970 (NBC)

Johnny Carson serves as "roastmaster" for this tongue-in-cheek tribute to Benny. Fellow comedians Milton Berle, George Burns, Dennis Day, Phil Harris, Alan King, and Ed Sullivan poke scathing fun at Benny's infamous personality traits. They are joined by Vice President Spiro Agnew, who discusses the government's view of Benny's fiscal policies.

Director: Dwight Hemion. Producers: Gary Smith and Dwight Hemion. Writers: Frank Peppiatt, John Aylesworth, Jack Burns, and Pat McCormick.

A Television Script for

The Jack Benny Program

This Benny show is the seventh program of the 1952–53 season. It was broadcast live at 4:30 P.M. (7:30 E.S.T.) from Television City in Hollywood, a CBS complex that had opened in November 1952. This was Benny's fifteenth program on television, but surprisingly it was only his second with a radio colleague, in this case Fred Allen. With the exception of Burns and Allen, Benny's previous guests were Hollywood film stars, including Claudette Colbert, Jimmy Stewart, and Barbara Stanwyck. Guests were also invited from fields other than entertainment, encompassing golf (Ben Hogan) and classical music (Isaac Stern).

One wonders why Fred Allen was not one of Benny's first guests. Their feud had been ongoing for years, and a visual confrontation should have generated enormous publicity. Ironically, during this show the pair is only on stage together for a few minutes. Although there are references to the feud, there is no explicit mention of radio.

The script is marked "as broadcast," but there are considerable changes throughout. Allen and Benny change words at the last moment, both of them searching for the word that compliments his style of delivery.

SUNDAY, APRIL 19, 1953
CBS 4:30–5:00 P.M. P.S.T.

The Jack Benny Television Program [Program #7 As Broadcast]

(AFTER COMMERCIAL JACK COMES OUT TO "LOVE IN BLOOM" AND APPLAUSE. HE IS WEARING GLASSES.)

Benny has always been cited as a master of identifying himself with the sponsors. In his opening statement he calls his series "The Lucky Strike Program," *not the official title,* "The Jack Benny Program." *He had been associated with the cigarette brand since World War II. In this particular program the sponsor will be thoroughly integrated into the plot.*

JACK: Thank you, ladies and gentlemen, welcome to the Lucky Strike Program . . . And tonight we have a show that we think is—oh, by the way—
(TAPPING HIS GLASSES)

Benny did wear glasses during earlier television shows, but that would not have set up the joke. His allusion to Mr. Peepers *is most odd.* Mr. Peepers *was a situation comedy about the travails of a shy science teacher played by Wally Cox. It debuted in July 1952 and was seen throughout its regular run opposite Jack Benny on Sunday nights. During the three years of competition, Benny's program consistently finished in Nielsen's top twenty, reaching as high as seventh place;* Mr. Peepers *was never among the top-rated programs of the season. In retrospect, one questions why the producers and network executive would have allowed any identification with* Mr. Peepers.

In case you're wondering about these . . . My producer insisted I come out wearing glasses. He said it wouldn't hurt if people thought I was Mr. Peepers.
(TAKES GLASSES OFF AND PUTS THEM AWAY)
He had another suggestion that I stand in the center of the stage while a two-ton block of cement dropped right on my head

---

Reproduction of Jack Benny's own script.

. . . He felt that this would appeal to the people who watch *You Asked For It* . . . He said he had thousands of requests . . . Anyway, I'm not gonna get upset about it because today I'm very excited. You see, right after my television show I leave for San Francisco, and I open at the Curran Theatre tomorrow night. I'll be there three weeks . . The reason I'm excited is that the first time I ever

appeared in public was in San Francisco. I played my violin. . . . Let me see . . . just where was that place? . . It was in the heart of town . . Let me see . . . I haven't been there for so long . . . Oh yes, it was on the corner of Taylor and Market. . . . I understand there's a theater there now . . After that I travelled. I played two weeks on a cable car . . . Anyway, as you probably know, ladies and gentlemen, Fred Allen is my guest star tonight . . Now a lot of people think that because of the feud that Allen and I have had on radio for years, that we hate each other. Well, this is not the truth . . Fred and I are the best of friends. Well, maybe not the best of friends, but friends . . Well, friends is not exactly the right word . . we're more . . . more . . . Maybe we *do* hate each other . . . I know I can't stand him . . . I want to tell

You Asked for It *was an audience participation show in which viewers wrote in to request difficult stunts to be performed. Again, this is another peculiar television reference.* You Asked for It *was broadcast on Sundays a half hour before Benny's program on ABC. Even in 1953 such programmers as Sylvester "Pat" Weaver understood the importance of audience flow: the first program a viewer tunes into is crucial to the determination of what network will be watched for the rest of the evening. Why make reference at all to ABC's 7:00 P.M. show? Some of the other series that followed* You Asked for It *in competition with Benny were* The Frank Leahy Show, *a discussion of Notre Dame football;* Hot Seat, *a live interview show with ABC newsman Stuart Scheftel; or some local presentation. It is noteworthy that the first two jokes during Benny's monologue were devoted to television. The assumption must have been that the audience had a working knowledge of the new medium. At this point 45 percent of American households had television. Two weeks earlier the regional editions of* TV Guide *had been launched after Walter Annenberg had bought out local publications. By the end of the year,* TV Guide *will have a circulation of 1.5 million.*

Benny decides to restructure his monologue and saves the discussion of San Francisco for the end. It is curious that Benny says his first public performance was in San Francisco. Any casual follower knew his early appearances were in the Midwest and later the East Coast. Perhaps Benny is uncomfortable with the joke, because he blows a crucial line. Instead of saying "it was in the heart of town" he remembers it was "in the shopping center," which reveals too quickly it wasn't in a recital hall. The blown line also fails to conjure up the image of a street corner, where there is now a theater. Benny's mannerisms do not fail him, however, and the audience laughs anyway.

The second section of the monologue is a discussion of guest star Fred Allen. What follows is a Benny symphony of hand movements, for which each movement is designed to effectively underscore the development of the joke. In many ways, this was the essential adaptation to a visual medium. In radio Benny stood behind a microphone and read a script. In television he had no such luxury. He would have to learn the monologue and make his points with body language. If the hands and words worked together, the visual counterpart of the Benny character would be established. What the viewer waited for week after week would be these signature gestures. The entire development of the joke lasts fifty seconds:

Right hand extended, with palm upward; left hand in trouser pocket
—"A lot of people think Fred and I are enemies"

Right hand fans the air
—"Fred Allen and I are the best of friends"

Fingers on right hand curl
—Benny waits for the audience chuckle

Both hands are out, palms toward the floor
—"Maybe I am overdoing it, just a little bit"

Hands are brought together and then spread apart with palms upward
—"I wouldn't say we are the best of friends"

Hands brought together and then quickly extended for emphasis
—"We are friends, friends"

Hands are clasped, rubbing together
—Benny waits for a laugh to develop

Hands apart as if conducting an orchestra
—"Friends might not be the exact word I am trying to say"

Hands moving back and forth
—"What I mean is we're more . . . ah"

Hands extended, palms skyward
—"Maybe we do hate each other"

Benny reaches the Bouché pose: hands clasp at waist, head turned to right with classic stare
—"I know, I can't stand him"

The final laugh.

you something about Fred Allen. A few years ago he came out here to make a Technicolor picture and they asked me if I'd play a small part in it. The name of it was, "It's In The Bag", or something, . . . Well, I said I would . . . then when we started to shoot the picture we found out that it couldn't be made in Technicolor because, due to a peculiar pigment in Fred Allen's skin, he photographed argyle . . . In fact, twice in my dressing room I tried to put my foot into his mouth . . . what a face . . . with those bags under his eyes he looks like a short butcher peeping over two pounds of liver . . . Anyway, he's going to be on my show, and—

Benny refers to Fred Allen's 1945 film It's in the Bag *in which he makes a guest appearance. He inadvertently says he wasn't paid for it, which is an extraordinary moment when the character slips and the man shows through; the character would never appear for free, especially to benefit his feud partner. Benny quickly tries to reassert the character's primacy by saying the movie was supposed to be in Technicolor and that he wanted to see his beautiful blue eyes on a large screen. This vanity about his eyes puts the character back in control. The joke also complements his comments about Fred Allen's eyes, a standard target in the feud.*

(STAGE MANAGER COMES OUT ON STAGE)

MANAGER: Okay, Mr. Benny, that's enough rehearsing on that . . . Raleigh, bring that boom in here so we can get that extra scenery in.

JACK: What's the matter?

MANAGER: You don't have to rehearse your monologue any more. It's just the right length . . . pardon me . . . Kill those lights in the back of the

JACK: Well, if we aren't going to rehearse my monologue any more, I think we oughta start rehearsing the sketch.

MANAGER: We can't do that. Mr. Allen hasn't arrived yet.

There has been no indication to this point that what we have been watching is a rehearsal. The backstage look at the Benny show was a favorite device of the writers. It allowed them to make inside jokes about television production, whether it be the placement of a boom microphone or the relationship between star and sponsor. This self-reflexivity about the medium was not uncommon: there was George Burns stepping away from the scene and commenting about the wacky involvements of his wife, although few recall that the entire 1952–53 season of Texaco Star Theater *was turned over to the travails of Milton Berle producing his show. During that season Berle is supposedly kidnapped and forced to watch Jack Carter as the new host of the series.*

JACK: How do you like that? I give a guy a job because I feel sorry for him, pay his bus fare all the way out here from New York, and he doesn't even show up for rehearsal.

MANAGER: Well, as long as we've stopped, we might as well break for lunch
(WALKING OFF, YELLING)
Lunch, everybody . . . Break for lunch!!

JACK: *(CALLING)*
Rochester . . . Rochester . . We're breaking for lunch!

So far the only jokes about the Benny character have been a suggestion of his inept violin playing and an offhand remark about his beautiful eyes. Now comes a series of jokes about Benny's stinginess, beginning with paying the bus fare for his guest star.

The bicycle/food-cart joke is perfectly realized. Rochester peddling the contraption immediately gets the audience laughing before a series of jokes about how Benny and his valet earn extra income.

(ROCHESTER ENTERS TO APPLAUSE RIDING A BICYCLE ATTACHED TO BOX-TYPE CART. ON THE SIDE OF THE CART IS PRINTED "BENNY'S MEALS ON WHEELS, WAGON NO. 7". ON EITHER SIDE OF THE LETTERING IS A PICTURE OF A HAMBURGER AND A HOT DOG.)

JACK: Have you got everything, Rochester?
(STAGE HANDS COME OVER TO WAGON)

ROCHESTER: What'll you have, Mr. Benny?

JACK: Never mind me, wait on the customers first.

ROCHESTER: Yes, sir.
(ROCHESTER HANDS EACH OF THE STAGE HANDS A SANDWICH . . THEY PAY HIM AND LEAVE. JACK WATCHES THE TRANSACTIONS WITH GREAT INTEREST.)

JACK: Rochester, why did you put so much catsup on those sandwiches?

ROCHESTER: It's just an idea I had for drumming up more business.

JACK: How could putting so much catsup on a sandwich bring us more business?

ROCHESTER: I figured if it drips on their shirts, we'll get to do their laundry, too.

JACK: Gee, I never thought of that.
(STAGE MANAGER ENTERS)

MANAGER: Oh, Mr. Benny—

JACK: What'll you have, ham or cheese?

MANAGER: I had my lunch. I just want to tell you that as long as Fred Allen isn't here, we'll have to skip the dialogue rehearsal, we have a lot of work to do on the lights, anyway. We won't need you for about two hours.
(STAGE MANAGER GOES OFF)

Rochester's explanation about the extra use of catsup is followed by several seconds of silence as Benny ponders the situation. Benny offers his trademark stare to the delight of the audience.

JACK: Two hours? I had an appointment to be at my sponsor's office at four o'clock and now I'll be late.

ROCHESTER: Well, boss, if you have two hours, why don't you go to see your sponsor now?

JACK: Say . . that's a good idea. You know this is the day he picks up my option.

ROCHESTER: *(WORRIED)*
Your option?

Meeting the sponsor is always a cause of anxiety for the Benny character. No matter how egotistical Benny appears, there lurks a fundamental insecurity about his position in show business and his value to a sponsor.

JACK: Rochester, there's nothing to worry about. It's just a formality . . they want to make sure they've got me. So I'll see you later. Oh, Rochester, sell all the sandwiches you can . . and give them a floor show, then you can add a cover charge.

ROCHESTER: Oh yes, Boss — yes sir. Get your sandwiches here . . Roast beef . . . ham . . . cheese . . . and Mr. Benny's home-made noodle soup . . . Come and get it.
(JACK EXITS)
(STAGE HANDS GATHER AROUND)
(ORCHESTRA STARTS . . ROCHESTER SINGS "SIDE BY SIDE" AS HE GIVES THE STAGE HANDS SANDWICHES, HE DANCES OVER TO THEM AND BACK TO THE CASH REGISTER . . AT END OF SONG ROCHESTER RIDES HIS CART OFF AS WE DISSOLVE TO MR. LEWIS'S OUTER OFFICE.)
(INTRO)

ROCHESTER: Oh we ain't got a barrel of money
Maybe we're ragged and funny
But we travel along
Singing a song
Side by side
We don't know what's coming tomorrow
Maybe it's trouble and sorrow
But we'll travel the road
Sharing our load
Side by side
Through all kinds of weather

Benny's departure for the sponsor's office gives Eddie Anderson as Rochester a chance to display his song and dance skills. Anderson had appeared in black revues as a teenager, eventually playing at the Cotton Club and Apollo Theatre. He starred in Vincente Minnelli's film musical Cabin in the Sky. *Unfortunately, his musical talents were almost never integrated into the radio show. His professionalism shines here as he both makes the sandwiches and delivers the song with a raspy charm. The final joke, not revealed in the script, is Don Wilson asking for his lunch and receiving a Dagwood sandwich.*

What if the sky should fall
Just as long as we're together
It doesn't matter at all.
When they've all had their troubles and parted
We'll be the same as we started
Just traveling along
Singing a song
Side by side
Last call—Ham - cheese - Mr. Benny's Home made noodle soup . . .
(PEDALLING OFF)
We'll travel along
Singing a song
Side by side.
(APPLAUSE)
(MR. LEWIS' SECRETARY, MISS ROCKFORD, IS SEATED BEHIND A DESK. AMONG OTHER THINGS ON THE DESK, THERE ARE THREE PHONES. AS THE SCENE OPENS ONE OF THE PHONES RINGS, *AND THE SECRETARY ANSWERS IT.)*

SECRETARY: Hello . . The American Tobacco Company . . I'm sorry, but Mr. Lewis can't be disturbed right now.
(JACK ENTERS AS THE SECRETARY CONTINUES TALKING ON THE PHONE.)
However, I'd be very happy to take a message.
(AS THE SECRETARY WRITES THE MESSAGE SHE IS GETTING OVER THE PHONE, JACK TRIES TO BE CALM, NONCHALANT AND PATIENT.)

SECRETARY: Yes . . . yes . . . uh huh. . . . uh huh. . . . yes . . . yes . . . yes, sir, I'll see that he gets it.
(SHE REPLACES THE RECEIVER AND LOOKS UP AT JACK.)
Yes, sir?

JACK: My name is—
(THE SECOND PHONE RINGS.)

SECRETARY: Excuse me.
(SHE ANSWERS THE PHONE.)

SECRETARY: Mr. Lewis' office. Oh yes, he asked me to take the information.
(SHE AGAIN STARTS WRITING AS SHE LISTENS)
Yes . . . . Yes . . . . yes. . . . uh huh . . . . uh huh . . . . Yes . . . yes . . . . . I've got it, thank you.
(SHE REPLACES THE RECEIVER AND LOOKS UP AT JACK AGAIN.)

SECRETARY: Yes, sir?

JACK: My name is—
(THIRD PHONE RINGS)

SECRETARY: Excuse me.
(SHE ANSWERS THE THIRD PHONE. AND JACK PICKS UP THE RECEIVER OF THE FIRST PHONE AND DIALS IT.)
Mr. Lewis' office. Yes . . uh huh . . . Yes . . Uh huh . . . I think so. . . . Yes . . . I see . . . Well, it seems that Mr. Lewis requested that—
(SECOND PHONE RINGS)

SECRETARY: *(INTO THIRD PHONE)*
Just a moment, please.
(SHE ANSWERS THE SECOND PHONE.)
Hello.

JACK: *(INTO PHONE)*
My name is Jack Benny, I have an appointment with Mr. Lewis. . . . Is he in?

SECRETARY: *(INTO PHONE)*
I'm sorry, Mr. Benny, but Mr. Lewis can't be disturbed right now. Can he call you back?

JACK: Call me back?

SECRETARY: Yes . . . are you at home or in Palm Springs?

JACK: I'm in Stockholm, Smorgasbord 7321 . . . Now Miss, if you don't mind, will you—

SECRETARY: *(LOOKING AROUND)*
Oh, Mr. Benny . . . I'm terribly sorry.
(THEY BOTH HANG UP)

The job of a secretary had recently become the subject of a television comedy with the premiere of Private Secretary, *starring Ann Sothern. That series was also sponsored by the American Tobacco Company and alternated with* The Jack Benny Program *on Sunday nights at 7:30 P.M.*

The comedy in all of this comes from the classic situation where the Benny character is ignored by someone he is trying to talk to, and we can all identify with his ensuing exasperation.

JACK: Now, Miss, I have an appointment with Mr. Lewis. May I see him?

SECRETARY: I'm sorry, Mr. Benny, but Mr. Lewis has someone in his office right now . . . and he left orders not to be disturbed.
(INDICATING A CHAIR)
Do you mind waiting?

JACK: Not at all.
(JACK SITS DOWN AND INTERESTS HIMSELF IN A MAGAZINE. AFTER A MOMENT, HE LOOKS UP.)

Benny's meeting with the sponsor will be satirized several more times during the series' run. The sketch invariably begins with a secretary who is totally unimpressed with the comedian. Benny's feigned smugness and self-satisfaction generate the initial laughs before the crucial meeting.

JACK: *(TO SECRETARY)*
You know, Mr. Lewis is going to pick up my option today. That's why I'm here.

SECRETARY: That's nice.

JACK: You know I've been with the American Tobacco Company for ten years and they're very happy with me.

SECRETARY: That's nice.

JACK: Of course, they should be because I'm acknowledged to be one of the greatest comedians in—

SECRETARY: Excuse me.

JACK: Certainly.
(AS SHE EXITS, JACK LOOKS HER UP AND DOWN)

JACK: Gee, I hope Mr. Lewis, isn't tied up too long. I've gotta get back to rehearsal.
(DISSOLVE TO MR. LEWIS'S PRIVATE OFFICE)

(MR. LEWIS IS SEATED BEHIND HIS DESK. FRED ALLEN IS STANDING FACING THE WINDOW, WITH HIS BACK TO THE AUDIENCE. AS HE STARTS TO SPEAK, HE TURNS AND THE AUDIENCE SEES WHO IT IS.)

ALLEN: As I was saying, Mr. Lewis—
(APPLAUSE)
. . As I was saying. It isn't that I want Mr. Benny's job. It's just that it's time you put him out to pasture.

LEWIS: Put him out to pasture?

ALLEN: Yes, for thirty years Benny's been milking jokes for an audience that is not contented . . . think it over, Mr. Lewis.

LEWIS: I don't know . . Taking a man like Jack Benny and . . er . . er . . putting him out to pasture. . . . So you think it'll work?

ALLEN: If Benny can spend his last years around anything green, he'll go for it . . . Take my advice, Mr. Lewis, let him go now. I'd be happy to take his place and finish out the rest of the season.

LEWIS: But I can't let Jack go just like that. We've given him a contract.

Fred Allen was one of the major radio stars who found no success in television. This sketch is written as if it were Allen's initial foray into the new medium. Unfortunately, this appearance actually follows a string of failures. Fred Allen had been a rotating host of two variety series, Colgate Comedy Hour *(1950) and* Chesterfield Sound Off Time *(1951–52). His verbal wit and caustic humor did not translate well to the visual medium. Allen's visage seemed too dour for the small screen, and he did not have an established character to compensate for it.*

Fred Allen had an ongoing battle against the overcommercialization of the media. He railed against the hucksterism that dominated the airwaves, most significantly in a 1946 Gilbert and Sullivan parody, "The Radio Mikado." NBC demanded extensive rewrites before the spoof was broadcast. As an inside joke Benny's writers decided that Allen should speak in the language of advertising. He refers to Benny "milking the same jokes for an audience that is not contented" (Carnation Milk reference) . . .

ALLEN: But, Mr. Lewis, you're a shrewd businessman. I'm sure that nestled somewhere in that legal document there must be a tobacco-picking clause.

LEWIS: Mr. Allen, why don't you sit down?

ALLEN: Sit down? Mr. Lewis, have you ever ridden thirty-two hundred miles on a bus? If the sun felt like I do, it would never set again.

LEWIS: Well, try that chair, it's very comfortable.

ALLEN: Okay.
(ALLEN SITS DOWN)

LEWIS: Mr. Allen, before I'd make any change, I'd have to be sure that it is one for the better. Have *you* any television experience?

ALLEN: Nobody has, even the Voice of Experience has no experience. However, I've studied the medium thoroughly. And because television has a comparatively small screen, I realize that the successful performer would be one who has trained himself to work in a limited space. So I did all my rehearsing inside a Bendix Washing Machine. I'm ready.

LEWIS: Inside a Bendix Washing Machine?

ALLEN: Yes . . . and to make that popular slogan even more popular . . . Now that Tide's in, let's let Benny out.

. . . rehearsing in a Bendix washing machine in hope that the "Tide's in" and Benny's out (Tide detergent) . . .

LEWIS: Mr. Allen, do you mind if I ask you a personal question?

ALLEN: Not at all.

LEWIS: I've seen you on occasional guest appearances. Does that pay you enough money to live on?

ALLEN: Oh, no . . . no. Fortunately, I have a unique talent that guarantees me steady employment . . . that is, three times a week.

LEWIS: Well, that's wonderful. What do you do?

ALLEN: I'm a taster for Dr. Ross dog food.

LEWIS: Dog food?

ALLEN: I'm the Fido who knows best. I'm known in Kennels from coast to coast as the Canine Duncan Hines.

. . . and he himself makes ends meet as a dog-food taster, "a Fido who knows best," a sly reference to the radio series with Robert Young that would transfer to television in 1954. Many of these advertising jokes seem somewhat demeaning to a comedian of Allen's stature.

LEWIS: *(IMPRESSED)*
A taster of dog food. That *is* unique.

ALLEN: I acquired the talent during the lay-off season. I knew a talking dog . . . He spoke highly of it, so I took it up.

LEWIS: Well, Mr. Allen, in regards to the Lucky Strike Program, I don't doubt for a moment that you are well qualified . . but I mustn't lose sight of the fact that in Benny we have a double asset. He's not only a comedian, but he also plays a musical instrument.

ALLEN: Are we not toying with words, Mr. Lewis? Let's just say he has a musical instrument. However, if it's music you want, I have come prepared. Let me tell you, Mr. Lewis, that in two minutes you won't know your office from Carneige Hall.
(ALLEN PICKS UP A CLARINET WHICH IS AT THE FOOT OF HIS CHAIR, AND THEN DEMONSTRATES HIS MUSICAL ABILITY BY PLAYING "LOVE IN BLOOM" JUST ABOUT AS LOUSY AS JACK WOULD PLAY IT ON THE VIOLIN.)

Allen was not known for his musical talents, although he and Benny in their radio days did perform a clarinet-violin duet of "Love in Bloom" in 1936.

ALLEN: Well, Mr. Lewis, I've given you all my qualifications. If you'll drop Benny's option and make me the star, I'll not only do a better job for Lucky Strike, but I'll give you a program that has no loose ends.
(A GROUCHO MARX DUCK COMES DOWN WITH A HUNDRED DOLLAR BILL IN ITS MOUTH, ACCOMPANIED BY SAME MUSIC AS ON GROUCHO MARX PROGRAM.)

LEWIS: *(EXCITEDLY)*
You said no loose ends, the Secret words.
(HANDING ALLEN THE MONEY)
This hundred dollars is yours.

ALLEN: *(BEWILDERED)*
Does Groucho know about this?

LEWIS: He installed it for me.
(DUCK GOES BACK UP.)

ALLEN: Well, Mr. Lewis, when do I start to work?

The secret word refers to Groucho Marx's quiz series You Bet Your Life, *which began on radio in 1947 and was adapted for television in 1950. Each week Groucho would inform the audience of the secret word and if one of the contestants said the word, he would win one hundred dollars. When the magic word was stated, a stuffed duck would drop from the rafters with the money. In four months Fred Allen would become a host of his own quiz show* Judge for Yourself, *a series that lasted less than a year.*

The script calls for Allen to hide behind a cardboard image of Dorothy Collins, although the joke was not realized in the production. Collins was a singer who first attracted attention by singing the "Be Happy, Go Lucky" jingle while placed inside a Lucky Strike bull's-eye. She was a vocalist on both the radio and television versions of Your Hit Parade. *Obviously there is a covert sponsor plug when Allen asks for a light.*

LEWIS: Mr. Allen, I appreciate your offer, but I'll need a few days while I think your proposition over. I have an appointment with Mr. Benny concerning his option, but I'll see if I can stall him off.

ALLEN: That's fair enough. And if you should decide in my favor, please let me know before nine o'clock Monday morning. It would be most embarrassing to be pulled out of line in the Unemployment office.
(THEY SHAKE HANDS. ALLEN GOES TO THE DOOR AND WHEN HE OPENS IT HE SEES JACK SITTING IN THE OUTER OFFICE . . . HE IMMEDIATELY CLOSES THE DOOR AGAIN.)

LEWIS: What's the matter, Mr. Allen?

ALLEN: It's Benny. He mustn't see me here . . . I better hide.
(ALLEN, LOOKING FOR A PLACE TO HIDE, NOTICES THE LIFE-SIZE CARDBOARD IMAGE OF DOROTHY COLLINS STANDING IN THE CORNER. HE STEPS OVER TO IT, GETS BEHIND IT, BUT IT IS TOO SHORT. HE PUTS HIS HEAD ON ONE SIDE, THEN THE OTHER . . . THEN HE BENDS BACK THE HEAD OF DOROTHY COLLINS AND STANDS SO THAT HIS HEAD REPLACES DOROTHY'S. LEWIS LOOKS AT IT CRITICALLY. ALLEN WALKS TOWARD A CLOSET.)

LEWIS: No, no, not that closet. Here, this one.
(ALLEN OPENS THE OTHER CLOSET DOOR, STOPS AND TAKES OUT A CIGARETTE.)

ALLEN: I may be in there quite awhile. May I have a light?

LEWIS: Certainly, certainly.
(LEWIS TAKES A LIGHTER OFF THE DESK, GOES OVER TO

ALLEN AND LIGHTS HIS CIGARETTE. ALLEN THEN GOES INTO THE CLOSET. LEWIS THEN FLIPS THE SWITCH ON HIS INTER-OFFICE PHONE.)

LEWIS: Miss Rockford, you may send Mr. Benny in now.
(CUT TO SECRETARY)

SECRETARY: *(INTO PHONE)*
Yes, Mr. Lewis.
(TO JACK)
Mr. Benny, you may go in now.
(JACK GETS UP AND GOES INTO LEWIS'S OFFICE.)

JACK: Hello, Mr. Lewis.

LEWIS: Hello, Jack. Sit down, sit down.

JACK: Thank you.
(JACK SITS DOWN)
You know, Mr. Lewis, I remember the very first year I worked for you. When it came option time, I was a nervous wreck . . . But since then it's been just a formality . . . I come in, you sign the option, and that's it . . . What a wonderful association.

LEWIS: Yes, it has been.

JACK: Been? . . . I mean, been? . . . Oh, yes yes . . . it has . . . and I'm confident that it will continue to be? . . what I mean is, it's been so much fun working for you . . . You're a wonderful sponsor. And, well, if I do say so myself, where could you find a better comedian than I am?
(A PUFF OF SMOKE COMES OUT OF THE CLOSET KEY-HOLE.)

JACK: Now, Mr. Lewis . . .
(SECRETARY COMES IN.)

SECRETARY: Mr. Lewis, I have the options you wanted to sign today.

LEWIS: Oh, good, good.

JACK: Yes, good, good.
(SECRETARY HANDS HIM THREE CONTRACTS . . . LEWIS SIGNS ONE.)

LEWIS: The Hit Parade.
(SIGNING ANOTHER ONE)
Ann Sothern . . .
(SIGNING ANOTHER ONE)
Robert Montgomery . . .
(TO SECRETARY)
And you'll see that these are in the mail so they can be counter-signed.

Mr. Lewis signs the contracts of American Tobacco's three biggest television accounts (excluding Jack Benny): Your Hit Parade, *a popular musical series with Snooky Lanson, Gisele MacKenzie, and Dorothy Collins;* Private Secretary *with Ann Sothern; and* Robert Montgomery Presents Your Lucky Strike Theater. *Although sponsored by the same company, both* Hit Parade *and* Robert Montgomery *appeared on NBC, a network competing with Benny's CBS.*

SECRETARY: Yes, sir.
(SHE TAKES CONTRACTS AND EXITS)

JACK: Mr. Lewis . . . Mr. Lewis . . . where's *my* contract?

LEWIS: Well . . . . .

JACK: I'm here, let me sign it. Let's get it over with. You know, let's have no loose ends.
(JACK LOOKS UP)
. . . . no loose ends.

LEWIS: Jack, what are you looking for?

Groucho Marx appeared once on The Jack Benny Program *in 1955 and spoofed his own quiz program and Jack Benny's vanity. Jack, disguised as a contestant on* You Bet Your Life, *must answer the question, "What is the real age of that famous comedian Jack Benny?" There is a classic use of silence as Benny ponders whether it is worth the money to reveal his correct age.*

JACK: You know what I'm looking for, Groucho told me . . . Now please, Mr. Lewis, where's my contract?
(JACK STARTS RUMMAGING THROUGH PAPERS ON LEWIS' DESK.)

LEWIS: Jack . . . Jack . . . please . . .
(JACK HAPPENS TO LOOK AT THE WASTEPAPER BASKET. REACHES DOWN AND TAKES OUT A LEGAL LOOKING PAPER AND LOOKS AT IT.)

JACK: My contract! . . . Mr. Lewis, what was my option doing in the waste-paper basket?

LEWIS: It must've blown off my desk. You see, when the window is open, there's a strong wind from the Northeast.

JACK: Hmm . . that's funny. Last year it was from the Southwest . . . Now look, Mr. Lewis, you don't have to beat around the bush with me . . . Anything we say is strictly confidential . . . After all, there are just the two of us here.

LEWIS: Now Jack, regretting your option—

JACK: What?

LEWIS: I mean, regarding your option . . .

JACK: Yes yes yes yes yes?

LEWIS: I'd like a little time to think it over.

JACK: *(GETTING UP)*
Mr. Lewis, I don't know why you're hesitating, but I'm getting the feeling that you want somebody else . . . Mr. Lewis, you can't turn me out just like that. After all, I've been with the American Tobacco Company for ten years.

LEWIS: That's true. When you first came to work for us, you were thirty-nine.

JACK: That's right . . . And for years now I've been doing a good job for the American Tobacco Company. . . . I've been selling the product . . . and two summers you even exercised the tobacco picking clause.

Although Benny promoted Jell-O for eight years on radio and one year as a cosponsor on television, and Lucky Strike cigarettes for a total of fifteen years, more than 40 percent of middle-aged Americans surveyed in 1973 still associated the comedian with the dessert.

LEWIS: We didn't exercise it, you held us to it.

JACK: Anyway, I came up here fully confident that you were going to pick up my option . . . but for some reason you seem to be stalling.

LEWIS: Jack, you're taking the wrong attitude. I haven't come to any decision about dropping your option . . . . . I merely asked you to wait awhile . . . Say four or five days.

JACK: Oh . . . Very well, I'll wait . . . Four or five days, eh?

LEWIS: Yes . . . where will I be able to get in touch with you?

JACK: Just call your secretary, I'll be sitting in the outer office . . . Goodbye, Mr. Lewis.
(STARTING TOWARD DOOR, NERVOUSLY)
Don't keep me waiting too long—you know—

LEWIS: Jack, that's the wrong—
(JACK OPENS THE CLOSET DOOR, EXPOSING FRED ALLEN.)

JACK: Fred . . . Fred Allen . . what are you doing in that closet?

This is the only sketch where Jack is seen with Fred Allen, and it is only for two minutes. Allen's appearance does not really update the feud for television. Perhaps the feud could only be sustained when both were at the apex of their careers. Here Fred Allen seems to be a defeated man; he is having obvious problems with the lines throughout the show. Making undue fun of Fred Allen now might be seen as excessively cruel.

ALLEN: *(STEPPING OUT)*
Believe it or not, I'm playing Post Office.

JACK: Post Office?

ALLEN: Kiss me.

JACK: Now wait a minute . . . there's something fishy going on here and I'm gonna get to the bottom of it . . . Mr. Lewis, what has Fred been telling you?

LEWIS: Jack, there's no need to get excited. As you know, the entertainment business is very competitive.

JACK: Wait a minute . . . So that's it . . . Fred, how could you do a thing like this to me? You ought to be ashamed of yourself . . . You, of all people, coming in here and trying to get my job.

ALLEN: Jack, I had to do something. I've eaten so much dog food, they wrote a song about me being in a window.

In a stretch to sustain the dog-food joke, Allen makes reference to a 1953 song, "Doggie in the Window," made popular by Patti Page. The advertising jokes become obviously stale with the strained "quotation" by shoe manufacturer and alleged poet Thom McAn.

JACK: Well, all I can say is you've got a lot of nerve.

ALLEN: All right, Jack, I'll admit that I'm a heel . . . But every heel is close to a good sole. That's a direct quote from the poet, Tom McCann.

JACK: Well, Fred, after that last line, I shouldn't forgive you, but I will . . . I know you're sorry for what you did, so let's forget it . . . Come on, we'll go out and have a bite to eat.

ALLEN: Okay.
(THEY START TOWARD DOOR.)

JACK: I'll be waiting to hear from you, Mr. Lewis

LEWIS: *(STANDING UP)*
Yes . . . yes . . .
(THEY GO OUT THE DOOR, LEWIS SITS DOWN . . THE OTHER CLOSET DOOR OPENS AND EDDIE CANTOR COMES OUT.)

CANTOR: I thought they'd never leave.
(APPLAUSE)

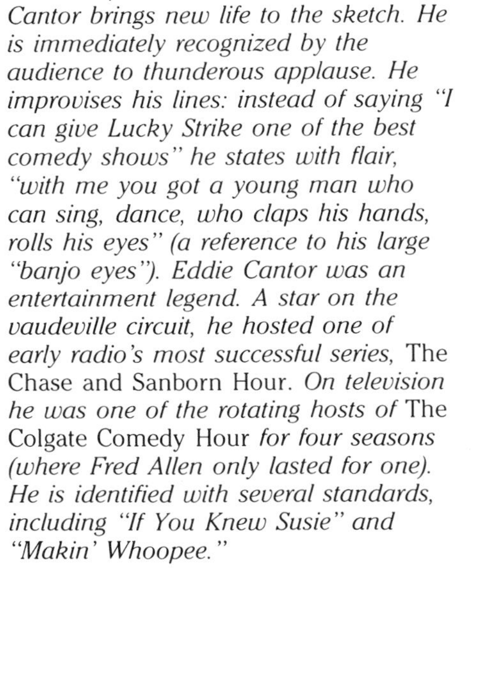

The unexpected entrance of Eddie Cantor brings new life to the sketch. He is immediately recognized by the audience to thunderous applause. He improvises his lines: instead of saying "I can give Lucky Strike one of the best comedy shows" he states with flair, "with me you got a young man who can sing, dance, who claps his hands, rolls his eyes" (a reference to his large "banjo eyes"). Eddie Cantor was an entertainment legend. A star on the vaudeville circuit, he hosted one of early radio's most successful series, The Chase and Sanborn Hour. *On television he was one of the rotating hosts of* The Colgate Comedy Hour *for four seasons (where Fred Allen only lasted for one). He is identified with several standards, including "If You Knew Susie" and "Makin' Whoopee."*

CANTOR: Now that they're both gone, Mr. Lewis, let's get down to business.
(CURTAINS START TO CLOSE)

CANTOR: I can give Lucky Strike one of the best comedy shows that was ever on radio, television, or the history of the entertainment business. With my talent, there's no limit where we can go—
(MUSIC)
(CURTAINS CLOSE)

DON: Jack will be back in just a moment, but first—
(TAG)
(AFTER COMMERCIAL, JACK COMES OUT TO MUSIC AND APPLAUSE)

JACK: Thank you very much, ladies and gentlemen . . . And you know, this whole scene about my sponsor not picking up my option was just a gag . . As a matter of fact, I've got a contract to be with the American Tobacco Company till I'm forty . . They didn't know what they were getting into . . . Say, did you see in the paper about Heifetz being slugged in the arm while he was playing his violin in Tel Aviv . . . It's funny, the same thing happened to me in Chicago and I wasn't even playing . . I was just carrying the violin case. Oh, Fred, will you come out here, please?
(FRED ALLEN OUT TO APPLAUSE)

JACK: I want to thank you for being on my show . . and I think you did a wonderful job.

ALLEN: Jack, you won't believe this, but I did my best to louse it up.

The show is running late, and Benny dispenses with the topical reference to Heifetz. He calls for his guest star in his inimitable manner: "Oh Fred, Fred Allen." After the dog-food joke is perfunctorily recited, Eddie Cantor takes a bow. There is obvious camaraderie among the three, and they begin to improvise. Benny gently refers to Allen as Fido, in a putdown of the whole running gag. Benny invites everyone to his home and as he begins to give directions he waves his hand in Cantor's face, who quickly pushes it down and complains "you're covering me." Everyone breaks up; a perfect off-the-cuff ending. Credits roll.

JACK: I believe it . . By the way, Fred, is it true about you eating dog food?

FRED: Yes, it is.

JACK: Well, doesn't it bother your stomach?

FRED: No, but eating out of that bowl is very hard on my knees.

JACK: I can understand that . . . Oh, Eddie Cantor . . will you come out here, please?
(EDDIE CANTOR COMES OUT TO APPLAUSE)

JACK: Eddie, I want to thank you for being on my show.

CANTOR: It was my pleasure, Jack.

JACK: No, no, Eddie, it was *my* pleasure.

CANTOR: No, Jack, it was *my* pleasure.

JACK: No, no, Eddie, it was *my* pleasure.

ALLEN: Ladies and gentlemen, this is what happens when two straight men get together.

JACK: What?

ALLEN: Why don't you give me my money so I can go?

JACK: No, no, Fred . . For being such good sports, I want both of you and your wives to come over to my house for dinner tonight.

CANTOR: Okay, Jack, thanks.

ALLEN: Well, Jack, I've never been to your house before . . . How do I get there?

JACK: Well . . . as you leave the studio, you go two blocks till you come to the California Bank . . . you turn right for five blocks till you come to the Bank of America. Then turn left for eight blocks till you get to the corner where the Security First National is. Then go straight out past the Citizens Trust Company till you come to the Beverly Hills Branch of the California Bank . . Then you ---- *(CUT OFF THE AIR)*

Credits as follows:

Directed by
Ralph Levy

Produced by
Hilliard Marks

Written for Television by
Sam Perrin
George Balzer
Milt Josefsberg
John Tackaberry

Music Director
Mahlon Merrick

Art Direction
Robert Tyler Lee

As credits roll, Don Wilson invites viewers to watch Private Secretary *next week and to listen to Jack Benny every Sunday night over the CBS Radio Network. He credits the sponsor and finishes: "This is Don Wilson saying 'Be Happy, Go Lucky.'"*

About the Contributors

LARRY GELBART has written for radio, television, the stage, and screen. He received an Emmy Award for the TV series *M*A*S*H* (which he developed for television), a Tony for coauthoring *A Funny Thing Happened on the Way to the Forum,* and Oscar nominations for his screenplays for *Oh, God!* and *Tootsie.* He received his second Tony Award for the book of the acclaimed Broadway musical *City of Angels.*

WILLIAM A. HENRY III is a senior writer and the theater critic at *Time* magazine. He has written extensively on television, having penned all or part of ten books on media issues as well as countless articles and reviews for *The Boston Globe, Life, The New Republic,* and *The Washington Journalism Review,* among others. His work has been awarded numerous distinctions, including the William Allen White Prize and two Pulitzer Prizes, one of which was in 1980 for "distinguished criticism" for his *Globe* writings about television.

DAVID MARC has been actively involved in the critique of popular culture for over ten years. A visiting professor at the Annenberg School for Communication at USC at Los Angeles, he has published two books on television—*Demographic Vistas: Television in American Culture* and *Comic Visions: Television Comedy and American Culture*—and is now at work on a third. He is also known for his work in *The Village Voice* and his regular feature in *The Boston Review.*

PETER W. KAPLAN, a writer and editor, was the editorial director of *Manhattan, inc.* magazine, as well as a cultural correspondent for the *New York Times* covering the television industry. He has written about television for *Esquire* and the *Washington Post,* among other publications.

RONALD SIMON is the curator of television at The Museum of Television and Radio. He serves as an adjunct professor at Hunter College and has lectured and consulted at the Cooper-Hewitt Museum, the Whitney Museum, the Museum of Modern Art, and the Smithsonian Institution. He is a member of the Editorial Board of *Television Quarterly.*

RICH CONATY is the former associate curator for radio at The Museum of Television and Radio. He has been the host and producer of WFUV-FM's *The Big Broadcast* since 1972 and was heard on WNEW-AM during 1983 and 1984. He is a regular contributor to *Video Review* magazine.

ELLEN O'NEILL is the senior editor of publications at The Museum of Television and Radio.

And now a word about our sponsor . . . "Jell-O, again. This is Jack Benny talking."

So began a Sunday night ritual that captivated millions of Americans for the better part of a decade. It was the cue for a nation numbed by the Depression to forget its troubles and settle in for thirty minutes of fun orchestrated by the possessor of that urbane and faintly self-mocking voice. Though his sponsors changed over the course of his career, it is with Jell-O that Jack Benny is still most closely associated, and Benny's "Jell-O" years saw his program at its popular and creative height. Until the launch of the *Jell-O Program* in October 1934, Jack Benny had endured two sponsorship switches in little more than one year. Although Benny had been a popular success from the start, he was the victim of sponsors who did not appreciate his act.

It took a while for Jell-O to come into its own, too. Peter Cooper, an inventor and patron of the arts, obtained the first patent for a gelatin dessert in 1845. But Cooper did nothing with his patent. In 1897, Pearl B. Wait, a Le Roy, New York carpenter, entered the growing packaged food business with a fruit-flavored adaptation of Cooper's invention, which Mrs. Wait dubbed "Jell-O." With insufficient capital and no sales experience, Wait's Jell-O floundered. In 1899, he sold the brand name and formula to the Genessee Pure Food Company.

Genessee's owner, Frank Woodward, didn't have any success with Jell-O until he launched an aggressive promotional campaign. In fancy horse-drawn rigs and snappy roadsters, Woodward's army of well-groomed salesmen became a familiar sight at state fairs, church socials, and picnics. These efforts were supported by colorful magazine ads and millions of Jell-O's famed recipe booklets, which soon became a fixture in America's kitchens. All of the promotions brought home the message that Jell-O was economical, easy to make, and a favorite of children. Seven years after Woodward acquired the product, Jell-O sales reached nearly one million dollars annually. In 1925, Woodward's business, renamed The Jell-O Company, Incorporated (and valued at sixty-seven million dollars), merged with the Postum Cereal Company to form the nucleus of General Foods.

So important was the Jell-O account to the fledgling Young & Rubicam advertising agency, that the firm moved from Philadelphia to New York to service it. While the second half of the 1920s saw a tremendous proliferation in radio stations, Y&R was relatively slow to get into the medium, and its initial efforts for Jell-O were limited to print advertising. When Jell-O did enter radio it was as the sponsor of NBC's daytime adaptation of *The Wizard of Oz* in 1934, the year that radio came into its own as an advertising medium. Jell-O moved into the evening hours with Jack Benny, whose third radio series had left the air September 28, 1934. Benny was not the first choice for Jell-O sponsorship, but he had a good track record in radio and was available. Benny's previous sponsor, General Tire, was willing to give him up from October 1934 through the middle of February 1935, with an option to get him back for another twenty weeks. General Foods committed $7,500 weekly for the thirty-minute program, in addition to the cost of securing NBC's Sunday night 7 P.M. time slot, chosen over 10 o'-clock Friday night in the hope of reaching Jell-O's prime market—children.

The October 14, 1934 debut of the *Jell-O Program* was designed to advertise an improvement in the six flavors of Jell-O, which had been arriving on grocery shelves throughout the summer. Much of it, however, remained on the shelves into December. Though an immediate ratings success, the *Jell-O Program* did not generate a corresponding increase in sales, and serious consideration was given to dropping Benny after an initial twenty-week run. Mary Livingstone told of how General Foods executives suggested a cut in the production budget, but Livingstone countered with an offer of her own: she and her husband would work for free until sales picked up, but the rest of the cast would continue to draw their current salaries. As it turned out, Jell-O sales increased dramatically during the first week of January 1935; they were the highest for any week since General Foods had acquired Jell-O ten years earlier. At a dinner party to celebrate their good fortune, General Foods presented the Bennys with a check amounting to the salaries they had given up. Benny was released from his General Tire contract, and the comedian signed a two-year pact with Jell-O.

Although Jell-O was not the first product to have its commercial messages integrated into a Jack Benny radio show, it was during Jell-O's tenure that the technique was perfected. This innovative, lighthearted method of advertising proved immensely appealing. Heywood Broun concluded a *McCall's* magazine article by declaring his hope that, "In days to come a grateful people would erect a statue to Jack Benny with the simple inscription: 'In memory of the first man to take the curse off radio commercials!' "

The November 3, 1935 *Jell-O Program* typifies how the commercials became an integral part of the broadcasts. The show opens with a collegiate cheer spelling out "J-E-L-L-O," then a peppy band number over which Don Wilson reads a fan letter, "The six delicious flavors stand out in front like a bolt of lightning on a dark and cloudy night. I can honestly and truthfully say that there is no other dessert on the market today that can live up to Jell-O's fine quality and delicious flavors!" As always, Wilson exhorts listeners to "look for the big red letters on the package. They spell Jell-O!" The scene switches to a barber shop, where Benny's exchange with "Pasquale" [bandleader Johnny Green] includes the barber's devotion to those six delicious flavors, "Ras-a-berry, straws-a-berry, cherry-berry, orange, lemon, and lime-a-berry!" Later, when Benny quizzes Don Wilson on his knowledge of "big words," the announcer replies, "Oh, just words like strawberry . . . raspberry . . . Jell-O." Benny points out that Jell-O isn't such a big word, but Wilson is prepared, "No, but it's the largest selling gelatin dessert in the world. And every day millions of people eat it!" "Well," Benny concludes, "I thought we dragged that in by the heels gracefully." "No," responds Wilson, "It didn't sound a bit obvious." Jell-O is even used to end a sketch. Above the roar of 10,000 elephants (provided by the show's sound effects man), Wilson points out that, like a pachyderm, "a Jell-O eater never forgets! Once you eat Jell-O you will always remember that extra rich fresh fruit flavor!"

These clever mentions were not overlooked by Jell-O's chief competitor, Royal Desserts, which sponsored Rudy Vallee's long-running Thursday night variety hour. The Royal Gelatin commercials of the Vallee program provide an interesting contrast to Benny's Jell-O spots of the same period. Unlike the *Jell-O Program,* Royal's messages are separated from the entertainment, but their tone and content is clearly a reaction to the Jell-O campaign. On Vallee's September 24, 1936 season premiere, his announcer boasts *"seven* delicious flavors" and reminds the audience, "Royal is spelled R-O-Y-A-L. Get some tomorrow!" Whether a reflection of the will of the sponsor, the advertising agency, or Vallee's formal sensibilities, the writing was flat, and so were the sales figures. Then, as now, Jell-O held more than a 75 percent share of the gelatin market.

The cast and crew of the *Jell-O Program* thrived in a high-charged atmosphere fueled by a generous advertising budget and Jack Benny's collaborative relationship with Young & Rubicam and *Jane* on CBS, but advertising dollars, like America's attention, were increasingly going to television. Jell-O was the sponsor of one of the first television talk shows, *The Author Meets the Critic,* as well as *The Seven Arts Quiz.* After an experimental visit to the medium in 1949, Jack Benny began to be seen regularly on television in 1950. Even though his Jell-O years were behind him, a March 1955 Lucky Strike telecast invokes Benny's memorable sponsor. As part of a sketch set in a carnival, the perpetually irritated Frank Nelson grabs Benny's arm, saying, "Is that your muscle or are you still plugging Jell-O?" It was not until 1962, however, that Benny once again was sponsored by Jell-O. In the eyes of the average viewer, though, Benny had always been synonymous with "America's favorite dessert." Just as on radio, the Jell-O commercials were integral to the program. In one show, Benny's conversation with guest star Jack Soo is interrupted by an intrusive overhead microphone. Benny confronts the irresponsible technician (played by radio alumnus Mel Blanc), who alibis the mishap by explaining that he's eating. "Eating! During *my* show!" Benny rails, "Well, that does it, you're fired!" Only when Blanc explains that he's eating

Jell-O does Benny relent.

On another program, Benny and his director confer about what to do for the commercial. Dennis Day cheerfully volunteers, then auditions Jell-O pitches as Edward G. Robinson, James Cagney, and, finally, John F. Kennedy. In the manner of a presidential news conference, Day's Kennedy announces that, "Jell-O has come out with two new delicious flavors: lemon lime and mixed fruit." Such scenarios, and Don Wilson's witty on-camera exhortations for Jell-O, brought the spirit of the radio years into the video age.

In a 1951 *Collier's* article under Benny's byline, the comedian commented on the secret to staying power in television. Benny wrote that there are some performers "you see regularly week after week for years and yet look forward to seeing on each succeeding visit." Such joyful anticipation mirrors America's devotion to the comedian himself and his most memorable sponsor. The simplicity, timing, and virtue of both Jack Benny and Jell-O have entered our collective psyche. Just as there's always room for Jell-O, there will always be a special place for Jack Benny.

General Foods's Charles Mortimer, who would later become the chairman of the board. In 1937, at the expiration of Benny's initial two-year agreement, he signed a new accord which paid him $10,000 per week plus nearly $600,000 annually for the production of the program. By 1940, General Foods devoted more than three-quarters of its Jell-O advertising budget to the Benny program, with Benny's personal salary in the $600,000 range. That 1940 season saw the program hit the peak of its popularity: a *Newsweek* article estimated that forty million people tuned in the *Jell-O Program* every Sunday. One of the show's enduring charms was Don Wilson's weekly rhapsody for those "six delicious flavors" of "America's favorite gelatin dessert," a "treat without equal!" Wilson even found a big, shimmering mold of Jell-O "one of the most attractive gifts of all!" and never left out his reminder that Jell-O was "economical and easy to make!"

During the Second World War, the Benny program dropped from first to fifth place, and both the company and the star began to consider a change. Additionally, General Foods found its sugar allotment restricted, so Jell-O production was cut severely. Any Jell-O that did show up on grocery shelves was sold without Benny's innovative plugs. For the 1942–43 radio season, Benny's sponsorship changed from Jell-O to General Foods's Grape-Nuts and Grape-Nuts Flakes. The switch was addressed comically on the *Jell-O Program* of May 10, 1942. After "learning" that he will not be broadcasting for Jell-O next season, Benny believes he has been fired. Only after a fictionalized visit to his sponsor, Charles Mortimer, does Benny relax. That's Don Wilson's cue to panic, "I won't do it, I tell ya! I won't do it!" So strong was Wilson's association with Jell-O that his comical reaction to the change was perfectly logical. "As long as they're at their grocers, can't they buy a little package of Jell-O, too?" he pleads. Even Benny's first Grape-Nuts broadcast reminds the audience of the Jell-O connection. It opens with the familiar Jell-O jingle and ends with Don Wilson incorrectly advising potential Grape-Nuts buyers to "be sure to look for the red letters on the box!"

After World War II, the production and sale of Jell-O escalated, but Benny had moved on to be sponsored by Lucky Strike cigarettes. For the 1948–49 radio season, Jell-O sponsored *mr. ace & Jane* on CBS, but advertising dollars, like America's attention, were increasingly going to television. Jell-O was the sponsor of one of the first television talk shows, *The Author Meets the Critic,* as well as *The Seven Arts Quiz.* After an experimental visit to the medium in 1949, Jack Benny began to be seen regularly on television in 1950. Even though his Jell-O years were behind him, a March 1955 Lucky Strike telecast invokes Benny's memorable sponsor. As part of a sketch set in a carnival, the perpetually irritated Frank Nelson grabs Benny's arm, saying, "Is that your muscle or are you still plugging Jell-O?" It was not until 1962, however, that Benny once again was sponsored by Jell-O. In the eyes of the average viewer, though, Benny had always been synonymous with "America's favorite dessert." Just as on radio, the Jell-O commercials were integral to the program. In one show, Benny's conversation with guest star Jack Soo is interrupted by an intrusive overhead microphone. Benny confronts the irresponsible technician (played by radio alumnus Mel Blanc), who alibis the mishap by explaining that he's eating. "Eating! During *my* show!" Benny rails, "Well, that does it, you're fired!" Only when Blanc explains that he's eating Jell-O does Benny relent.

On another program, Benny and his director confer about what to do for the commercial. Dennis Day cheerfully volunteers, then auditions Jell-O pitches as Edward G. Robinson, James Cagney, and, finally, John F. Kennedy. In the manner of a presidential news conference, Day's Kennedy announces that, "Jell-O has come out with two new delicious flavors: lemon lime and mixed fruit." Such scenarios, and Don Wilson's witty on-camera exhortations for Jell-O, brought the spirit of the radio years into the video age.

In a 1951 *Collier's* article under Benny's byline, the comedian commented on the secret to staying power in television. Benny wrote that there are some performers "you see regularly week after week for years and yet look forward to seeing on each succeeding visit." Such joyful anticipation mirrors America's devotion to the comedian himself and his most memorable sponsor. The simplicity, timing, and virtue of both Jack Benny and Jell-O have entered our collective psyche. Just as there's always room for Jell-O, there will always be a special place for Jack Benny.

Selected Bibliography

Adamson, Joe. *Groucho, Harpo, Chico and Sometimes Zeppo.* New York: Simon and Schuster, 1973.

Allen, Steve. "Jack Benny." In his *More Funny People.* New York: Stein and Day, 1982.

Barnouw, Erik. *A Tower in Babel.* New York: Oxford University Press, 1966.

Benny, Jack, and Joan Benny. *Sunday Nights at Seven: The Jack Benny Story.* New York: Warner Books, 1990.

Benny, Mary Livingstone, and Hilliard Marks (with Marcia Borie). *Jack Benny.* Garden City, N.Y.: Doubleday, 1978.

Blanc, Mel, and Philip Bashe. *That's Not All Folks!* New York: Warner Books, 1988.

Buxton, Frank, and Bill Owen. *The Big Broadcast.* New York: Viking Press, 1972.

De Cordova, Frederick. *Johnny Came Lately.* New York: Simon and Schuster, 1988.

Dunn, Gary A., Larry Gassman and John Gassman. *Jack Benny Radio Log.* 1990. Unpublished.

Dunning, John. *Tune in Yesterday.* Englewood Cliffs, N.J.: Prentice-Hall, 1976.

Dygert, Warren B. *Radio as an Advertising Medium.* New York: McGraw-Hill, 1939.

Fein, Irving. *Jack Benny: An Intimate Biography.* New York: G. P. Putnam's Sons, 1976.

Giddins, Gary. "This Guy Wouldn't Give You the Parsley Off His Fish." In *The Best American Essays 1987.* Edited by Gay Talese and Robert Atwan. New York: Ticknor and Fields, 1987.

Gilbert, Douglas. *American Vaudeville: Its Life and Times.* New York: Dover Publications, 1953.

Goldman, Herbert G. *Jolson: The Legend Comes to Life.* New York: Oxford University Press, 1988.

Josefsberg, Milt. *The Jack Benny Show.* New York: Arlington House, 1977.

Lee, Laura, ed. "39 Forever: The Ultimate Log of Jack Benny Radio and Television Shows." 1989. Unpublished.

Lewine, Richard, and Alfred Simon. *Songs of the Theater.* New York: H.W. Wilson, 1984.

MacDonald, J. Fred. *Don't Touch That Dial!* Chicago: Nelson-Hall, 1979.

Shepherd, Donald, and Robert F. Slatzer. *Bing Crosby: The Hollow Man.* New York: St. Martin's Press, 1981.

Sobol, Louis. *The Longest Street.* New York: Crown Publishers, 1968.

Stein, Charles W., ed. *American Vaudeville as Seen by Its Contemporaries.* New York: Alfred A. Knopf, 1984.

Sudhalter, Richard M., and Philip R. Evans (with William Dean-Myatt). *Bix: Man and Legend.* New Rochelle, N.Y.: Arlington House, 1974.

Summers, Harrison B., ed. *History of Broadcasting: Radio to Television.* New York: Arno Press and *The New York Times,* 1971.

Taylor, Robert. *Fred Allen: His Life and Wit.* Boston: Little, Brown and Company, 1989.

Wertheim, Arthur Frank. *Radio Comedy.* New York: Oxford University Press, 1979.

Acknowledgments

The Museum of Television and Radio gratefully acknowledges the support and cooperation of all who helped make this exhibition and publication possible. The Museum wishes to thank a number of organizations and individuals for helping us to acquire and get clearance for the Jack Benny television and radio programs.

UCLA made available their collection of Benny radio and television broadcasts, many of which are included in the Museum's exhibition. In December 1967, Jack Benny donated to the UCLA Library's Department of Special Collections an archive of materials covering the entire span of his illustrious show business career. In addition to 1,344 radio scripts, 284 television scripts, numerous photographs, and other documents, this gift included 1,087 radio transcription discs and 206 kinescopes and telefilms which were later turned over to the UCLA Film and Television Archive. At the archive, we would especially like to thank Robert Rosen, Director; Edward Richmond, Curator; Dan Einstein, Archivist; and Ronald E. Staley, Radio Collections Manager. And at the Department of Special Collections, University Research Library, we would like to acknowledge Anne Caiger, Manuscripts Librarian, and Jeffrey Rankin, Supervisor of Reader Services.

The Museum of Television and Radio, the Library of Congress, and NBC share ownership of the 175,000 disc NBC Radio Collection, which is preserved at the Library of Congress. Our deep appreciation goes to the Motion Picture, Broadcasting, and Recorded Sound Division of the Library for its excellent transfers from transcription disk to audiotape of programs from the NBC Collection. These transfers represent more than one third of the radio broadcasts in the exhibition. We would especially like to thank Samuel Brylawski, Reference Librarian; Wynn Matthias, Reference Librarian; Mike Donaldson, Lead Recording Engineer; Dina T. Fleming, Public Services Coordinator; Steve Leggett, Public Services Assistant; and Nicole Douglas, Clerk-Typist.

The American Heritage Center at the University of Wyoming loaned the Museum television programs and scripts from its collection. We have included many of these programs in the exhibition and have reprinted in this book the script that features Fred Allen. The American Heritage Center at the University of Wyoming maintains a collection of Jack Benny correspondences, scripts, and manuscripts (1931–74) from weekly radio and television programs, specials, and guest appearances as well as Benny photographs, films, and records. Special thanks go to David L. Baker, Director; Thomas Wilsted, Associate Director/Operations; and Debra Slaughter, Documentation Officer.

We are also grateful to Maureen Angelinetta of MCA Television who arranged for the rights to and copies of *The Jack Benny Program* that they distribute; Walter Iwinski, Manager for Audio and Visual Production of CBS Inc., who helped us tremendously with access to the CBS collection of programs with original commercials; Larry Kiner of Spokane Records, for donating dozens of Benny radio programs and guest appearances; Shokus Video, which donated several shows; and Ron Kirk, the General Manager of Video Craftsman, and Steve Bell, Senior Vice President and General Manager of KTLA/Los Angeles, both of whom provided excellent transfers and technical expertise.

It is an enormous task to amass a collection of photographs for a book such as this, and we are grateful to many people for their efforts: Paul McGuire, Director of Photography, and Jay Kaplan, Photo Files Coordinator, at NBC, Inc.; Ray Whelan, Jr., Vice President, at Globe Photos, Inc.; Jim Carlson, Photo Archivist, at the American Heritage Center at the University of Wyoming; Martin Silverstein, Director of Photo Operations; Krystina Slavik, Manager of Photo Services, and Shirley Jones, Photo Assistant, at CBS Inc.

We are very grateful to MCA Publishing Rights, especially Nancy Cushing-Jones, Executive Vice President, and Yvonne Kartak, Executive Assistant, for their cooperation in helping us obtain permissions. We would particularly like to thank Sid J. Sheinberg, President of MCA Inc., for facilitating our acquisition of these photographs.

We are also grateful to the following individuals for their time and patience in the sometimes complicated and lengthy process of obtaining clearances to reproduce the network photos: Virginia Frey, Manager of Business Affairs, CBS Entertainment; Karen Levitt, Paralegal, CBS Law Department; Jan Kreher-Policastro, Director of Marketing, NBC Business Affairs; and Marilyn Roberts, Assistant to the Director of Marketing, NBC Business Affairs.

Special thanks to Edie Adams, Lucie Arnaz, Milton Berle, George Burns, and Sid Caesar for their blessings on certain photos.

A number of individuals helped the Museum in various important capacities. We are indebted to Jeff Abraham for both his enthusiasm and research which helped us to find and transfer materials on the West Coast; to John Behrens, Supervisor, CBS Program Information, who opened his extensive files to us, allowing us to confirm many air dates; to Kenneth Anger for donating valuable *Radio Guides;* to Vince Giordano for the loan of the sheet music photographed in the book; to Betty Ruder for her support in the early planning stages of the exhibition; to Greg Williams for his first-rate fact-checking; and to Arthur Klebanoff, for all his help and advice as our literary agent.

At Kraft General Foods, Inc., the sponsor of our exhibition, we wish to gratefully acknowledge the enthusiasm, involvement, and support of Brian G. Laragh, Group Vice President (retired); Stephen I. Sandove, Group Vice President, Desserts Division; Dana M. Gioia, Marketing Manager, Jell-O Desserts; and, Anne Ivanhoe, Product Manager, Jell-O Desserts.

An exhibition and publication of this magnitude required the efforts and talents of the entire Museum staff. The following people in particular were integral to the completion of this project:

Michael Waitzman, Television Researcher; Mary Beth Williams, Curatorial Assistant; Stephanie Wolk, Curatorial Assistant; Susan Fisher, Director of the Curatorial Department; Andy Halper, former Director; Bill Beam, Director of Technical Operations and Engineering; Adrian Cosentini, Audio Editor; Stephen Blot, Audio Editor; Seth Chang, Audio Dubber; Tom Fleming, Video Editor; Diane Lewis, Director of Public Relations; Dana Rogers, Public Relations Assistant; Sean Daly, Editorial Assistant; Joseph Zarinko, Editorial Assistant; Lou Dorfsman, Art Director; and Frank Skorski, Designer. Randy Dolnick, Assistant Curator, Television and Roberta Panjwani, Publications Associate for Clearances deserve a special note for their contributions.

Above all, this publication would not have been possible without the talents and dedication of Ron Simon, Curator, Television; Rich Conaty, former Associate Curator, Radio; and Ellen O'Neill, Senior Editor, Publications.

Permissions

Note: The following items have been reproduced with permission as stated below. We have carefully researched and obtained these permissions in writing. Any error or omission herein is unintentional.

Jack Benny Estate
Script for the *Jell-O Program Starring Jack Benny;* April 20, 1941.
Script for *The Jack Benny Program;* April 19, 1953.
Article written by Jack Benny entitled "From Vaudeo to Video via Radio," first printed in the March 24, 1951 edition of *Collier's* magazine.
Photographs from Jack Benny's personal collection at the American Heritage Center at the University of Wyoming.
The Bouché drawing of Jack Benny.
All used by permission.

MCA Publishing Rights
Radio and television photographs reprinted with permission by Universal Pictures. Copyright © by Universal Pictures, a Division of Universal City Studios, Inc. Courtesy of MCA Publishing Rights, a Division of MCA Inc.

CBS Entertainment; A Division of CBS Inc.
Script for *The Jack Benny Program;* April 19, 1953.
All CBS photographs.
Script and photographs courtesy of CBS Entertainment.
Used by permission.
Photographs on pages: ii, vi, 3 (top), 4, 6, 7, 8, 9, 10, 14, 17, 18, 19 (both), 20, 21, 22, 24, 25, 27, 28, 29, 30, 34, 35, 36 (both), 40, 43 (top), 44, 45, 46, 52, 56, 64, 66 (both), 68 (top), 70, 71, 73, 74, 75 (both), 76, 94 (top), 98, 102, 111 (both), 112 (top), 113, 118 (bottom), 120, 121 (top), 122 (both), 124 (both), 127, 130, 155, 157, 158, 162, 163, 183, 184, 185 (both), 186, 187, 188, 189 (both), 190, 191, 193, 194, 195 (both), 196, 197, 198, 199 (both), 200, 201 (bottom), 202, 203 (both), 204, 205 (both), 206, 207 (bottom), 208, 209, 210, 211 (both), 212, 213, 215 (both), 216, 217, 219 (both), 220, 224, 225 (both), 226, 236 (all), 238, 239 (top), 240, 241, 242–243, 248, 250, 252, 253, 255, 256, 257, 261.

National Broadcasting Company, Inc.
Script for the *Jell-O Program Starring Jack Benny;* April 20, 1941.
All NBC photographs.
Script and photographs courtesy of the National Broadcasting Company, Inc.
Used by permission.
Photographs on pages: 2 (top), 3 (bottom), 15, 16, 32, 42, 43 (bottom), 54 (both), 55, 57, 58, 59, 61, 63, 65, 67, 68 (bottom), 72, 79, 80 (both), 81, 83 (bottom), 84 (both), 86 (top), 87 (both), 88 (both), 90, 91, 92 (top), 93, 97 (all), 100, 101 (top), 103, 104, 106, 107, 108 (bottom), 110, 114, 115 (both), 118 (top), 119, 121 (bottom), 126, 128, 132, 136, 137 (both), 138, 141, 148, 150, 153, 156, 159, 160, 161, 164–165, 167, 168, 169, 171, 172, 174, 221, 228, 229, 230, 231 (both), 232, 233, 234 (all), 235.

American Heritage Center; University of Wyoming
Script for *The Jack Benny Program;* April 19, 1953.
Photographs from Jack Benny's personal collection. Photographs on pages: 2 (bottom), 12, 32, 38, 50, 53 (bottom), 77, 82, 85, 86 (bottom), 92 (bottom), 94 (bottom), 96 (both), 99, 101 (bottom), 108 (top), 112 (bottom), 116, 140, 153, 154, 201 (top), 239 (bottom).
Used by permission.

Kraft General Foods, Inc.
Script for the *Jell-O Program Starring Jack Benny;* April 20, 1941.
Jell-O advertisements (pages 62, 89 (both)). Used by permission.
Note: Jell-O, Grape-Nuts, and Grape-Nuts Flakes are registered trademarks of Kraft General Foods, Inc.

Department of Special Collections, University Research Library; UCLA
Script for the *Jell-O Program Starring Jack Benny;* April 20, 1941.
Used by permission.

Globe Photos, Inc.
Photograph (pages 147, 150, 153) reprinted by permission.

Culver Pictures, Inc.
Photograph (page 124 (top)) reprinted by permission.

Stephen Cox
Photographs (pages ii, 13, 125); photograph on page 23 by Clarence Sinclair Bull.

Max Wilk
Photographs (pages 27, 67, 199 bottom)

Hope Enterprises Inc.
Photograph on page 11.

Bouché drawing

Drawing courtesy of The National Portrait Gallery, The Smithsonian Institution, with a special acknowledgment to Mrs. René Bouché.

All sheet music covers reprinted with permission by the Jack Benny Estate and the following:

"The Bee" (page 133)
Warner/Chappell Music, Inc.
Permission also granted by the Trustees of the Boston Public Library on behalf of the Fred Allen Estate.

"Why Should I Cry Over You" by Ned Miller and Chester Cohn (page 53 (top))

"Rock 'n' Roll" (page 83 (top))
Bourne Co. Music Publishers